THE DREAMER

AND

THE DOCTOR

Washington Jacob's-ladder
Polymodium pectinatum

THE DREAMER AND THE DOCTOR

A FOREST LOVER AND A PHYSICIAN ON THE EDGE OF THE FRONTIER

JACK NISBET

Illustrations by Jeanne Debons
Maps by Joe Guarisco

SASQUATCH BOOKS
SEATTLE

Printed in the United States of America

Published by Sasquatch Books

23 22 21 20 19   9 8 7 6 5 4 3 2 1

Editor: Gary Luke
Production editor: Nicole Burns-Ascue
Design: Tony Ong
Illustrations: Jeanne Debons
Maps: Joe Guarisco
Copyeditor: Rachelle Longé McGhee

Library of Congress Cataloging-in-Publication Data is available.

ISBN: 978-1-63217-202-0

Sasquatch Books
1904 Third Avenue, Suite 710
Seattle, WA 98101
(206) 467-4300
SasquatchBooks.com

For Claire

CONTENTS

▽▽▽▽▽▽▽▽▽▽▽▽▽▽▽▽▽▽▽▽▽▽▽▽▽▽▽▽▽▽▽▽▽▽▽▽▽

▽▽▽▽▽▽▽▽▽▽▽▽▽▽▽▽▽▽▽▽▽▽▽▽▽▽▽▽▽▽▽▽▽▽▽▽▽

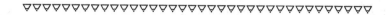

AUTHOR'S NOTE

Although many botanists pronounce the Leiberg name with a long *i*, oral accounts from around Lake Pend Oreille testify that neighbors always called them John and Carrie LEE-berg. As with other aspects of this book, local knowledge wins the day.

All common plant names are taken from the USDA PLANTS database. Those interested in current Latin taxonomy can match the equivalent names at Plants.USDA .gov.

Place names can be traced on the USGS web site at GeoNames.USGS.gov.

INTRODUCTION

There was a moment in August of 1890 when John Leiberg almost became a widower. "My wife has been very ill," he wrote to a friend. "Did not expect her to recover." For days on end, he acted as doctor and nurse during a constant vigil in their tidy cabin beneath imposing mountains at the southern tip of Lake Pend Oreille.

The lake provided a magnificent setting at a juncture that held uncertainty and promise for the couple. The Leibergs were both in their late thirties that summer, and both had left behind other lives in the Midwest. John, one among hundreds of prospectors trying to cash in on various mining booms around the region, had invested three years of hardscrabble work with no guarantee of any return. Carrie was a physician who practiced a difficult art in a place with minimal medical resources. Idaho had just been granted statehood that July, and their part of the new state was changing fast. Towns along the nearby railroad were coming into their own as centers of agriculture, logging, and mining supply. Hotels were rising along scenic Panhandle lakeshores to serve tourists. Efficient rail routes encouraged Carrie to set up a practice along a spur line and allowed John to communicate regularly with consultants on the other side of the country.

John was the more visible member of the couple, a talker who traveled far and dreamed of leaving a scientific legacy. He not only read widely in multiple languages but also absorbed local knowledge from the spectrum of people who crossed his path. He pursued plants with a sensual joy, pressing his face into rain-soaked mosses to capture their essence. In the mineral realm, he struggled mightily to find tangible wealth among the rocks. He was a man who embraced the freedoms of Western life while lobbying vehemently for regulations on public lands. "I have the preservation of the forests much at heart and so write of it," he told a friend. "Alas here I am but one in a multitude."

Carrie Leiberg left a much quieter imprint than that of her husband. While reams of his thoughts rest in various archives, only a dozen or so examples of her writings are known, and not a single letter between the two of them has ever come to light. Yet it is clear that she nurtured a personal ambition that matched his, as well as a complementary skill set. Along a trail of correspondence, herbarium sheets, medical journals, newspaper clippings, and court proceedings; of fruit trees, assay pits, alpine ridgetops, and faint oral memories, the Leibergs emerge as a modern couple at the ragged end of frontier times. They were forced by circumstances to live apart for long stretches, yet always aching to reunite; fully committed to the place where they landed, yet prepared to depart for new lands and start all over again. "You can send anything else to my wife exactly as to me," John once wrote when he knew he would be out of touch for a while. "We are one in all affairs in life."

John did not provide any details concerning Carrie's illness that August, but two months after the crisis passed, he reported that she was improving a little bit every day. She lived on to face the world beside her husband for another quarter century, through a dizzying variety of situations. "We try to bear good or ill fortune as bravely as we can," she wrote. That philosophy would be put to the test as Carrie and John's quest for good fortune propelled their saga far beyond the lakeside cabin where Carrie languished in bed that summer of 1890, waiting for the scales to tilt.

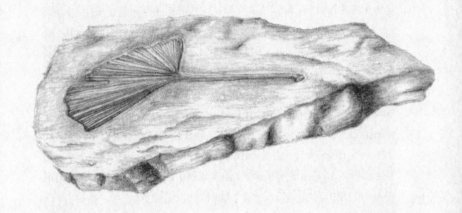

Fossil ginkgo leaf

∇∇∇∇∇∇∇∇∇∇∇∇∇∇∇∇∇∇∇∇∇∇∇∇∇∇∇∇∇∇∇∇∇∇∇∇∇∇

FIRST RIDE

∇∇∇∇∇∇∇∇∇∇∇∇∇∇∇∇∇∇∇∇∇∇∇∇∇∇∇∇∇∇∇∇∇∇∇∇∇∇

The story begins in Malmö, the busy Swedish port where Johan Bernhard Liberg was born in 1853. "My father was a sea captain," he wrote, "and the first remembrance I have of anything in this world was one morning being carried out in my mother's arms from the cabin on deck. There are few things I love better than the heaving ocean." As a boy, he apparently endured a conventional education under teachers he remembered as aged and intimidating: "How my heart used to thump against the ribs when brought before one of these solemn old owls to be examined on some abstract problem in Latin or Greek grammar or some equally useless point in geometrical lore—problems that the mind of a boy could grasp about as well as a pig can understand the mystery of the nebula in Orion." At some point in his youth, he escaped those owls to spend two years sailing with his father, who was hunting pirates among the islands of the South China Sea. For the rest of his life, Captain Liberg's son would remember the excitement of visiting remote parts of the world and yearn for more. That appetite for adventure might explain why Johan joined a wave of Scandinavians departing for the New World soon after he graduated from secondary school in 1868. His emigration record classified him as a *yngling* (youth), six months shy of his fifteenth birthday, and noted that he was traveling alone to America.

There is a nine-year gap in his story here. He resurfaced in Seney, Iowa, some thirty miles northeast of Sioux City and far from his beloved sea. During those missing years, he Americanized his name to John Bernard Leiberg and learned enough English to land a job with the St. Paul and Sioux City Railroad. On the January day in 1877 that he sealed his American assimilation by marrying seventeen-year-old Mattie B. Johnson, a friend testified that "the excellence of character and unblemished reputation of the groom make him well worthy of his lovely bride." By the end of the year, the Leibergs announced the arrival of a son they named Godfrey; shortly thereafter, John was sworn in as a naturalized US citizen. Employed as a ticket agent and inspector for the railroad's grain elevator, he became a well-known figure around the hamlet of Seney, with the local paper carrying occasional tidbits about the "popular station agent" and his wife.

Meanwhile, in the rolling prairies outside town, John indulged a serious interest in botany. "The desire to collect and preserve plants with me is simply perfectly irresistible, and I do not remember the time when it was not so," he later wrote. Although his parents had frowned on this boyhood hobby as an impractical waste of time, his fascination had persisted. He pressed wildflowers and grasses for the Davenport Academy of Science, whose members were compiling a list of Iowa's native flora. Among his finds was a distinctive switchgrass that became the first of many plants to be named for him: *Panicum leibergii.* In the process of compiling his personal herbarium, he wrote to other collectors, seeking specimens from the Midwest and beyond.

In the late summer of 1881, Mattie gave birth to a second son, christened Cassiel (the archangel of tears and temperance). Within weeks of his birth, the family moved to the much larger town of Mankato, Minnesota, where John had earned a promotion with the railroad. The area presented new botanical offerings, and over the following two years, he collected plants of all sorts at a furious rate in Blue Earth and Pipestone Counties. Upon encountering a puzzling duckweed in a small pond, he installed an aquarium at home to cultivate cuttings. By this time, he had acquired a microscope and could observe minute growth stages to aid in identification. He sent his conclusion to a professional botanist for corroboration, and when that contact offered a different opinion, Leiberg displayed a stubborn streak that manifested itself in a series of queries to several "Masters of Science" and ceased only when the eminent naturalist George Engelmann of St. Louis agreed with his determination.

John also corresponded with scientists from the Geological and Natural History Survey of Minnesota and donated specimens of native plants to the state museum. He

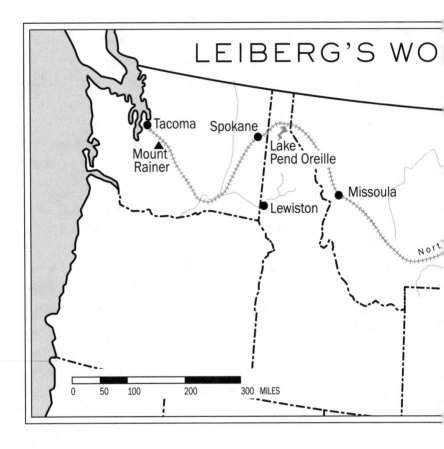

journeyed eighty miles to Minneapolis to attend meetings of the Minnesota Academy of Science, where topics such as the theories of Charles Darwin were discussed. He was elected a member in February 1883 and a month later presented his first paper to a gathering of twenty-four people. In fluid prose that betrayed no hint of a writer laboring in a foreign language, Leiberg described several species that had not been previously recorded in Minnesota, including a grass, an alga, and a liverwort.

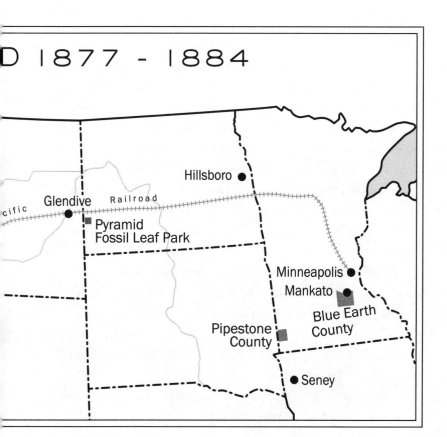

That same year, his botanical interests coincided with a job opportunity for the Northern Pacific Railroad, which was in the midst of an ambitious experiment in the Dakota and Montana Territories. Their tree-planting department was setting out deciduous saplings to create windbreaks and snow fences along the tracks, as well as ornamental groves to make the treeless plains more attractive to settlers. While traveling west to the Yellowstone River to supervise plantings, Leiberg studied the rise of prairie wildflowers such as the tufted phlox that blanketed the arid steppe beyond the

Missouri River. He noted how perennials with long root-stocks, like locoweeds and biscuitroots, could withstand the intense seasonal droughts characteristic of the northern plains environment. He snacked on gooseberries, surprised to find them sweet and juicy despite the extremely dry soil in which they grew. The midsummer temperature fluctuations proved shocking; one hot July day, he watched scorching winds completely desiccate lush green prairie grasses within two hours. Leaves wilted on trees, and stalks of flowers dried up before his eyes. Two evenings later, the thermometer dipped below freezing.

Fossil tree stumps peeking through the prairie sod further excited his curiosity. In Eocene lignite beds around North Dakota's Pyramid Park, he counted hundreds of petrified logs with butts up to twelve feet in diameter. John pulled pebbles from streambeds that proved to be fossilized pieces of wood, each grain and knot perfectly preserved. He split soft sandstone to find imprints of leaves, some recognizable as the kin of familiar Midwest hardwoods, while others, such as ginkgo, evoked the exotic. "It is a rather novel and strange arrangement," he remarked, "that the settler upon these prairies should, in order to clear his farm, be obliged to pull the stumps of trees that flourished perhaps fifty thousand years ago." But what could have destroyed these ancient forests, and what had prevented them from growing back? Conventional wisdom held that fires had wiped them out in the distant past, and that intermittent prairie fires continued to destroy seedlings before they could grow into trees. Leiberg was not so sure about that explanation.

While he puzzled over fossil stumps in the summer of 1883, Northern Pacific crews in central Montana laid the last miles of track to complete the railroad's cross-country route. In September, Leiberg took advantage of an opportunity to ride all the way west to Washington Territory, where he collected a rockcress and a wallflower from the slopes of Mount Rainier. On the return trip, he watched the dense coniferous forests of the Cascades and Rockies diminish east of the Continental Divide and speculated on the relationship between tree growth and precipitation. He envisioned a deep geologic past before the Cascades and Rockies had risen to their present heights, when rain clouds from the Pacific could flow unimpeded to the prairies. The resulting moisture could have nurtured the vast deciduous forests whose fossilized remains he had witnessed. As epochs passed and the mountains rose, their increasing height would have blocked the Pacific air currents, stifling the annual rainfall on the plains and killing the ancient Dakota forests. With this process in mind, he wondered whether the western ranges were still rising, as suggested by the smoking volcanoes of the Cascades and the thermal springs of interior basins. In contemplating these phenomena, he revealed an awareness of geological theories that were still in their infancy in the 1880s, and the general drift of his reasoning has proved remarkably sound.

The following spring found Leiberg mounting a horse in the unlikely location of Lewiston in central Idaho Territory, an eighty-mile steamship ride from the nearest rail line. News of gold strikes around the Clearwater River and Prichard Creek off the North Fork of the Coeur d'Alene River had apparently piqued his interest. He headed east into the mountains with the intention, he wrote, "of ascertaining the prospects of mineral wealth in this region." Although precious metals provided the incentive for his journey, John devoted plenty of attention to plants along the way.

Following a narrow trail up the Clearwater and through the Nez Perce Indian Reservation, he passed a profusion of wildflowers, including several varieties of the spring biscuit-roots that formed a key part of the tribe's diet. The track ascended to a series of arid plateaus well populated by ponderosa pine: "this species forms parklike forests, the trees growing at distances varying from twenty to fifty feet apart, the ground free from underbrush and covered with a luxuriant growth of grass." Although Leiberg did not realize that the tribes managed such parklands by regularly running ground fires through them, he did recognize the high quality in the yellow, coarse, resinous wood of mature trees. Because of the wide variety of habitats where the ponderosas thrived, he believed that they might be successfully transplanted east to the prairies of Montana and Dakota Territories, where their deep roots could withstand the constant wind.

The farther upstream Leiberg traveled, the wetter the conditions became. More species of conifers entered the forest mix. He maneuvered his horse through thickets of grand fir with branches as sharp as porcupine quills, and dismissed lodgepole pine with its unsightly black cones as having no value for fuel or timber. But he stepped back in awe of Douglas-firs whose trunks rose like magnificent pillars, estimating that no other tree could provide more board feet per acre of ground. He measured ancient cedar trunks at ten feet and more in diameter. After crossing a divide from the Clearwater north into the Coeur d'Alene Basin, he came upon western white pines growing straight and tall. On several slopes that had been wiped clean by recent fires, the white pine seeds had sprouted quickly, producing doghair stands that hampered his progress.

As he penetrated deeper into the Coeur d'Alenes, Leiberg navigated a series of steep ridges separated by deep ravines, where he was often astonished at the prodigious amount of deadfall timber. One morning he counted 135 fallen trees within fifty feet of his campsite. For hours the only sounds besides his ax were woodpeckers and carpenter ants working on snags. It was a relief to break into a clearing where life exploded with an abundance of grazing deer and fluttering birds. "In one part of the meadow huge snow drifts are rapidly disappearing under the influence of the hot sun," he observed with delight. "Gay flowers are blooming up to the very edge of the retreating drifts, while swarms of butterflies alight on the traveler."

Such poetic reveries were accompanied by cool assessments of the business at hand. He had traversed a region of complex geology with promising prospects for a variety of minerals, but the rugged terrain would make exploration and development doubly difficult. The recent strikes around Prichard Creek had produced some gold-bearing placers and quartz veins, but many of the hopeful men who had flocked to the area were either unable to find work in the existing camps or were unprepared for the realities of prospecting. "For a while every trail leading out from the mines was crowded with small squads of half-starved men eager to reach civilization and a 'square meal' once more," Leiberg wrote. He blamed their failure on wild hopes of acquiring sudden wealth, and he did not intend to join the ranks of those hard-luck cases.

After a train trip to North Dakota, Leiberg doubled back to Lewiston in time to make extensive plant collections around Lake Waha on the edge of the Nez Perce Indian Reservation. Ballhead waterleaf, orange globe mallow, giant blazing star, and two beautiful penstemons were among the dozens of wildflowers he pressed and mounted during the summer. Whether he engaged in any mineral prospecting is not known, but according to Godfrey and Cassiel Leiberg, there was another explanation for his presence in Lewiston that year. His sons later claimed that the family had moved to Idaho to escape the "seductive acts" practiced upon their father by a Minnesota woman.

Her name was Caroline Marvin, and she was more familiarly known as Carrie. A year older than John, she had been born to a deep-rooted Loyalist family from Quebec and New England. Her father, like many northern New England farmers of the time, had drifted west, and the family eventually settled in Blue Earth County, Minnesota. According to family lore, Caroline's girlhood ambition to be a physician was initially thwarted by a lack of funds, then revived by an older man's offer of education in exchange for marriage. Whatever the truth of this story, at the age of nineteen she did marry James Marvin, almost twenty years her senior. The 1880 census found the Marvins and a seven-year-old adopted son living in Blue Earth County; Carrie's occupation was listed as "keeping house."

That same year, she entered the Woman's Medical College of Chicago, one of the few American institutions where a woman could train to become an accredited physician.

Carrie's training included technical practice in surgery and histology, as well as obstetrics, gynecology, and diseases of children. The commencement address for the twenty-three members of her graduating class, delivered in March 1882 under cold and rainy skies, focused on the subject of cleanliness: "When the filthy hovels, the miserable dark and musty basements, with their foul back-yards, cease to be the habitations of human beings, there might be a decrease in both crime and disease." While sanitation was certainly one of the issues the newly minted doctors would have to confront in their careers, they also had learned to wield a scalpel and prepare a slide for microscopic examination.

At some point around 1882, Carrie Marvin encountered John Leiberg. At first they were friends, then lovers. Mattie Leiberg apparently learned of the affair and, in an attempt to protect their marriage, she and John moved to Idaho in late 1883 or 1884. Meanwhile, Carrie left her husband and adopted son and relocated to California. She received certification to practice medicine in that state, but her residence there was short-lived. Godfrey and Cassiel later declared that she pursued their father to Lewiston and persuaded him to abandon his family. There is no record of either John or Carrie's account of these events.

In May 1885, a census taker for the village of Alexandria in Douglas County, Minnesota, recorded the presence of John B. Leiberg and Carrie E. Leiberg, Wife. John must have still been working for the railroad, because he also appeared on a count the following month as a wheat inspector residing in a boarding house in Hillsboro, Traill County, Dakota Territory. That November, Carrie gave birth to a son named Bernard in Minnesota. Apparently she was still in touch with her estranged husband, for years later she would maintain that Bernard was James Marvin's son. But the infant was sickly, and Marvin did not want responsibility for his care. Instead, he promised Carrie that he would leave half of his estate to Bernard if she would raise the boy. This account raises the question of paternity: why would Marvin bequeath an inheritance unless he believed he was the child's father? Why would Carrie name the boy Bernard unless she was honoring the real dad? At any rate, Marvin initiated divorce proceedings shortly thereafter.

Meanwhile, in Nez Perce County in Idaho Territory, Mattie Leiberg had hired an attorney. In September and October 1885 the *Lewiston Teller* published a legal summons notifying John Leiberg that his wife was filing for divorce on the grounds of willful desertion. In December, after noting that John had failed to answer the summons, the district court decreed that the parties were freed from the bonds of matrimony and awarded Mattie sole charge and custody of their two children. She soon remarried a respectable rancher and remained in Lewiston with eight-year-old Godfrey and four-year-old Cassiel. By their account, they never saw their father again.

The following summer, John, Carrie, and the infant Bernard boarded a train in Minnesota and headed west, where John had determined to try his hand at prospecting. "Mining is an occupation that demands skill and knowledge of the highest order, also capital and patience," he had written at the close of his packhorse trip through northern Idaho. "With these requisites, success in this region is almost sure in the end." The sources of his skill and capital remain unknown, but he had seen promising outcrops during that 1884 trek, and the Panhandle held the additional lure of free land and sparse settlements. Surely this was a place where a couple with a smudged reputation could forge a new identity.

Leiberg's waterlily
Nymphaea leibergii

CHAPTER TWO

THE LAKE

▽▽▽▽▽▽▽▽▽▽▽▽▽▽▽▽▽▽▽▽▽▽▽▽▽▽▽▽▽▽▽▽▽▽▽

Heading northwest out of Montana, the Northern Pacific Railroad sweeps along the Clark Fork River. After that stream receives its sister Flathead at Camas Prairie, the tracks parallel the river's beautiful run across open rolling plains before cutting into the southern flank of the Cabinet Range to roll through a valley lined with ice-scarred Precambrian cliffs. As the river pours snowmelt from a considerable stretch of the northern Rockies into Lake Pend Oreille, the rail line arcs north to clear the braided delta, pressing against steep uplifts on the mountainside. A rocky point masks the lake for a couple of miles before water breaks into view again near the station town of Hope.

LAKE PEND OREILLE 1886 - 1888

Cabinet Mtns.

Sandpoint

Hope

Pend Oreille R.

Indian Meadows

Clark Fork Delta

Clark Fork R.

Northern Pacific Railroad

Green Monarch Ridge

Packsaddle Mtn.

Granite

Cape Horn

Leiberg Point

Lakeview

Athol

Limestone Quarries

Athol-Leiberg Tr.

Bernard Peak

Chilco

Chilco Saddle

Little

Rathdrum

Iron Gulch Cr.

Rathdrum Prairie

N. F. Coeur d'Alene R.

Cascade Cr.

0   5   10 MILES

(or) Traille River

Monument Mtn.
(Bare Knob Peak)

When the Leibergs made this journey in the early summer of 1886, the windows of their coach would have offered spectacular views beyond Hope as the tracks traced a semicircle around the northern shore of the lake. They crossed the Pack River's wetland on a long trestle, then bent southwest to the nascent town of Sandpoint. Another bridge over the lake's outlet at the Pend Oreille River continued the turn south, following the great tectonic cleft of the Purcell Trench from forest land into a pleasant grassland prairie where ranching and farming were beginning to take hold. The train rolled through whistle-stop stations at Granite, Athol, and Chilco on the way to the county seat of Rathdrum. With a population that had recently swelled to almost a thousand souls, this town was a mining hub that provided equipment and offered stagecoach service into the Coeur d'Alene ore districts. Only two seasons before, Wyatt Earp himself had disembarked there on his way to the gold fields to get in on the action.

By the time the Leibergs arrived on the scene, the gold properties that Earp purchased on the North Fork of the Coeur d'Alene River were petering out. But the previous fall a prospector named Noah Kellogg had stumbled upon rich galena ore on the South Fork, and now the lure of "white metals"—silver, lead, and zinc—was drawing people in droves to the Silver Valley. John Leiberg was painfully aware that he had missed a rare opportunity during his 1884 excursion: "When I first came to 'spy out the land' and determine the seat of my operations, the hoofs of my horses trod the veins, then unnoticed and unknown, in the South Fork of the Coeur d'Alene districts," he lamented. "Plenty of these claims are worth now from one to two millions of dollars each. I was 'green' in those days, and imagine my chagrin when now I contemplate these rich mines and reflect they might have been mine." Despite his regret at missing out on the silver boom, he felt certain that there were plenty of undiscovered riches in other parts of the Panhandle. But first he needed a home for his family.

He had already scouted a spot the previous summer on the southern shore of Lake Pend Oreille. A tidy bay there formed the setting for a port called Pen d'Oreille City, founded during the Fraser River gold craze of the 1860s. Supplies for that rush had been shipped via steamboat across the lake and north to the British Columbia strikes. Commerce had been slow since the Fraser fever cooled, but the president of the Northern Pacific still docked his personal steamer at the little-used landing.

Leiberg's choice for a homestead lay on a forked tongue of land that split the lake's southwestern tip. He estimated that the peninsula of glacial drift comprised about twelve hundred acres, fully half of it a natural parkland dotted with large ponderosa pine, Douglas-fir, and tamarack. Since no surveys had been made in the area, John knew he would be taking a chance to settle there—the railroad controlled every other section of land around the lake's south end, ceded by the government as an incentive for laying track. Anyone who built on one of the railroad's sections would have to purchase the property from the Northern Pacific at whatever price the company chose to ask. Despite that risk, he and Carrie began pouring sweat into the peninsula that would come to be designated Leiberg Point on early maps. They called a wall tent home while they built a small cabin, then John put up a barn and fenced a meadow to pasture the horses he needed for prospecting. At some point he added a hen house and a blacksmith and carpentry shop to the compound. They planted a garden and envisioned a fruit orchard on two promising terraces.

Lakeside Ranch, as the couple called their place, opened onto a vast expanse of water and mountains. At the lake's southern terminus, a dome that they named Bernard Peak loomed above them. The rugged cliffs of Green Monarch Ridge, sculpted by the Purcell Lobe of the last continental ice sheet, curved north to the Clark Fork Delta. The Leibergs could look east across a neck of water to Gold Creek and the tent city of Lakeview, where the first raw kilns of a cement business were being built to process native limestone deposits. The double horn of Packsaddle Mountain, a thousand feet taller than any near neighbor, stood behind the Green Monarch Ridge, and on clear days the Cabinet Mountains, whose peaks rose above seven thousand feet, were visible on the northern horizon.

Leiberg reveled in the singular wonders of Lake Pend Oreille. He declared that the climate was nearly perfect between May and October and that the temperatures remained mild most of the year. Calypso orchids and Idaho goldthread were abundant; mosquitoes were a rarity. In early winter, the snow often came down in flakes the width of a man's hand that locals called "sheepskins." It piled up to thirty inches and more beside the lake before thawing rapidly in the face of chinook winds. There were plenty of fish to be caught on an afternoon's rowboat excursion, and plenty of deer to fill the family larder. Their end of the lake had not yet been polluted by the "wreckage" of civilization: "You see I am not a lover of crowds, but rather a Thoreau in my love of solitude," he wrote. Like Thoreau, John had the ability to ignore some of the human reality around him. Directly across the narrow bay lay a winter village of Salish people who fished near his homestead and traveled the same trails he followed into the mountains.

With his family safely quartered at Lakeside, Leiberg was ready to seek his fortune. He had formed the Idaho Mining and Prospecting Company as an indication of his optimism, and in spring 1887 he set off in search of the ore veins that he felt certain would lead to success. His destination was an unmapped tributary of the North Fork of the Coeur d'Alene River that he called the Traille River, apparently in homage to the North Dakota county where he had served as a wheat inspector. This stream (now known as the Little North Fork) flowed from the ridges south of Bernard Peak through an isolated tight canyon for more than thirty miles. The outcrops Leiberg saw along its length seemed to hold the same kind of colorful, quartz-laden promise that had proofed out for big money farther downstream.

For years to come, Leiberg would lead a string of packhorses and a small crew up Lewellen Creek to Chilco Saddle, then drop into the Little North Fork, where his dream of monetary wealth lay in wait. On the steep climb to the divide, he often experienced a precipitous change in climate. "In 1887 on the first day of May, the snow on the Leiberg trail on the Chilco ranges was twenty-five feet in depth," he recalled. "It was so hard and compact that our horses with packs or riders scarcely made any impression." In time, his route over Chilco Saddle became so well known that as late as 1948 the "Leiberg-Athol Trail" still appeared on US Forest Service maps.

The establishment of a legal mining claim required a two-step process. The first involved marking boundaries on the ground with flags, distinctive landmarks, or actual stakes. After Leiberg "staked" a likely outcrop, he made his way to the Kootenai County Recorder's office in Rathdrum, where he described the perimeters in concise language:

> 8 July 1887 John B. Leiberg and Idaho Mining and Prospecting Company
> This claim is further described as follows:
> situated in Iron Gulch, a valley of the Traille River, one of the tributaries of the North Fork of the Coeur d'Alene River about fourteen miles southeast from Lake Pend Oreille and about eighteen miles east from Chilco station on the Northern Pacific Railroad.

During the next decade he would file a total of twenty-eight claims, some registered with Carrie or a couple of business partners. Like many prospectors, he anointed his sites with names pulled from whimsy or hope: Big Moccasin, Steadfast, Anniversary, and None Sutch Lodes; Bernard and Bernardino Lodes; even the Godfrey and Cassiel Lodes in acknowledgment of his two eldest sons. Most of these claims fanned across the remote small tributaries of the Little North Fork.

At that time, the only geographic reference line set by government survey in the region was the Boise Meridian, which followed longitude 116 degrees west, passing near the capital of Idaho Territory and running north to the forty-ninth parallel. The line lay just to the east of the Little

North Fork drainage, and although the marker blazes were not well maintained in the steep, densely forested terrain, Leiberg was adept at finding them. "Boise Meridian" often appeared as an indicator on his claims, along with place names that he bestowed on local landmarks. One of these was a mountain that he called Bare Knob Peak. If a person stands on Chilco Saddle today and points a spyglass south toward the main stem of the Coeur d'Alene River, the obvious candidate for that bare knob is a lumpy ridge marked on modern maps as Monument Mountain.

A few days spent creeping along muddy Forest Service roads or bushwhacking through John Leiberg's Iron Gulches, Flat Creeks, Bare Knob Peaks, and Cascade Canyons prove that he had a stout pair of legs and a very stubborn will. He and his associates were determined prospectors, humping through seriously steep terrain, winding back and forth to inspect every promising outcrop. "There are different ways to explore a country," John wrote. "There is as wide a difference between the way in which official explorations are carried on and the way a prospector examines a country as there is between night and day." He was obviously proud of the ground he covered during those heady years and the lessons he learned about the land. "A prospector's life is a dog's life but oh, the knowledge one gains of the mountains." His tenure is reflected in names that endure today: his Flat Creek, which he used several times as a claim site locator, appears on the current Coeur d'Alene National Forest map as Leiberg Creek, and it runs off Leiberg Ridge, just below Leiberg Peak.

From the time of his first recording in 1887, John remained wary of claim jumpers, periodically checking on all his registered sites to make sure they remained secure. One spring he snowshoed 130 miles carrying a ninety-pound pack on his inspection tour: "I was on foot, traveling through snow, deep forests over high ridges, along deep canyons with roaring streams far below me, working my way slowly along 70 and 80 degree hillsides covered with brush or jutting crags for miles."

The steep dark canyons harbored few flowering plants, and in any case, there was no room in his saddlebags for blotting papers or bulky specimens. But everywhere he looked—on the faces of rough cliffs, the trunks of trees, the crumbling bark of decaying logs, and the surfaces of streamside boulders—he saw mosses of every conceivable variety. More and more, he focused his attention on their luxuriant forms. "I cannot tell you of the dense and gloomy forests that cover this basin, nor of the *immense* accumulation of vegetable debris of all sorts that has been gathering for many centuries in these deep ravines. The rainfall and general atmospheric humidity are excessive. This basin is *the* place for mosses," he wrote. Luckily, damp mosses are easy to transport without damaging their essential parts, and whenever Leiberg went out, he hung stout hand-sewn canvas bags from his saddle and stuffed them full. "To examine these mountains thoroughly, whether it be for minerals or mosses, requires an accurate knowledge of mountain life and surroundings, an iron constitution to whatever the necessary exposure, and an unflinching determination and will," he declared.

Leiberg was sometimes frustrated by the sheer volume of the mosses crammed into his canvas bags. By the time he returned home he often had so many species that it was "well nigh impossible for any but a professional bryologist to arrange specimens true to name." He needed to send his collections to botanists for determination, to take advice on which specimens might be important. The closest post office was in Rathdrum, which meant a horse or wagon ride of over twenty miles, on roads so rough that his dried moss specimens were often pounded to dust. The Northern Pacific depot at Granite lay only seven miles away, but there was no postmaster there, so John talked freight conductors into dropping off and picking up his mail at the Granite station.

Waiting for the train to come in one day, he wandered to a pockmark pond near the Granite depot and spotted a prim little waterlily that he did not recognize. The plant's single white flowers, none more than an inch or two in breadth, graced the water's surface at the end of naked stems and bristled with dozens of bright yellow stamens. Each leaf rose from a stout rhizomal root to float alongside the flowers. John thought he might have stumbled upon an undescribed treasure, and soon found some expert advice to help him identify the plant. Dr. J. H. Sandberg was a fellow Swedish immigrant living in Minnesota, where he practiced medicine and avidly collected plants. The physician, whom John might have met at one of the Academy meetings in Minneapolis, traveled widely in search of new species. When Sandberg took the train west to Idaho in 1887, John showed him the waterlilies at the Granite pond. The pair then ventured into the mountains beyond Chilco Saddle, allowing Sandberg to return to Minnesota bearing a parsley-family specimen unknown to science but that soon carried the name of Sandberg's biscuitroot.

In their June 1888 issue, the editors of the Botanical Society of America's *Botanical Gazette* printed a letter from

Mr. John B. Leiberg postmarked "Camp Lakeside, at the south end of Lake Pend Oreille, North Idaho." John had been providing curious plants to the society for some time, and this letter announced that he was shipping seventy species of mosses that he had collected within two miles of his home. As spring ate the snow away, he intended to travel to the Traille River tributary in the Coeur d'Alene Basin, a moss paradise of "high peaks and deep, dark canyons and chasms, waterfalls, and cascades." He could not resist touting his virgin botanical territory: "While this is a difficult country, one at least has the satisfaction of knowing he is on ground on which *no one* has ever before collected."

The ebullient letter described several promising plant locations along the lake, beginning with a large silt bar at the delta of the Clark Fork River. In shallow water above the bar, he had watched green algae flourish in profusion. On a precipitous granite ledge south of there, he had found a tuft of one of his favorite mosses "fruiting abundantly!" In fact, that spring had brought a parade of unfamiliar species to the front faster than he could identify them.

The previous issue of the *Gazette* had announced that the white waterlily from the pond near Granite had been officially described as a new species, named Leiberg's pygmy waterlily. John expressed his gratification, then declared his amazement that such a distinct lily should have remained undiscovered by western botanists: the plant was abundant in the little pond where he collected it, surrounded by yellow pond-lilies and spatterdocks, and he believed that it must be widespread around the region. He signed off with the promise of more to come.

A few days after the publication of the *Botanical Gazette*, Leiberg received a letter from one of its subscribers: Elizabeth Knight Britton, a young bryologist who edited the *Torrey Botanical Club Bulletin* out of New York City— apparently the first woman in America to head an established scientific journal. As a girl, she had spent considerable time on her grandfather's sugar plantation in Cuba, where she became fluent in both the Spanish language and tropical flora, knowledge which led to dozens of collecting trips in the Caribbean and Latin America. She graduated from Hunter College at the age of seventeen, stayed on for a while to tutor natural science, then joined the Torrey Club in 1879, just as she turned twenty-one. Possessed of a strong personality as well as a formidable intellect, she excelled in her chosen field of mosses and liverworts. In 1885 she married Nathaniel Lord Britton, a Columbia College instructor of geology and paleobotany who shared her ardor for plants.

Mrs. Britton was well connected within botanical and scientific communities and was authoring articles on all manner of flowering and non-flowering plants at the time she wrote to John Leiberg in July 1888. She had read his letter with great interest and wanted to know if he would be willing to trade specimens of plants from the Idaho mountains for ones from her herbarium. She expressed a desire for one of his waterlilies, if possible, and was curious to know more about the flora of the region.

"Dear Madam," Leiberg replied. "I shall be very glad to furnish any plants I have from this region in exchange for others." Besides mosses, he was especially desirous of grasses, sedges, algae, liverworts, and lichens—tribes mostly ignored by the majority of amateur botanists. This eccentric list must have struck a chord with Britton, and they began a long and fruitful relationship. As she began to tease apart his Idaho mosses, John fired off effusive letters containing intense bursts of taxonomic information interspersed with bits of local news, personal revelations, and botanical questions. "Can you tell me where this species was first reported from this country and any localities where it is now found?" he asked about a flax he found growing at one of the nearby train depots. "At the station where I collected it the past two seasons, it grows but very sparingly and after next year will doubtless be destroyed entirely as the ground will be occupied by streets and buildings."

Britton responded in kind, often including magazine articles and small gifts for his family. She posted a portrait of the pioneering American botanist Asa Gray, who had only passed away the previous year; Leiberg was thrilled, having never seen the great man's likeness. When John wanted to send a living specimen of his eponymous waterlily to London's world-renowned Kew Gardens, Britton told him to route it through New York so she could hydrate the plant prior to its ocean voyage.

Within a few months of their initial contact, Britton made a pointed request. She found the moss specimens he sent most satisfactory and would like to see more. She also wanted the opportunity to make the determinations on (that is to say, to name) any new species and publish formal accounts of them. But first she needed to know exactly what kind of arrangement Leiberg had with Professor Charles Barnes, a University of Wisconsin professor who served as one of the editors of the *Botanical Gazette* and had published a manual of moss identification. Leiberg's friend Sandberg had sent some of the mosses they collected in Idaho to Barnes to identify, and when Barnes asked for more, Leiberg had supplied several dozen. Since almost a year had gone by with no reply, Leiberg assumed the professor was too busy to give attention to his latest shipments.

"I have made no promises to him or any other party of any sort," Leiberg responded to Britton. "Now, if you will agree to see that material from me is properly worked up within a reasonable time, I will promise to furnish it to you, exclusively, first of all and to no one else until you have had time to work it up." This was obviously agreeable to Britton, for packages of plants began to crowd mail cars traveling between Lake Pend Oreille and New York City.

In addition to the boxes of specimens, Leiberg averaged two or three letters each month, covering page after page in his serviceable script as he described the difficulties of plant hunting in northern Idaho. He had no library access, and only a single reference manual that was too large to carry while he slogged through the mountains searching for minerals. He had never used specimen labels as a way to order his meager collections but at some point in the future, after he achieved his dream of full-time botanical employment, he intended to print his own personal labels and collect full sets of Northwest plants. For the time being, he took great pleasure in sharing descriptions of his hunting grounds around the lake, including the imposing uplift of Green Monarch Ridge: "Along the face of this granite wall for a distance of four or five miles is the collecting ground par excellence for mosses and lichens of this region . . . I hardly ever row over to this locality but that I find some species new to me." Other intriguing habitats he had seen along the many miles of lake shoreline included a maze of abandoned channels within the Clark Fork Delta, where tens of thousands of captured logs lay festooned with tree mosses. He recounted his trips into the densely timbered forests, broken only by a mosaic of scars from wildfires that had roared up steep slopes and along ridges. He estimated that in time he would find up to five hundred different species of mosses within the emerald paradise. Today, a quick glance at the Panhandle National Forest's still-growing list reveals that his guess was not far off.

He also shared his struggles to identify the scores of specimens he was accumulating. Moss identification is an esoteric skill that requires learning a new vocabulary of anatomical parts that bear little similarity to those of familiar flowering plants. In addition, stems and leaves can be miniscule, and developing spores within a capsule require observation on the cellular level, especially in regards to the architecture of elements such as the peristome, a fringe of sixty-four teeth that cap the larger structure. John Leiberg, like some scientific Lemuel Gulliver, wrestled with very large subjects, such as evolution and geologic time, and with minute life forms that could only be viewed through a microscope. Through diligent practice, he taught himself to enter those tiny worlds, to notice subtle variations and often sublime beauty. He had long experience with magnifying lenses and a steady confidence in his ability; even though Elizabeth Britton was a renowned expert, he did not hesitate to spar with her over difficult details. At the same time, he absorbed her knowledge like a sponge and was fond of extrapolating the micro world of mosses into ecological lessons on a grand scale. "With every change in climatic conditions, some slight alteration takes place in the species of mosses," he postulated.

Most of his letters to Britton contained several mysterious new specimens, and he delighted in their difficulty: "The Moss Flora of the mountains of western North America is a delusion and a snare, a pitfall for the intellect of man to fall into, out of which it cannot emerge unscathed." He chose to compare himself to Don Quixote, saying that his pursuit amounted to "a fine field to break lances in—tilting at shadows."

This challenge served to stimulate Leiberg's busy mind as he fluctuated between frustration and triumph with each new subject he gathered. "How the mosses do come crowding in as my mental horizon and power of discrimination widens!" he told Britton. "Forms new to me on all sides every day." After wandering into a side canyon near the steamboat landing, he declared "I do not yet know the *ABC* of the moss flora of my immediate surroundings. Such a latitude of species and such vigor of growth my eyes never yet saw." To celebrate one New Year's Day, as he and Britton refined their ever-expanding list of northern Idaho collections, he addressed a poetic snippet to his teacher and muse: "May the mosses flourish in the coming season and may our list from this western country surge into rotund proportions."

Part of the botanical interest during this era involved developing facility with a microscope. The *Observer*, a popular natural history magazine, ran a regular column called "Practical Microscopy." Related articles with titles such as "Luminous Mosses" often accompanied the column, and Elizabeth Britton published a series of tutorials titled "How to Study the Mosses." These pieces were interwoven with advertisements for affordable mail-order microscopes teased with tag lines such as "The microscope is not a mere extension of a faculty—it is a new sense."

Leiberg possessed a compound microscope with a Crouch stand that held excellent definition up to a magnification power of five hundred. "Even with such modest equipment," he reflected, given "plenty of time at one's command, considerable work can be accomplished." His unassuming statement hid a secure belief in his own abilities. To keep mosses alive at home, he constructed an "air box" where specimens could thrive and produce the fruiting bodies often necessary for identification. For his dissecting scope, he pirated the lens from an old pair of field glasses, which provided the necessary flat field of vision under adequate magnification. For the stage beneath that lens he sawed a smooth pine board, solid enough to take constant cuts but easy to replace. He made delicate dissecting blades from fine tool steel so he could grind and temper them to his desired qualities. "You see," he explained to Britton, "when one does not have access very readily to the opticians' or instrument makers' shops, one has to rely upon one's own individual efforts or do without."

In addition to these acquired skills, John felt that he had been born with a distinct advantage. "I also enjoy a 'microscopic eye' that is due to an optical deformity, my left eye being extremely myopic while the right is normal," he wrote. "In proper light and the object not too transparent, I can often see pretty clearly things not above the 10,000 of an inch in size. It has been that way for years, and the deficit causing no inconvenience, I do not try to remedy it in any way. It has often been very useful as to enable me to see many objects totally invisible to normal eyes."

Finally, John Leiberg was a competitor. He seldom met a collector who could keep up with him in the field, and he bowed to no one when it came to knowledge of the Panhandle. When Elizabeth Britton proposed that he compare his annual moss list with that of British Columbia botanist John Macoun, a legend among his peers who had been sampling Rocky Mountain flora for many years, Leiberg did not flinch. "I should be glad to accept Mr. Macoun's challenge and march on to certain victory . . . He has the advantage of me in power of discrimination, but I undoubtedly possess more strength of leg and knowledge as to how to slip over the mountains and through the forests."

Leiberg knew that he was operating in a period of dynamic change in the study of botany in the Americas. For some decades, the long-lived Asa Gray had towered over the discipline, with his Harvard herbarium firmly established as the hub of American botany. As Gray faded from the scene, new centers of influence sprang up around the country. Elizabeth Britton and her husband played a seminal role in creating the keystone New York Botanical Garden. Each fresh institution held its own taxonomic principals, and each one wanted new and significant collections.

The plant world has always attracted enthusiastic amateurs, and along with John Leiberg there were other self-trained collectors supplying Pacific Northwest plants to university centers of learning. Thomas Jefferson Howell, based in Portland, William Cusick of northwestern Oregon's Wallowa Mountains, and Wilhelm Suksdorf, a German immigrant who had passed through Iowa on his way to the

Columbia Gorge, were all major talents who spent decades studying regional flora. Robert Statham Williams, who rode the Northern Pacific back and forth across the Rocky Mountains in Montana, was also interested in mosses, and also in touch with Elizabeth Britton. But the work of these collectors left plenty of room for Leiberg to make a name for himself in the slice of territory that stretched from Idaho's Salmon River north to British Columbia, across mountain and shrub-steppe habitats that spilled into Montana, Washington, and Oregon.

That vast area remained relatively untouched by collecting botanists, and Leiberg wanted to be the man who illuminated it. "I mean to work up a bigger list of species of mosses from the Western slope than any single collector has done heretofore." John's ultimate ambitions, in fact, reached much further than that. "I do not wish to be regarded as a mere 'herbarium maker,' for nothing is further than the truth," he confided to Britton. *"Between ourselves strictly,* I have a desire and have had it for years, to place my mark in some shape on some department of American botany that shall never be effaced."

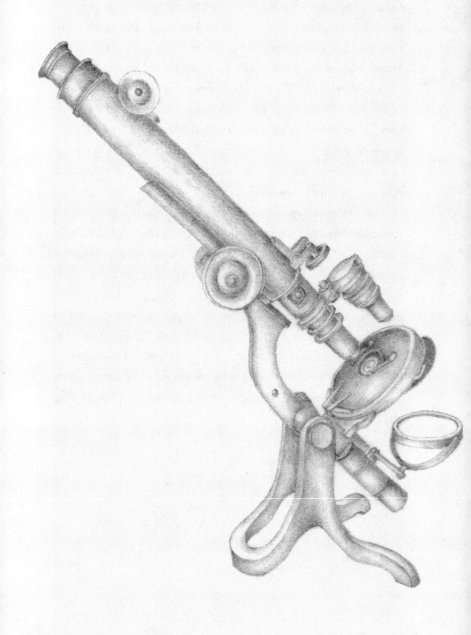

1880s microscope with Crouch stand

CHAPTER THREE

FAMILY PRACTICE

▽▽▽▽▽▽▽▽▽▽▽▽▽▽▽▽▽▽▽▽▽▽▽▽▽▽▽▽▽▽▽▽▽▽▽▽▽▽

John Leiberg was peering through his microscope at a curious moss he had found on the edge of an old beaver pond in early April 1889 when a package arrived from Elizabeth Britton, addressed to Carrie and containing not plants but a copy of *Harper's* magazine. The issue covered the inauguration of Benjamin Harrison, who the previous fall had defeated incumbent Grover Cleveland by winning the electoral vote even though he lost the popular count. For a politically divided nation, the result marked the second presidential split decision in a dozen years, and Carrie was eager to read opinions about the state of the union. "Many thanks for your thoughtfulness," she wrote

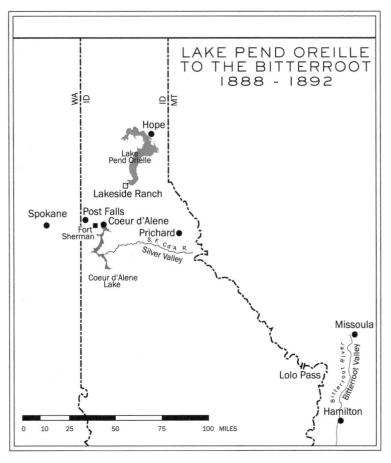

LAKE PEND OREILLE
TO THE BITTERROOT
1888 - 1892

Hope

Lake
Pend Orielle

Lakeside Ranch

Spokane
Post Falls
Coeur d'Alene
Fort
Sherman
Prichard
S. F. Cd'A. R.
Silver Valley

Coeur d'Alene
Lake

Missoula

Bitterroot River
Bitterroot Valley

Lolo Pass

Hamilton

0   10   25   50   75   100 MILES

to Britton. "We are so remote from civilization and its influences that an occasional glimpse of the world outside of these vast mountains is agreeable and interesting." Thus began an occasional exchange between two women on opposite sides of the continent, and it is through Carrie's surviving correspondence that a more complete portrait of Leiberg family life emerges.

In one spring letter, Carrie mentioned that the first buttercups of the season had just sprung up, and she was pleased to discover that little Bernard remembered the

name of the flower and could point out its petals and stamens. John undoubtedly took part in this teaching, perhaps
to compensate for the disdain his parents had shown toward
his own youthful interest in plants. "I only hope my boy will
take to botanical studies as I have tried to do," he wrote. "If
so, he shall have all the material and moral aid and support
I can give."

John's own botanical studies were flowering that spring
as well. "An Enumeration of Mosses Collected by Mr. John
B. Leiberg, in Kootenai County, Idaho" appeared in the April
edition of the *Bulletin of the Torrey Botanical Club* and covered no less than ninety-three different species that he and
Elizabeth Britton had identified. Dr. Barnes of Wisconsin,
who had been sitting on several of the same specimens for
almost two years, was not happy that Britton had published
their descriptions ahead of him. John thought it all petty
jealousy and suggested that Britton pay no attention to the
criticism—he considered her a more careful and painstaking
botanist, and intended to stay the course. "I enclose a characteristic letter from Dr. Barnes," he wrote to his bruised
friend. "Please read and consign it to the wastebasket . . .
When Dr. Barnes endeavors to pour out his vials of spite on
me, he is simply wasting time, ink, and paper."

As the snow began to recede from the foothills, Carrie
was wishing for a change of scenery, so John placed her on a
horse with three-year-old Bernard, whom they called Pixie,
and took them on "a picnic trip into the mountains . . . no
mosquitoes and an abundance of 'aqua purex' and a thousand and one interesting sights." Back at Lakeside, his
thoughts returned to mining. He mailed a box of ore samples
to Elizabeth Britton with a request that she pass them along

to Dr. J. S. Newberry, Professor of Geology and Paleontology at Columbia and an accomplished field geologist who had worked in eastern Oregon. John had shown the unusual samples to several local assayers, but their knowledge did not extend beyond the common run of gold, silver, lead, and copper, and he hoped that Newberry would be able to analyze them further. "The vein they came from carries cobalt and bismuth with other minerals," John wrote. "There is also evidence of the presence of some other mineral which I have tried in vain to have determined out here." The identity of that mystery element would give him a clue about whether the outcrop merited further investigation.

As his understanding of the geology of the Little North Fork deepened, John believed that the 1889 mining season would reveal the true worth of his holdings. For the past three years he and his crew, "by large expeditions and a great amount of work," had thoroughly explored the fifty-mile length of the drainage. They had cut many miles of trails to access their target outcrops, and the previous fall they had sunk a fifty-foot shaft on one promising claim: "I discovered the key to the distribution of the metalliferous veins in the basin, and since then you may be sure I have turned that key assiduously and turned it hard, until now I own miles of great metallic veins." The trick, as he well knew, was that "there is a vast difference between paying mines and the ownership of great veins." He would have to prove their value himself, with pick and drill and dynamite. He spent that late spring and summer staking more claims in an area with an abundant growth of ceanothus, whose intertwined branches possessed "the power in abundance of inflicting the most exquisite torture imaginable" upon anyone traveling the ridges. At the end of July he apologized to Britton for his neglect of the mosses: "You see we are turning the 'Wheel of Dame Fortune' with all our might. We *think* we are sure to draw the lucky number, which would mean abundance of time and unlimited means for prosecuting botanical studies, but as yet we don't *know* with certainty. Mining is like a game in which Mother Nature is the opponent and she does hide her cards effectively." He felt certain that his efforts would eventually pay off, but that success, when it arrived, would have come at a personal price: "All the money, be it ever so much, that they will produce can never repay me for the pain of being separated from my companion," he confessed.

John's hopes were cut short when the basin began to roil with more smoke than he had ever seen. He retreated to the Lakeside cabin, but 1889 turned out to be a historic fire year. In early August he wrote that flames were raging in the mountains all around the lake. "A London fog is as nothing compared with the dense cloud of smoke that envelopes us and makes existence almost unendurable," he complained. "No rain is due in this latitude for six weeks or more, so we have to suffer a while longer with red eyes, depressed spirits, etc.," a sentiment with which anyone who has lived in the American West could nod in sympathy. He cursed the careless prospectors and timber men who had started most of the blazes, and he fretted about the destruction: "It will be many years before the mountains at this end of the lake will regain the mossy carpet that covered them a few weeks before."

Although the Leibergs' ranch was never threatened, that tinder-dry summer did put pioneer homes and towns constructed of wooden buildings at terrible risk. On August 4, a fire raged through the city of Spokane, destroying most of its core. The following week, Leiberg took the short train ride west to view the smoldering ruins of the "great conflagration," and it wasn't until a full month later that he could set aside the charred images and return to his usual cheer: "Three days of rain has put out the forest fires, cleared the air from smoke, and made Lakeside look like itself again—the most beautiful spot on Earth I ever saw."

Far from forgetting about the fires, Leiberg kept track of the lessons they could teach. At the height of the ensuing winter, a series of killer avalanches buried two Silver Valley mining settlements. "They are now reaping what they have been sowing for many years," he told Britton, referring to the wanton destruction of the forests with fire and ax during the last decade. The summer fires had exacerbated the devastation, "until now but small patches of wretched lonely-looking trees remain. So comes the avalanche and the landslide and a whole long train of ills." He recognized the essential role of trees and herbage in preventing slides and controlling runoff, and he encouraged his fellow prospectors on the Little North Fork to work together to manage the forest wisely. The mountains around that basin had steeper slopes and received heavier snowfall than those of the Coeur d'Alene's South Fork but remained slide-free for years. John credited that stability to his campaign against unnecessary tree cutting and wasteful fires and felt that it proved a few hard-working men could still accomplish some good. When he visited the Little North Fork the next spring, he found that although wildfires had run through the area, the overall damage to the forest was not extreme, and the soil remained healthy.

Perhaps Elizabeth Britton meant to lift Carrie's spirits during the anxious smoke-filled weeks by offering to send her a portrait of John James Audubon. As a champion of some of the early conservation movements in the United States, Britton supported the newly formed Audubon Society's campaign against killing long-legged wading birds for decorative hat plumes and was apparently trying to recruit a new member. John replied that his wife was not especially interested in ornithology, but she did believe that all life was sacred and would only kill animals in self-defense or for study: "Least of all would she indulge in the foolish habit of using for personal adornment the wings of slaughtered birds." He reckoned that made Carrie a member of the Audubon Society in sentiment, if not in fact.

Dr. Leiberg had more pressing concerns than hat feathers that fall. Bernard turned four years old in November, and she was ready to return to work. She had filed her medical school graduation certificate with the Kootenai County Recorder in Rathdrum, which allowed her to practice medicine in Idaho Territory. Late in 1889, Carrie opened an office in Post Falls, a growing town eight miles south of Rathdrum on the Spokane River that was close to Fort Sherman, where a military family that the Leibergs had known in Minnesota was posted. Winter's onset found her and Bernard boarding in town. "The dear little chick is sound asleep now, one little fat hand tossed over his head, the other tightly clasping an impromptu rag doll, made out of a towel, but which is very dear to his heart nevertheless," she wrote one evening.

John, meanwhile, had headed south to look at a mining property near Baker City, Oregon. While the gold claim in the Powder River Mountains did not work out, he did get his first look at the snow-capped Wallowas, as well as some spectacular country for dryland plants. By the turn of the year 1890, he was back at the Lakeside Ranch, and Carrie wrote that she was sad that he would have to spend so much of the winter alone there. She worried that he didn't have enough to occupy his time until the flowers began to reappear with spring, and mused to Britton that permanent names should not be bestowed on people until maturity, because then her husband would surely not be saddled with such a plodding name as "John." She thought her husband the noblest, truest, most manly man she ever knew. "Every year I love him better, and more appreciate his worth," she confided. She ached for his unfulfilled ambition, stranded in the wild with no one to talk to who could understand his dedication.

"You are right about it being lonesome here sometimes," John admitted in his own missive to Britton. He felt compelled to stay on the ranch until the land was surveyed and they could obtain a legal title. "No one can tell when somebody may come along and finding the place unoccupied simply 'squat' on it. Therefore we never stay away very long at a time," he explained. For diversions he read botanical journals, worked on his plant specimens, and snowshoed to bare stony ridges where he thought he might be able to find some interesting mosses. But he missed his wife dreadfully; she was "a perfect helpmate if God ever made one, a most charming and lovable woman." Expressing his appreciation in blushingly romantic terms, he praised Carrie's mind and heart, her broad and liberal views, and her noble character. His world, he wrote, was "but as dust and ashes compared to the happiness of her companionship."

One stormy February evening, Carrie and Bernard huddled in Post Falls while John tended the ranch. As strong gusts lashed rain against the windows, Carrie sat awake, worrying about a case of peripheral peritonitis that had kept her up for two nights running. "It is a terrible thing to see a little brood of children which a few hours may find motherless," she wrote. "Even the best of physicians are so powerless! It is no wonder that one with either knowledge or conscience dreads the responsibility." She slept better than expected that night and awoke to find the sun shining brightly. "My spirits always rise with the barometer," she reported. They rose higher when she found that her peritonitis patient had survived the night. The doctor gave her charge a fair prospect of recovery but couldn't quite shake her blues of the previous evening. "The study of medicine is grand," she wrote, "but the practice is so full of responsibility and labor that it is very, very hard. I shall be glad when our ship comes in so I can retire from the field."

On a happier note, Carrie reported that Bernard was delighted with a book of photoengravings that Britton had kindly included in a recent package of new moss slides. Carrie, who had studied histology in college, was impressed with the careful preparation of the slides, and knew that John would soon be eagerly poring over them. "I watch him, sometimes, as he sits for hours at the microscope," she wrote, "and a great motherly sort of pity fills my heart for him, trying to master the difficulties without a soul to help him, or even necessary books. He would make such a grand man if he had a chance."

Carrie wished for a day when they would be free from money concerns so that John could devote himself entirely to plants. He believed that his good judgment, hard work, and geological knowledge would prevail, unlike prospectors who took their inspiration from a whiskey bottle. Carrie, on the other hand, felt that luck played an outsized role. "It is a fact that by far the great majority of rich and important discoveries in the West have been made by riffraff and the outscourings of the Earth," John observed. "Mrs. Leiberg says that's because the majority of prospectors are composed of that class of men, and I presume she is right."

In early March 1890, buttercups were again bringing a hint of spring when Bernard came down with a rash that Carrie diagnosed as scarlet fever. Knowing how quickly the disease could spread, she decided to quarantine herself and her son. She knew of an old shanty about a mile outside the village of Post Falls and sent workmen to line its walls with thick paper to keep out the wind, then had them deliver a cot, stove, and chair. She borrowed a farm sled, bundled Bernard in blankets, and drove him quickly to the makeshift infirmary with no ill effects. "It was *very* desolate there I assure you," she wrote. "All alone, with a sick child, so far from anyone. A chore boy from the hotel brought food once a day." The source of the disease, according to John, was "one of those foolish and careless persons who seem to delight in constituting themselves traveling centers of infection. A bag of buttons used as a plaything by a child that died from the disease, then brought five hundred miles or more and given to Bernard to play with."

While the notion of germs lurking in a velvet bag has been disproved by modern science, in Carrie's time it still held sway. Fortunately, Bernard's attack turned out to be a mild one, and as soon as Carrie deemed him no longer contagious, she moved him to more comfortable quarters with her friends at Fort Sherman. There he continued to recover, though there was still the danger of sequelae—the secondary effects known to haunt scarletina patients with symptoms that ranged from irritating sores to dangerous rheumatic fever.

By the end of March they were able to return to Post Falls, where Carrie found a note from Elizabeth Britton expressing her sympathy for little Bernard's illness. "Somehow your letters always give me a sense of friendliness and womanliness which is very agreeable," Carrie replied. "I should like so much to know you, and hope that some time our little paths may cross." For the time being, though, she was back to her "daily routine of work, and worry, and heart hunger for husband and home." Changing the subject, she asked if her friend could spare a picture of herself. Britton had mentioned that she was buying a Zeiss camera for her work, and Carrie was interested in the recent advances in photography. As technology began to make the transition from glass plates to film, the first handheld cameras were becoming popular, and Carrie was thinking of getting an amateur outfit of her own. "If I do, my friends will be flooded with 'views.' May I include you in my list of victims?"

When Britton requested a photograph of John for her botanical club, he complied with characteristic flourish. "Herewith I send you a likeness of the prison house in which we travaileth these six and thirty years," he wrote in an accompanying letter. "I am not very fond of having my photograph taken. It was done at the request of Mrs. Leiberg at a time when strolling along Coeur d'Alene Lake we happened to meet a photographer." The full-length portrait was taken in front of a painted studio backdrop. In the foreground a stoutly built, obviously fit fellow props one leg on a flimsy rail fence. He wears a suit complete with vest and watch chain, a white shirt buttoned up to the neck, and a narrow-brimmed fedora. Dark hair sprigs out from beneath the hat to complement a healthy mustache. Leiberg's right hand grips a short walking stick firmly, and his dark eyes stare out with stark intensity. In the photograph John looks very much the same as he sounds in his letters, like someone on a mission.

No comparable portrait of Carrie has ever come to light, but a grand-niece recalled her aunt as an imposing, tall woman with a fine figure and very erect posture. "Stern" was a word that came to mind. Carrie never smiled and always wore black, yet somehow related a sense of warmth, and the young niece felt certain that her aunt enjoyed her company.

John's letters of 1890 displayed ever more fervor for plants, for prose, for mining, and for money. He hoped that Elizabeth Britton would find his collections much superior to those of past years because she had taught him so much about technique. He began to accumulate lichens alongside the mosses, as many as his canvas bags would hold. He rhapsodized about meandering all day in search of new plants, "stretching out on the ground or rocks among them, watching a single form for many hours, noting its peculiarities and variations." He wore practical clothing so that he could "creep through the mazes of the forests or roll among the rocks with freedom and ease and impunity." And he loved to go botanizing in the rain, when "the mosses, lichens, etc. stand forth in all their beauty and vigor . . . That is the way to study botany and to obtain the knowledge that books, always imbued with the idiosyncrasies of its authors, never can give."

Leiberg's letters of that particular summer were riddled with literary allusions. He compared the back canyons of the Little North Fork with Dante's *Inferno* and "all the elementals of Rosicrucian lore." He called out Jupiter Pluvius for sending down endless rain. The situation was always highly dramatic, as when he retold the story of Noah Kellog's initial Silver Valley strike: "Fact: the discovery of the real nature of these veins was made by a genuine long-eared donkey." John invariably returned to the subject of his own luck: "Success in our game with Fortune here means millions, defeat means nothing. We don't know yet who will win. . . . Great sums of money, the most debasing thing this world holds, are necessary, and we do our level best to bend things to our will."

Leiberg's level best meant that by July he was camped in a rough ravine forty miles south of his home, where he directed a crew of men punching an adit into his most promising claim, a lode named for little Bernard. "Everything is wild, lonely, and the stillness of death pervades everything," he wrote. "Crossing this canyon runs a mighty quartz vein, everywhere splotched and dotted with masses of the yellow sulfuret of copper and beautifully mottled and streaked with the green and blue carbonates and red and black oxides of this metal."

Leiberg's quartz claims of that season trace to Cascade Creek, a feeder stream that rushes through a tight canyon not far above its junction with the Little North Fork of the Coeur d'Alene. The place still has a wild feel—many parts of the Little North Fork retain that sense because of the steep metamorphic landscape, despite well over a century's worth of prospecting and logging—and the outcrops that line the ravine still contain equally wild variations of color and crystalline form. For years, in fact, the Panhandle National Forests employed a land manager whose job was dedicated to mitigating abandoned mining claims. Today, most of them have been incorporated back into the forest, and their remnants of digging, blasting, sluicing, and hauling have quietly settled into the duff of open woods. Many former tailings piles, including some on Cascade and Leiberg Creeks, now support a rich variety of wildflowers, and the timbered beams of several collapsed adits have melted into shaded mossy hillsides.

During periods when he was not working the Bernard Lode, Leiberg devoted himself to his moss collections. He continued to trade numbers and traits with Britton as they inched toward a supplemental list of northern Idaho mosses to complement their 1889 publication. "I spend every moment of my time when at home sorting, noting, drawing—and they simply drive me wild sometimes . . . but you can be perfectly sure that every point I receive from you in botanical matters is treasured and appreciated," he told her.

His summer work was interrupted when Carrie fell dangerously ill, and following her recovery, she decided not to return to Post Falls. She celebrated the new year of 1891 by again requesting a photograph from Elizabeth Britton. "I should so much like to have it," she explained, "to help me imagine what you are like." At medical school, she had measured bumps and protrusions with outsized calipers according to the discipline of phrenology, which at that time had plenty of professional supporters. Carrie had come to see the practice as "the veriest trash," but she still believed that a person's appearance offered clues to their character. In lieu of an actual visit, a photograph might help.

Britton asked about their mail service, and Carrie described their seven-mile row to a new post office at the settlement of Lakeview, where the limestone business was flourishing. If she was staying at their Lakeside Ranch alone, she usually waited for a neighbor to bring the letters across every ten days or so, because even though she had biceps as strong as any average man, the wind and waves on Lake Pend Oreille could make for a harrowing journey. Now that her husband had returned from his mining camp, they would pick it up on a more regular schedule—"he is so large, so strong, so vigorous, that he makes the boat dance through the water lively."

Britton had expressed her desire to send Bernard a holiday gift of Grimm's fairy tales or a writing slate, but Carrie regretted to tell her that the boy's whole soul was wrapped up in engines, railroad cars, and steamboats. He entertained himself by emptying the wood box to build train tracks and shuffling chairs for boxcars. "He is alternately brakeman, engineer, steam valve, and whistle, and the racket he keeps up is astonishing and half maddening," she wrote. It is hard to tell whether Carrie was speaking affectionately or out of exasperation, since at that moment her six-hundred-square-foot log house harbored John's complete herbarium, laboratory, and office as well as Bernard's railroad station. She suggested that Britton send dominoes instead of a book, because at least the boy could line those up like a train. His vitality amused his mother, for she had worried that he might retain his temperament from infancy. When he was little, she explained, he had such a sour disposition that his Irish nurse had called him Pickles, but he had cheered up considerably since then.

Soon after the turn of the year 1891, John and Carrie decided to rent a cottage in Hope so that Bernard could go to school there. Since the Northern Pacific had elevated Hope to the status of division point three years before, the town was beginning to prosper. In addition to a school, a fine new hotel lured train travelers and tourists. Carrie restarted her medical practice there while John continued work on forging his future in the mining realm. A steamboat ran to the south end of the lake, making it convenient for him to reach the ranch and outfit himself for the mountains. As with so many prospectors, he remained certain that a rich strike was imminent, and that the coming season would be the one that made all their toil worthwhile.

It was not to be. By mid-season, John realized that a great deal of digging remained before he could determine the true worth of the Bernard Lode. He took some small solace in a notification from the secretary of the Torrey Botanical Club that he had been elected as a corresponding member of the society. "Have no doubt this is due to your kind office," he told Elizabeth Britton. "Many thanks."

As his mining projects ground slowly on, John began fishing for botanical employment. He declared he would go anywhere in the world but was particularly interested in the tropics. "Of late our looks and aspirations are turned southward, even so far as Guiana or Brazil," he wrote. "We both dislike snow and cold exceedingly, and always enjoy better health and enjoy life better in the real hot days of summer." Most of all, he looked forward to wrestling with tropical flora. Carrie suffered from sea sickness, but what was a little discomfort for true explorers? It would be a while they were ready to depart, for he still had mining operations to tend to.

As John and his crew returned to Cascade Canyon, serious labor troubles were erupting just over the next ridge in the underground mines of the Silver Valley. Organizers formed a workers' union that summer, and a contentious strike followed. When the companies brought in scab replacements, violence broke out at the Bunker Hill Mine, one of the major silver producers of the region. Those actions led to a lockout, federal troops, more violence, and a flurry of court decisions that generated political and economic upheaval across the Intermountain West for years to come. Leiberg may have been thinking of this turmoil when he wrote to Britton that October with an update on his personal progress. He had men under contract to probe Cascade Canyon until the spring of 1892. As long as his enterprise remained on tenterhooks, he would make weekly trips along his trail to keep track of his laborers and lurking claim jumpers.

Meanwhile, Carrie had begun to pursue an ambitious project of her own. "At present Mrs. L is in Spokane Falls, prospecting places for the establishment there of a

Maternity Hospital and Training School for Nurses," John wrote to Britton in October. "There is not in the whole of Idaho or in Eastern Washington an institution of the kind, and there is a great need of it." In fact, two local hospitals were beginning to direct more attention to women's health issues around Spokane. Over that winter of 1891 to 1892, one of them opened a school for nurses staffed by two women from the Chicago Training School, and a maternity hospital was in the works.

During her research, Carrie would have met Dr. Mary Latham, who had gained a medical degree in Cincinnati at age forty-two and moved to Spokane to start a practice in 1887. Latham's husband, Edward, also a physician, chose to remain behind for some years, so Mary made her own way, working out of her home at first. She soon developed a strong following among both women and men, and when the August fire of 1889 incinerated the downtown Spokane building that held her office, she forever endeared herself to the city by opening a makeshift dispensary with the pledge to treat any fire victim who could not afford care free of charge. At the time when Carrie was making inquiries about a maternity hospital, Dr. Latham served as the obstetrics specialist for an institute based on a faddish blood health theory known as "biochemics" while continuing to maintain a private office at the Blalock Building in downtown Spokane. Early in 1892, as Latham was lauded for her work with the downtrodden in a local magazine, Carrie Leiberg rented space in the same building, apparently dividing her time between Spokane and Hope.

In late spring 1892, John Sandberg, the Minnesota physician whom John Leiberg had taken for a mountain excursion five years previously, revisited Lake Pend Oreille while working as a field agent for the US Department of Agriculture. He and two assistants, including a young New Yorker named Amos Heller, were bound on a plant collecting expedition, cruising territory that Leiberg knew well: west on the Northern Pacific line through Montana and down the Clark Fork to Hope, then south to Lewiston and the Nez Perce country.

John was miffed that Sandberg had not invited him to join the expedition, especially since he had the home base, the horses, and the local knowledge to be of great service. It was obvious that if he wished to work as a field botanist, there were government protocols to learn and personal connections to make. There were financial considerations as well: he still had a crew to pay, and in order to take part in a collecting trip, he would have to hire a straw boss to oversee his operations at a cost of ninety dollars a month. Sandberg's assistants, he learned, were making a hundred dollars per month plus expenses, and John decided he could accept that. "It would have squared the financial matter very nicely and given me a summer's work *wholly* in botany, in which my soul delights," he told Britton.

Leiberg did rendezvous with Sandberg's survey team when they returned to Lake Pend Oreille some weeks later. Over a three-day period, he piloted the party to the top of Packsaddle Mountain, the landmark peak that rose above Green Monarch Ridge. During that venture, he was impressed with Heller. "I consider him to be a close, careful, and painstaking collector, and a good companion in botanical excursions." On the way up Packsaddle, John showed the young assistant a bittercress that Amos Heller later described as a new species named *Cardamine leibergii.*

That fall, Elizabeth Britton informed John that, having published a detailed addendum to their original Kootenai County moss list, she no longer had time to identify bryophytes for him. While the pair continued to correspond sporadically over the next two decades, Leiberg would miss their animated discussions: "Your correspondence and knowledge so freely imparted to me at all times have proved of extreme value to me and make me all the more conscious of the loss I will sustain in being deprived of your counsel and learning," he wrote to her that fall.

John's letter was postmarked from Hamilton, Montana, a town at the southern end of the Bitterroot Valley that had been booming since a railroad spur line connected it to Missoula five years before. He found himself in a bustling center of ponderosa pine sawmills, with spring log drives on all the major creeks and draft teams pulling tremendous loads into the yards. From the streets of Hamilton he could gaze up at some of the West's most spectacular scenery—east to the main range of the Rockies, west to the enormous crags and precipices of the Bitterroot Mountains. His presence there involved a bit of intrigue. Another transcontinental railroad was headed west, and the company had hired Leiberg to explore some of the ranges for a practical passage. *"This is confidential,"* he emphasized to Britton. The thing he enjoyed most about his new job was the opportunity to see fresh mountain scenery. He remarked that it hadn't taken long for him to appreciate the travails that Lewis and Clark had experienced during their slog over Lolo Pass, and he quickly recognized the richness of the Bitterroot and Clearwater drainages in the realm of flowering plants. In the end nothing came of the proposed railway route, but he hoped that at some point he might put his alpine experience to use.

The previous summer, Dr. Sandberg had advised Leiberg to write to the assistant botanist at the US Department of Agriculture if he was interested in working on government field surveys. Two days after Christmas, Leiberg mailed a letter that would steer his livelihood into botanical pursuits. "What are the probable chances of going as collector for the [department] this coming summer?" he asked the assistant botanist, adding that he was willing to lead a party, take on the task by himself, or be attached to an expedition. In any case, his knowledge of the western mountains would prove most useful to the department. A postscript listed his references: "Mrs. E. G. Britton, Columbia College, would gladly speak in my favor. So would Dr. J. H. Sandberg."

Washington Jacob's-ladder
Polymonium pectinatum

CHAPTER FOUR

CROSSING THE COLUMBIA PLATEAU

▽▽▽▽▽▽▽▽▽▽▽▽▽▽▽▽▽▽▽▽▽▽▽▽▽▽▽▽▽▽▽▽▽▽

W hen one looks over towards these immense mountain fastnesses that fill such a large portion of
Idaho and which have never been explored botanically, it makes me wild with desire to penetrate them and
reap the harvests that undoubtedly lie in there," Leiberg
wrote in February 1893. As he sat in Hamilton, dreaming
of alpine plants, Carrie was completing a winter visit to
Chicago, where she split her time between the Woman's
Medical College and the Chicago Polyclinic. "Anatomy and
surgery are her delights," John explained. Both institutions
were at the forefront of recent medical advances, including the shift from home to hospital birthing. At that time,

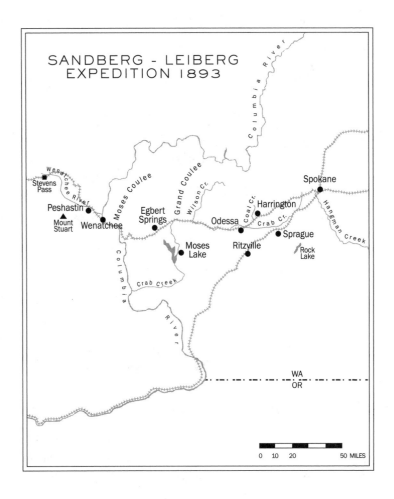

SANDBERG - LEIBERG
EXPEDITION 1893

Columbia River

Stevens Pass

Wenatchee River

Peshastin

Mount Stuart

Wenatchee

Moses Coulee

Grand Coulee

Wilson Cr.

Egbert Springs

Columbia River

Crab Creek

Moses Lake

Odessa

Coal Cr.

Crab Cr.

Harrington

Ritzville

Sprague

Rock Lake

Spokane

Hangman Creek

WA
OR

0   10   20   50 MILES

the Polyclinic was one of only four hospitals in the city that offered "lying-in" facilities, so it would have provided a perfect learning ground for Dr. Leiberg's idea of starting a maternity hospital in Spokane. But her timing was unfortunate. By the time she and John were reunited in Hope in March, the economic crisis known as the Panic of 1893 was brewing. One of the catalysts was overproduction by western silver mines, especially in Idaho's Silver Valley.

The price of silver fell, and by the spring of 1893, the Bunker Hill Corporation, along with several other large operations located on the Coeur d'Alene River's South Fork, was deeply in debt. The Sherman Silver Purchase Act of 1890 had been intended to offset that glut by requiring the US Treasury to purchase a certain amount of silver, using notes backed by either silver or gold. But when speculators began demanding gold in exchange for their silver notes, the Treasury Reserve reached its limit for the minimum amount of gold. In order to support the traditional gold standard, the government was forced to borrow tens of millions of dollars' worth of bullion from J. P. Morgan and the Rothschild banking family of England. This angered members of the Populist Party, many of whose most ardent supporters were western miners and farmers from the Midwest and South. The inauguration of Grover Cleveland, a big-business Democrat who promised to repeal the Silver Act, only added to the sense of panic.

As the limit of silver-for-gold exchanges was reached, demand for silver notes fell precipitously. When the price of that commodity plummeted, it began to erode the bond market. Bank failures followed, then four major railroads, including the Northern Pacific, went into receivership. National unemployment headed for 20 percent, with much higher rates in the mid-Atlantic and Great Lakes states.

Such uncertainty would have discouraged Carrie's plans for building a maternity hospital, and with silver prices at an all-time low, John's mineral prospects didn't look any better. He had given up hope that the USDA would sponsor his proposed expedition and was thinking of mounting his own trek into the Bitterroots when an unexpected letter arrived in mid-April. Frederick Coville, newly appointed as chief of the USDA's Botany Division, was proposing that Leiberg join Dr. Sandberg on a botanical survey of the Great Columbia Plain (also referred to as the Columbia Plateau or the Columbia Basin) from Spokane to the eastern slope of the Cascades. Along the way, the team would determine the eastern and western boundaries of the treeless area inside the Columbia's Big Bend. To cap off the trek, they would attempt to summit one or two of the volcanic peaks in the central Cascades. Although this was not quite the excursion that Leiberg had envisioned, he quickly accepted the assignment from the new chief botanist.

Twenty-six-year-old Frederick Coville had spent most of his young career at the department herbarium in Washington, DC, but he was not lacking in field experience. Two years previously, he had participated in a rigorous collecting trip to Death Valley, then authored a full report on its flora. A mountain climber at heart, he yearned to scale some of the Cascade volcanoes himself. Coville's interest in subjects as diverse as the commercial potential of wild blueberries and the ethnobotany of western aboriginal peoples mirrored Leiberg's own eccentric concerns, and over the next two decades the pair would share each other's obsessions with good cheer as they exchanged many dozens of letters.

John Leiberg was forty years old when he received his first official plant-hunting commission, and he could hardly wait to get started. He recommended to Coville that they begin the survey as soon as possible; as someone who tracked the weather in that part of the world, he knew that spring rains came and went quickly, as did some of the most interesting plants. If they did not start before June, they would miss an entire blooming cycle. The chief botanist complied with his new employee's advice and moved the starting date two weeks earlier, instructing Leiberg to proceed to Spokane and find Dr. Sandberg, "under whose direction you will work until further orders."

On May 10 Leiberg met Sandberg in Spokane, which had rebounded from the disastrous 1889 fire thanks to its status as a rail center that supplied materials across the breadth of the Interior. Here they rented a wagon and purchased provisions, then rumbled a mile down the Spokane River to the mouth of Hangman (also called Latah) Creek, where whole acres were clothed with sky-blue silky lupines. Leiberg remarked on the vegetable plots and fruit orchards along lower Hangman Creek that supplied the city's markets. Thick riparian growth followed the stream course, with ponderosa pine mixed among the more expected willow, aspen, and cottonwood. Those pines continued upslope as an open scattered forest, and Leiberg assumed from seeing several abandoned sawmills that somewhat denser stands had existed before the city rose. A variety of native bunchgrass species thrived beneath the remaining trees.

On May 15 the men pitched their first base camp six miles up Hangman Creek from its confluence with the Spokane River. The site lay at the foot of a long curving section of bluffs that had been created by the region's extensive Ice Age floods. In his field notes, Leiberg noted the stratified gravel of multiple water events and pondered their origin. He also stepped back to an earlier geologic epoch, scouting Miocene basalt outcrops and visualizing the way hot oozing lava had "overflowed" the visible layers of clay.

John had been correct in his itchiness to get started and found spring's herbaceous vegetation already well advanced.

Even so, the flora still offered plenty of variety. The first day, he collected a lovely blue clematis and saw golden currant blooming along the stream banks. All the familiar constituents of a healthy ponderosa pine regime, including innumerable clumps of arrowleaf balsamroot, top-heavy whorls of largeflower triteleia, and a variety of showy penstemons, appeared on his list. "Many species appear to be very localized, and a short excursion in any direction from camp is sure to be rewarded by new plants," he remarked. Over the first week, they collected three hundred or more specimens every day, until a lingering spell of rain forced them inside their wall tent to dry dozens of damp blotter papers in front of the fire—"very slow and tedious work."

Dr. Sandberg was lame in one leg, and the pair quickly fell into a division of labor: the doctor spent most of his time in camp sorting and pressing specimens while his energetic junior partner did most of the fieldwork. It was Leiberg who tended the horses and wagon that hauled their gear as they trudged from Spokane to the Cascade Divide. It was Leiberg who tabulated the numbered collection list and, most importantly, kept a field journal detailing their daily progress. "This work made an extraordinarily 'busy man' of me for four months," he wrote. "It is a fact that my time was so fully occupied that only but barely could I snatch a few minutes to write to my wife."

After taking the measure of lower Hangman Creek, Leiberg rode eight miles southwest to the resort town of Medical Lake. He described the basalt and granite setting of an extensive marshy basin and noted that all the water, including the flow from farmers' outhouses, seeped directly into the central lake. He felt that the entire network held the same solution of salts that were "extolled for their cura-tive properties" in Medical Lake proper. He also found a mix of invasive weeds creeping along the edges of every field and marshland nearby. Several of the aliens on his list, includ-ing dandelion and woolly mullein, remain on the scene today, joined by successive waves of new invaders such as knapweed and rush skeletonweed.

Near the end of May, the men rolled twenty-seven miles southwest to establish a second campsite beyond Medical Lake. Along the way, Leiberg delineated an ancient lava sheet pocked with numerous lakes and ponds that would help determine the eastern limits of the Great Columbia Plain. Rounded hills composed of the rich wind-blown volca-nic soils now called *loess* made for rich hay and pastureland. Settlers had blasted ditches to keep water flowing through Ice Age flood channels, and their recently erected barbed wire fences had greatly restricted some excellent grazing ground composed of bunchgrasses and sedges.

Following the lay of the land, the expedition's wagon rattled across the rocky lithosols that locals called "scab-lands" long before geologists used the term to describe how large tracts of soil had been stripped away by the ancient floods. John would trace a rift in the lava as it expanded into a shoestring lake, remarking on the way terraces sloped down to the water's edge in some places while ver-tical cliffs rose a hundred feet in others. The cliff basalts had cooled from oozing lava into hexagonal columns, and loosely eroded talus accumulated as rubble up to a quarter of their total height. He quickly identified talus as the place to find the good plants. Like many Columbia Plateau explor-ers, Leiberg lost himself in the luxurious vegetation until he tread across a southern exposure that served as a winter den, or hibernaculum, for large concentrations of snakes. Now those serpents were coming awake with the warmth of spring. When John found himself faceup with a slowly gliding rattlesnake, his startled stone throw was answered by the rattles of a hundred others from the loose blocks of rock, and the Sandberg-Leiberg Expedition beat a hasty retreat.

Rock Lake, fifteen miles east of their camp, was worth a special collecting trip. In places, the layered basalt walls rose 250 feet above the water, hiding sparse stands of Douglas-fir in the shade of the upper terraces. At a prosperous farm in the bottomlands along the lake's east shore, a rancher stirred Leiberg's prospecting blood by showing him an outcrop cut though with uniform quartz veins. The rain that had slowed their progress on Hangman Creek continued to pour down, and as springs and creeks began to spill their banks, wagon travel became more and more difficult. Yet between Rock Lake and the shallow ponds of the scablands, the collectors picked up thirty-five new species for their presses, including a yellow lady's slipper orchid that still peeks up occasionally in the same vicinity today. On the other end of the spectrum, John noted that some alkaline ponds were fringed with dwarf hesperochiron in such abundance that they whitened the ground like a recent snowfall.

When the men moved camp again, Leiberg gained his first view of the open treeless plain that was their goal. The new ground was spotted with well-spaced sagebrush and antelope bitterbrush, and basalt escarpments were frequently exposed in the depressions between gently rolling hills. Wherever he encountered deep enough soil, he met settlers trying to raise crops of dryland wheat. They told him that the flow of water through the basalt fractures was so unpredictable that no one even tried to irrigate except for small garden patches. Although droughts did occur, most years saw enough precipitation to make a harvest.

It was early June when Leiberg and Sandberg pitched their tent a couple of miles east of the railroad town of Sprague. John quickly recognized carved water features all around him, which today are known as the result of those same Ice Age floods. Depressions in the lava flows, breeched basalt dikes, and island-like mesas left standing high above the hollows gave evidence of powerful erosive action. Dozens of water-rounded boulders lay strewn over the hillsides and the plains. Some settlers had created fertile ground by draining the shallow ponds and wet meadows, but Leiberg noted that crops planted in such depressions seemed vulnerable to frost damage. In order to feed their cattle and horses, many farmers were cutting wheat straw before the grain matured or scything the coarse sedges and rushes that fringed the ponds for hay; John thought they would do better to introduce cultivated grasses such as timothy.

Ten miles southwest of Sprague, he observed bands of rusty-red calcareous tufa capping the basalt flows and wondered if it might be reduced to valuable iron ore. He theorized that this mineral might be responsible for the alkalinity of the soil and water. Mixed currants and willows formed dense thickets around ponds where the soil was not too alkaline, but wherever a white salty crust prevailed, veiny peppergrass and white cryptantha dominated other species. Each lithosol seemed to contain its own floral mix, with some species completely absent for miles at a time. One plant that thrived on the craggiest of scablands was bitterroot, now at the peak of its flowering season: "The bare basaltic rocks that support nothing else are now gorgeously red and pink with masses of the handsome and showy flowers of this species."

From their Sprague camp, John made a couple of supply runs southwest to the town of Ritzville. These yielded more wildflower pleasures, including the Washington Jacob's-ladder, common then but very restricted now, plus fameflower and deerhorn clarkia. In this area, standing water dwindled away, and any seeps or wet depressions served as cattle wallows. On one of his Ritzville excursions, Leiberg collected the first known specimen of cheatgrass found south of British Columbia—an ominous initial record of the invasive grass that has become the symbol of noxious weeds and wildfire fuel across the arid West. In conversing with the few farmers who had cleared the shrub-steppe for cropland, John found that dry summer winds tended to kill all but the hardiest grains. Even in this unusually wet year, he judged their fields of rye to be in only fair condition. He saw numerous abandoned homesteads and marveled at how quickly a low complex of shrubs reclaimed possession of idle ground. These species were well adapted, he reasoned, to both the arid climate and to the particular fertility of the soil.

On June 12, the expedition lumbered almost thirty miles north to camp near the wheat-farming town of Harrington. This track took them through the upper Crab Creek drainage, where they found the greater portion of the upcountry under successful cultivation. At the crossing of Crab Creek's main branch, they saw their first "tree claim," where some enterprising soul had planted box elders for lumber and fuel. Most of the plantings had grown vigorously for a foot or two, then died back. In addition to that discouraging vista, Leiberg also reported that the untilled portion of the country around the tree claim was covered with introduced grasses. He and Sandberg devoted much time at their camp near Harrington to drying blotters and cataloging plants, then desperately hanging onto their tent poles in the face of intense rain and gale-force winds. Leiberg imagined the poles snapping loose and several thousand drying papers flapping away with the wind, but they managed to keep the wall tent upright. The two men packed a box of their gleanings, addressed it to Frederick Coville at the USDA, and shipped it from the Harrington post office on a chilly mid-June afternoon.

As they rolled west through Coal Creek Coulee, they passed newly cultivated ground enclosed by stout barbed wire fences. Local farmers told them that this was shaping up to be the best year they had seen in a while, but Leiberg worried that the fine ashy loam in which those crops were growing would be baked hard by the hot dry winds of high summer. What those settlers needed, he thought, was a cultivated grass that formed a turf rather than the scattered native bunchgrasses that dominated the landscapes they had seen so far. The route through Coal Creek Coulee to its junction with Crab Creek, at the present-day town of Odessa, led them through sagebrush steppe broken by white-crusted alkaline flats that bristled with greasewood, shadscale, and the brilliant red-orange glow of globe mallow. Instead of trying to grow grain on the coulee slopes, the settlers hugged the valley of Crab Creek. Thirsty cows tended to remain close to the creek, resulting in some severe overgrazing.

The men made only one brief camp before reaching the settlement of Wilson Creek. The flora in this vicinity contained many unfamiliar species, and John wandered farther and farther afield as he added to his collections. One day he followed a route twenty miles west-northwest to the astonishing alkaline lakes of lower Grand Coulee, including Soap Lake and Lake Lenore. He covered seven journal pages in an attempt to describe the "mass of shifting sand" that swallowed Coulee Creek (now covered by Billy Clapp Lake). All of the features he had previously seen paled before the massive ravine of lower Grand Coulee. Its perpendicular walls made access to the benches above Lake Lenore's west side nearly impossible, and the bedded dip of those terraces revealed basalt layers of 150 feet and more as they angled down to the opal-blue waters of Soap Lake.

John soon discovered that those stunning waters were not so easy on the tongue: "The first sensation is a salty taste followed closely by a soapy one, as though it were a dose of concentrated lye." Although in need of refreshment after a hard day on the trail, neither of his horses would drink, so he decided to remain through the afternoon to watch how local livestock handled the situation. Toward evening, several groups of horses ambled down the coulee and spread out on the fine gravel beach, about fifty feet away from the lake's edge. There they pawed down two feet and more to reach the water table. After a patient wait, they sipped the liquid that filtered into their hoof-scraped pools. When Leiberg tried this method himself, he found the accumulated water to be free of the salty-soapy taste but still extremely bitter. One of his horses drank freely from the puddle without any ill effects; the other flatly refused. He took a different route back to the camp on Wilson Creek and was rewarded when the trail led him up to rolling heights. "From the hills around the lake fine views of the Cascades were had of their summits about 120 miles away," he wrote. "Long ridges broken now and again by steep snow-crowned peaks."

Upon their arrival at Wilson Creek, Sandberg and Leiberg had catalogued around 240 different plant species; before they departed on July 1, they had added nearly a hundred more to their list. Among them were weeds as familiar as dalmatian toadflax, which farmers still grind their teeth about today, and natives as shadowy as coyote tobacco, an important cultural plant that remains elusive across the Columbia Plateau. Leiberg also recorded numerous "'kitchen middens' with all the old litter usually accompanying them," including ancient artifacts. Around many of these archaeological sites, he noted that a white sand verbena flourished, "which seemed to have been introduced by ancient dwellers purposely or spread from their old camping grounds."

The men next moved their wagon fifteen miles west, camping on the bed of a dry lake where they again dug through the gravel to obtain brackish drinking water. They spent only one night there before heading for the well-known oasis of Egbert Springs (present-day Ephrata) at the base of the Beezley Hills. "The grass on these hills is the best and most abundant we have as yet seen along our route," Leiberg wrote, a fact well known by cattlemen since the 1850s.

Their route crossed Crab Creek once again. After having flowed underground for a dozen miles, the stream magically reappeared at this point, more than two feet deep and almost twenty feet wide. As the reborn creek bent south toward Moses Lake, the landscape changed dramatically. "Crossing the creek, we emerged on a plain covered with boulder drift," Leiberg observed. "The boulders of very large dimensions and the drift composed of basalt and granite. This drift sheet has a northerly and southerly trend, and where we cross it is about four miles in width. It appears to have come directly through the great fissure in which lies the alkali lake previously noticed in trip of June 26." The "great fissure" was Grand Coulee, and Leiberg was describing the end result of Ice Age flood events. "The plain over which we were traveling abounded in long, low ridges, all forming part of some great stream which once flowed here from north to south," he penned in his journal.

Today geologists call this feature the Ephrata Fan, a massive flood bar created between twenty and fourteen thousand years ago. During several different episodes, the advancing Okanogan Lobe of the Cordilleran ice sheet rerouted the Columbia River east through Grand Coulee, creating a channel that was further scoured by outbreaks from Glacial Lake Missoula hundreds of miles to the east. As floodwaters and debris-laden ice chunks tore through the confines of lower Grand Coulee to reach more open country around Soap Lake and Ephrata, untold tons of boulders, rocks, gravel, and sand that had been carried downstream dropped according to weight and flow speed. "The vegetation among these masses of boulder and gravel drift was so far as the eye could reach west and south nothing but big sage-brush," Leiberg wrote. "Scarcely a tuft of grass anywhere."

John observed that the flood droppings decreased in size to smaller boulders, then rocks, then gravels, and finally the extensive dune system that circled Moses Lake. He recognized that the lake had no visible outlet; rather, its south end was closed by miles of drifting sand dunes. Local settlers told him that the old outlet had been filled long ago, and two miles of lakeshore had disappeared beneath an advancing sea of sand within their memory. John estimated the height of some advancing dunes at seventy-five feet and noted how the ragged front edge settled into regular swells and troughs, trending northwest to southeast. This sea of blowing sand is today mostly drowned beneath the waters of Potholes Reservoir, but its memory lives on in oral histories that describe how active dunes occasionally dammed or released the lake in different places.

From Egbert Springs, Sandberg and Leiberg pointed their wagon west, making for the Columbia Valley. It would be their first look at the big river's main stem, and they worked across a level plain with fertile soil that was covered with big sagebrush—some of the most promising farmland they had seen since they set out, lacking only water to be productive. A large quantity had been purchased by a Seattle company that proposed to plant fruit trees and vineyards, then irrigate them "by way of the ancient channel of the Grand Coulee . . . taking water from some point north on the Columbia River. Surveys have been made but the result is unknown." It took another half century to set these grand schemes in motion, but the company's original plan of replacing the Columbia Plateau's shrub-steppe with orchards and vineyards has been progressing relentlessly ever since.

The wagon trail descended from Babcock Bench via a steep winding ravine to touch the Columbia at Crescent Bar.

From there the team proceeded upstream to pitch camp at Rock Island. The river remained high with late-season run-off, tearing past the basaltic island at seven miles an hour. From their camp, Leiberg made collecting forays into Moses Coulee, where he clambered up steep basalt walls to watch thunderheads build over the high Cascades.

Taking advantage of the readily available water from a growing system of irrigation ditches, the slopes between Rock Island and Wenatchee were already well cultivated in an array of soft fruits and a few small grain fields. Farmers informed John that vineyards and the business of wine-making were on the rise. Beneath the cloak of new vegetation, Leiberg recognized that the uplifts beyond the Columbia's west bank marked the beginning of the Cascade foothills. Although the slopes remained nearly bare of timber until higher elevations, changes in the flora indicated increased precipitation. He and Sandberg boxed their latest collections, posted them East, and moved up the Wenatchee River past more fruit trees and laboriously dug sluiceways. July's heat had baked the green from the native flora above those watered fields, but scattered ponderosa pine graced the sagebrush slopes. They watched farmers scythe the stalks of robust balsamroot to supplement their grass hay. After traveling through Columbia Basin basalts for the whole journey, the rocks beneath the men's feet had shifted to a granitic conglomerate.

Near the town of Peshastin, as the valley began to narrow and its cultivated area dwindled, the first western redcedar appeared along the river, and Douglas-fir began to fill tight draws. The men continued upstream past Leavenworth through Tumwater Canyon, where the Wenatchee River breaks through a granite gorge as "a succession of long cataracts tumbling over roaring masses of foaming water . . . with towering masses of rocks and vast chasms and precipices." John took a side trip to ascend Icicle Creek and collect on the slopes of Mount Stuart, reaching forests of Pacific silver and subalpine firs at an elevation of seven thousand feet. Leiberg, who loved nothing more than to run a long mountain ridge, found the high country to be surprisingly dry and the timber surprisingly small—due, he thought, to frequent fires that had swept through the area. He still managed to find Tweedy's lewisia and snow douglasia, a pair of small but beautiful alpine genera first collected by Meriwether Lewis and David Douglas, two pioneering naturalists whose legacy he was determined to expand.

At the end of July, he and Sandberg pushed over thirty miles along the route of today's Chumstick Highway, passing Lake Wenatchee to a camp on Nason Creek, just below Stevens Pass. Along the way, Leiberg saw the first timber that really impressed him—a mix of pines and firs that were large in size and clear of lower branches. Settlements were already established on several spots along Lake Wenatchee's shoreline, and above them he could see that the ridge summits and large portions of the slopes "had been repeatedly savaged by the common curse of . . . forest fires, and were therefore quite bare of timber." He was convinced that the majority of these blazes were either intentionally set by prospectors as a way to expose outcrops or accidentally touched off by passing trains and careless farmers. Although the weather was clear, fires at lower elevations made for hazy viewing. The scene reminded him of the senseless damage he had witnessed in North Idaho.

John had already designated three distinct floral regions across the Columbia Plateau. Now he began to delineate forest zones according to elevation, noting distinct changes that culminated in the high country in a mix of subalpine fir, dense thickets of rhododendron, and scattered whitebark pine. Above the tree line, he reveled in open meadows of fescue spotted liberally with spring wildflowers. Many of these bloomed right up to the edges of frozen snowbanks that on north slopes still measured more than a dozen feet deep.

August was well along when Sandberg and Leiberg established their westernmost camp on Stevens Pass, at an elevation of nearly four thousand feet. They slept adjacent to the tracks where the Great Northern line crossed the divide via a very long and tortuous switchback. Leiberg combed the forests of Pacific silver fir to find the first mountain hemlock and Alaska yellow cedar of the trip. He was in the process of sorting out the variety of huckleberries within the understory when the weather socked them in, precipitating one of his few low entries: "We are immersed in mud and everything, no matter how well covered, is damp . . . Investigations are unable to lighten the gloom of the camp. Mosquitoes and gnats hover around us in myriads and help make life a burden . . . on the whole a dismal day."

John's mood lifted when he began to ponder why his horses did not take to the abundant fescue grass in the high meadows. As he talked to passersby, he learned that this curious circumstance was known to everyone who traveled in the high Cascades: "their horses starve to death on this species of grass." He never mentioned how he kept his horses healthy, but he did return to his work with gusto, noting signs of past glaciers around their camp in the form of small cirques and obvious moraine lines. When the skies finally cleared to reveal the mass of Glacier Peak, standing tall among numerous unnamed mountains in the range, he gauged its distance to be about thirty-five miles. "The peak presents the common view of so many of the extinct volcanoes in the Cascades, a truncated cone."

Following Coville's instructions to attempt to scale one of the volcanoes, Leiberg ascended to a prominent ridge and wandered through a world of alpine lakes for two nights of rough camping. He found the peaks that loomed more than two thousand feet above him to consist of rounded granite masses, "often exceedingly precipitous, and in the main, very difficult to explore." In search of something more approachable, he returned to the town of Peshastin to take a second shot at Mount Stuart. His first attempt, made on the way upstream five weeks earlier, had been thwarted by heavy snow. This time he tried a route up from Icicle Creek, but again turned back in the face of unpassable precipices. Probably with the help of a local guide, he skirted the base of the mountain for eight miles east, then caught a steep spur that led directly to the central peak. After camping at a good watering hole only 1,300 feet below the mountaintop, he was able to spend much of August 29 collecting on and around the summit.

Leiberg's journal entry describing this excursion has come under some question because of the steep terrain. The first ascent of Mount Stuart is an honor generally ceded to US Geological Survey field-worker Sam Gannett, who left a cairn at the summit in 1895. Although several faces of the peak offer technical challenges for mountain climbers today, Gannet wrote that his survey party followed a main ridge up the southeast side, exactly as Leiberg described in his day-book. With local knowledge or assistance, the climb would have been a feat of stamina rather than mountaineering.

Beyond that consideration, Leiberg was interested in plants, not routes or first ascents. He was chasing mountain-top species and declared himself mightily disappointed to find that Mount Stuart's highest slopes had been recently burned over. Even worse, they were not at all alpine in their character—he had seen much more snow above Stevens Pass at half the elevation. He placed the blame on Stuart's position in the Wenatchee Range, east of the Cascade crest and thus too close to the heated air of the Columbia Plateau. Even so, he collected a rich flora on his way down the mountain, plants that thrived in extensive meadows not yet altered by livestock or agriculture. He also noted a number of serpentine dykes that traversed these slopes from north to south and displayed a flora very different from the more familiar granites of the Wenatchee Range.

When Sandberg and Leiberg returned to their Peshastin camp, they were nearing the end of their contract and decided it was time to wrap things up. They tended to their most recent collections and shipped specimens to Coville before breaking camp. Sandberg boarded a train bound for Minneapolis, while Leiberg made one final weather report for September 2, in which he found the sky clear and the wind southerly. He then closed his field journal and steered his brace of horses and battered wagon east toward Lake Pend Oreille.

As far as Coville and the USDA were concerned, the 1893 expedition demonstrated that John Leiberg had combined his prospecting experience from Idaho with botanical rigor to develop a procedure that worked in the Intermountain West. He minded the task at hand, wrangled his own horses, followed instructions with a practical flexibility, adhered to the intended schedule, and kept a close eye on his overall costs. Leiberg also pushed beyond his basic instructions, probing the geology for its mineral potential and assessing timber stands with a logger's eye. He chatted with local farmers and stockmen, listening as they described soil conditions, moisture, and crop yields. He studied the development of dryland and mountain flora not only in terms of a given season, but also from the viewpoint of plant associations and their evolution in relation to climate and geology. He documented the ways in which overgrazing and weeds were conspicuously altering the plant communities of the Plateau and foresaw the ramifications of careless human-caused fires along the east slope of the Cascades.

Ecologist Richard Mack has pointed out that the plant hunters who preceded the Sandberg-Leiberg Expedition—from Meriwether Lewis and David Douglas to Johnson and Brackenridge of the Wilkes Expedition, from the German wanderer Charles Geyer to American railroad surveyors Cooper and Suckley, and forward to Leiberg's late-nineteenth-century contemporaries William Cusick and Wilhelm Suksdorf—either skirted the edge of the Columbia Plateau or produced little beyond a diary of the plants seen each day. The deeper ecological story of this shrub-steppe arena begins, belatedly, with John Leiberg's account of his summer journey with Dr. Sandberg. Leiberg was not trained in any specific field, and his theories could leap from spot-on to shaky within the space of a sentence. Yet he understood the deep underlying connections in the landscape, noting that "geological considerations and deductions are not to be ignored in determining the causes that govern plant distribution and growth." The breadth of his curiosity provided a starting point not only for more than a decade of his own government surveys, but also for the more comprehensive geographical investigations of the twentieth century.

Railroad handcart ca. 1890

CHAPTER FIVE

TRACKS

▽▽▽▽▽▽▽▽▽▽▽▽▽▽▽▽▽▽▽▽▽▽▽▽▽▽▽▽▽▽▽▽▽▽▽▽

W hen Leiberg arrived back in Hope in mid-September, Carrie thought her husband looked quite thin and haggard, but while John may have been physically tired, the rigors of his summer expedition had only stimulated his indefatigable mind. As soon as he could sit down at his desk, he began planning a series of colored charts to illustrate the summer's data on geology, topography, climate, distribution and range of flora, and agricultural factors. His wide-ranging scientific aspirations were reflected in articles about plants and mosses that he had published in botanical journals for over a decade. In fact, a short piece illuminating aspects of ninebark flowers had just appeared that summer.

Those ambitions took a leap forward with the arrival of the September 22 issue of *Science* magazine. As the official publication of the American Association for the Advancement of Science, the weekly stood as one of the most respected scientific journals on the scene, and this particular number contained a one-page article titled "Petrographs at Lake Pend d'Oreille, Idaho" by John B. Leiberg. (The term petrograph is an outdated synonym for petroglyph.) A central illustration credited to the author showed an array of bear paw prints mingled with geometric forms and cryptic animal shapes.

The article began with a few general observations that revealed Leiberg's ignorance of the local Salish culture. He quickly found firmer footing when he read the clues left by slow-growing rock lichens on undisturbed cairns to establish that people had been living in the vicinity and making petroglyphs for countless generations. The outcrop under discussion, located on the north shore of Lake Pend Oreille, consisted of bedded schist with a dramatic dip of about eighty-five degrees, "broken apart and stood upright by the wear of the lake in former ages." When Leiberg tried to mark on it himself, he found the hard stone extremely difficult to peck, even with the tempered steel chisels that he used at his quartz claims.

The figures incised on the panel occupied a space almost twenty feet long and more than six feet high in places. John counted twenty-eight images that he thought represented bear paws, although he noted a variety of styles and different numbers of toes on the feet. Three figures looked to him like cougar tracks, and one animal shape seemed to be a mountain goat. He counted one arrowhead, several small round holes centered within distinct circles, and two more abstract designs. Nearly all of the images were thickly overgrown with close-clinging rock lichens, which made them easy to overlook except when cast in favorable sunlight.

The petroglyphs consisted of deep, wide grooves engraved into the rock. The sides of the grooves were so smooth and free of chips that Leiberg felt certain they must have been cut by friction rather than rough chiseling. He speculated that a bow drill fed with sharp sand and steadily doused with water could have created the round holes. In the same manner, a person working sand and water with a piece of shaped wood might wear regular grooves into the surface, but it would have required diligent labor. The author hoped that readers of *Science* more familiar with this subject than he would weigh in with their knowledge both about the methods of carving and the meaning of the figures.

The bear paw petroglyphs that so intrigued Leiberg were located along the edge of a long narrow grassland that lay across the railroad tracks from Hope. Locals called the area Indian Meadows because for as long as anyone could remember, a wide mix of tribes, especially the Interior Salish-speaking groups known as Kalispel or Pend Oreille, had camped there in late summer and early fall. The annual encampment continued to take place for all the years that the Leibergs lived in Idaho. From Indian Meadows, families went out to gather tule rushes for mats and Indian hemp for cordage. They caught whitefish and bull trout for food, and ascended into the mountains to hunt deer and gather huckleberries. They then returned to the meadows to dry meat, fish, and hides on racks outside their lodges. Some of these people had left their marks on nearby outcrops. John found additional troves of rock images nearby; some were hidden beneath a mass of humus in the forest, and he thought he might be able to use botanical clues to determine their age. These finds were dwarfed by the slab containing the remarkable bear paws, which remains the largest known group of figures on the lake. Leiberg's *Science* article was the first published description of this significant cultural feature.

In 1898 Carrie Leiberg brought her camera to the Indian Meadows encampment, where she took several photographs of lodges, drying racks, horse-drawn buggies, children running along worn-down trails, girls on horses, and family groups. Kalispel historians have identified individuals in the shots and matched oral accounts with the pictures. Botanists have studied the riparian habitat that fringed the meadow. Depression-era aerial photos set side by side with Carrie's work provide perspective on the relation of the encampment to seasonal water levels around the Clark Fork Delta.

The annual tribal gathering continued for another six decades, until the Albeni Falls Dam raised the level of Lake Pend Oreille by several feet, flooding Indian Meadows and drowning petroglyphs on nearby islands and rocky points. The bear paw panel described by John Leiberg remained dry. As managers of the dam, the Army Corps of Engineers assumed responsibility for cultural sites along the perimeter of Lake Pend Oreille. With tribal assistance, they catalogued numerous sites in the 1980s and since then have worked with the Kalispel people to protect the images. One concern was the possible effect of rock-loving lichens (the same ones noted by Leiberg a century earlier) and whether they might "eat" into the stone and gradually erase the grooves that formed the bear paw shapes. A committee of Kalispels, botanists, and geochemists ultimately recommended that the best course of action would be to leave both the lichens and the petroglyphs alone.

In the fall of 1893, within a few days of his return from the Columbia Basin, Leiberg headed to Lakeside Ranch, where he repacked his kit for a ride across Chilco Saddle to examine his mineral claims on the Little North Fork. Carrie and Bernard remained in Hope, where they rode out the first big storm of the season. "The lake roars like the very ocean, and gusts of wind and rain dash against our little cottage," Carrie wrote as she watched her son curled up in an armchair before the fire, munching a cookie and telling her of some wonderful things he was going to do when he was a man. Instead of his dreams uplifting Carrie, she found it "sad that we always live in the future and never learn to be happy in today."

She was about to call it a night when a loud knock sounded on the door. She opened it to find a streaming-wet man holding a lantern. "He said his wife had been in labor for three days, and they thought she was dying, and wanted me to come right away. I was soon ready and out in the fierce storm." Although Carrie did not mention it, the Leibergs obviously had made some provision for Bernard's care so she could get away at times like this. At the Hope railroad station, she and the frantic husband hopped onto a handcar and pumped ten miles up the track to a small hut. Inside, Carrie found an exhausted woman surrounded by several hungry children. The situation was indeed dire, and the doctor had to attempt a high forceps delivery: the baby was wedged above the birth canal, which required the longest instrument in her bag. The procedure culminated in the delivery of a deformed, stillborn child.

Carrie tended to the unfortunate woman until her condition stabilized around noon the next day. Then she and the patient's husband pumped ten more rainy miles back to Hope on the handcar. At home, she changed into dry clothes and made herself a cup of tea. She had been finishing a letter when the knock had come on her door the previous evening, and now she poured out her feelings in a postscript. "I think none but a physician can realize so keenly the folly, weakness, and utter contemptibility of the great majority of the human race," she told Britton. "If one could but reform the world and take from it a portion of its *needless* misery!"

In mid-October, freshly returned from the Little North Fork, Leiberg pounded away on a typewriter that he had recently acquired. He informed Frederick Coville that he was making steady progress on the plant catalog and general report of his summer expedition and hoped to soon forward them to the Department of Agriculture. That optimism evaporated a few weeks later when he received a letter from Minnesota indicating that Dr. Sandberg intended to write the final report himself. To that end, he requested the plant list and field notes that Leiberg had compiled. John bristled at this development, for he had understood that he would be the one to author that document.

Leiberg was still unsettled when he relayed this news to Frederick Coville, noting that it was Sandberg's privilege as expedition leader to render such a report. But Leiberg made it clear that he wanted credit for his extensive work. The draft he had already forwarded to the department included a great deal of information based on his own experience and research, and he wanted to make sure that "other parties" did not coopt his data. Coville must have agreed, because he never hired Sandberg for any more field assignments, and the department never published Sandberg's report.

Leiberg, meanwhile, used a new burst of enthusiasm to compose a proposal for an ambitious plant survey, one that promised to achieve "more thorough and closer work in the field and greater results generally than have yet been reached in any previous expedition of this sort into the Northwest." With John Leiberg, as Carrie said, the best was always yet to come.

His eight-page proposal outlined a survey of eastern Oregon, where vast landforms remained practically unknown botanically. John explained that previous explorers had covered only a small part of the territory and that modern collectors were working almost exclusively on the west side of the Cascades. Based on what he had learned from his summer's expedition in Washington, he felt he was ready to tackle the region south of the Columbia River.

In order to carry enough supplies to collect twenty-five complete sets of plants, plus five more of mosses and lichens, he estimated that he would require more than a ton of gear. This would include "pack saddles, riding saddles, camp paraphernalia, botanical supplies, one portable folding boat, and one Kodak camera of the largest size available." He also requested a soil-testing laboratory for his excursion, plus permission to retain a portion of the collections, especially fossils, that he expected to gather along the way. He wanted to load all this gear on a covered wagon made in Portland and "designed to carry at least 3,000 pounds over any sort of ground where a wagon can go." The carriage would be shipped by rail to a station at Heppner, Oregon, which lay on a Union Pacific branch line that he could reach from Spokane. Leiberg would supply a span of draft horses and three riding horses for the crew, which would include himself, a cook for camp duty, plus an assistant botanist to share the specimen work. John figured that he should receive $150 per month for managing the outfit, that an assistant was worth $100, and that he could procure a cook and camp assistant for $50 in Heppner, thereby saving one rail fare.

They would run a bare-bones operation, and the route would be a rigorous one, beginning at Heppner in mid-March to catch the early spring bloom as it rolled through the western uplifts of the Blue Mountains toward Prineville. From there they would curl south past Bend to the marshlands around Klamath Lake, where the folding boat would come in handy for aquatic plants. The horses would remain fit by wintering in the Klamath wetlands so that the following spring they could move east through the Harney Basin toward the Malheur country to catch the crucial vernal flora. In Leiberg's opinion, the most efficient course would be to extend the trip to four years. That would allow him to spend a third season engaged in mountain work, embracing the floras of the southern Oregon Cascades from Crater Lake across to the Willamette Valley. He and his crew could cover the Warner Valley and Steens Mountain when they recrossed the state one final time on the way home.

Upon reading Leiberg's desire to comb the vegetation of every significant drainage in eastern Oregon, Frederick Coville waited several days before replying that he found the proposal admirable, but certain changes would have to be made in the details. For the moment, he offered John a three-month contract in Washington, DC, to help staff members sort out the Sandberg-Leiberg collections. The department was prepared to reimburse Leiberg's round trip fare and to offer a salary of $50 per month for his time away from home.

John telegraphed his acceptance and prepared to depart at a moment's notice but was delayed while the department sorted out his legal residence for their records. Did he live in Hope, Hamilton, or Lakeview? Leiberg explained the multiple mailing addresses on file: Lakeview, the new post office closest to his homestead on the south end of Lake Pend Oreille; Hamilton, used during a work stint in the fall and winter of 1892; and Hope, which would be the correct one for the present. As soon as that was clarified, the paperwork for his commission went through, and John boarded an eastbound train.

When Leiberg arrived in Washington, DC, he learned that Frederick Coville had whittled the multi-year Oregon proposal down to a single season, then lobbied hard to fund it. John indicated that he would gladly accept a contract for the coming summer. When they began their herbarium work, Coville paired him with an assistant taxonomist of high regard named Joseph Rose, who helped make many of the thorny determinations from the Sandberg-Leiberg Expedition. Rose specialized in plants of the umbellifer, or parsley, family, which included all the biscuitroots that Leiberg so admired. "Have you noticed how beautifully these early flowering low umbellifers form a chain from the highest to the lowest elevations in this region?" John asked. "As I view them, the low umbellifers are so very characteristic of our region." Rose wholeheartedly agreed—in fact, he would in time complete a monograph on the family. While poring over their specimens, the two developed a close rapport, and John became a regular guest at the Rose family home. Leiberg learned a great deal in his time inside the herbarium, especially in regard to "the vast difference between studying plants in their mummy [pressed] state and when they are flaming with life. I have used my eyes and ears to best advantage, however on the mummies, and my mental botanical horizon is very much broadened." He also absorbed the latest ideas about lumping and splitting species, lamenting that so many erroneous designations in the past rendered it impossible to understand the taxonomy of Western plants with any certainty.

Outside the plant laboratory, Leiberg met several other government naturalists working in DC, including C. H. Merriam, chief of the USDA's Bureau of Biological Survey and a down-to-earth man with the same square build—five foot nine, two hundred pounds—as the Idaho visitor. During the time Leiberg was working his quartz claims on the Little North Fork, Merriam had been performing mammal surveys from a buckboard in the southern Appalachians.

He was close with Theodore Roosevelt and Ernest Thompson Seton, had helped to found *National Geographic* magazine with his friend Henry Gannett, and directed the Biological Survey as his own personal fiefdom.

Merriam had spent the past several years talking to his cohorts about "biological life zones" as he developed habitat concepts first put forth by Alexander von Humboldt a century earlier. After an 1890 foray into Arizona's San Francisco Mountains, where such zones shift dramatically across constant elevation bands, Merriam had refined a method of describing local plant associations and ecological evolution. Leiberg longed to apply these ideas to landscapes he knew in the Northwest and was thrilled to learn that Merriam intended to make a mammal-collecting trip through eastern Oregon the upcoming summer. Perhaps they would cross paths.

Meanwhile, John's winter work kept him so busy that he only strayed from the lab long enough for a one-day run through the Museum of Natural History and the Army Medical Museum. He initially planned on returning home via New York City so he could meet Elizabeth and Nathaniel Britton and tour their botanical gardens. As time for the visit approached, however, he sent his regrets; spring had broken, he explained, and he found himself "hungry for the giant old mossbacks of far-off Idaho's mountains."

Cous
Lomatium cous

▽▽▽▽▽▽▽▽▽▽▽▽▽▽▽▽▽▽▽▽▽▽▽▽▽▽▽▽▽▽▽▽▽▽▽▽

CHAPTER SIX

HIGH LAVA PLAINS

▽▽▽▽▽▽▽▽▽▽▽▽▽▽▽▽▽▽▽▽▽▽▽▽▽▽▽▽▽▽▽▽▽▽▽▽

I n late April of 1894, John Leiberg hopped aboard a passenger car at the Hope station and set off for Heppner to
begin his fieldwork in eastern Oregon. Ordinarily it would
have taken this train about nine hours to chug through
Spokane, angle south-southwest to meet the Columbia at
its confluence with the Snake, then sweep around the river's clockwise curve to Wallula Junction. This time it took
four full days. John blamed the delays on "the industrial
armies," by which he meant Jacob Coxie's United States
Industrial Army—an Ohio businessman's attempt to create
jobs through government road projects. Coxie's Army had
gained many western sympathizers since the Panic of 1893,
and that month its troops had caused disturbances across

the Pacific Northwest. When several hundred Portland enlistees were denied train access to travel east and join Coxie's main group in Washington, DC, they marched along the railroad tracks through the Columbia Gorge, disrupting traffic up and down the line. Leiberg did not appreciate the delay, referring to the marchers as "hordes of tramps." While he paced impatiently in the shrub-steppe that surrounded the Wallula depot, he admired mule-ears sunflowers that were just beginning to bloom and looked east to see great masses of snow lingering high in the Blue Mountains—conditions, he hoped, that would keep many spring plants in flower until he could reach them.

When he finally arrived in Heppner two days later, he took possession of a heavy-duty wagon shipped from Portland that was designed to carry a ton and a half of gear over rugged ground. He picked up an aneroid barometer and a War Department map of Oregon at the post office, then took a hard look at his outfit. "I have several horse trades on tap," he informed Coville as he shipped half his collecting supplies on to Prineville and hired a local man to keep camp. Together they hitched the wagon and moved north seven miles before they found land that had not been severely grazed by sheep. As soon as they reached better ground, Leiberg collected the type specimen of serrate balsamroot, a lovely, single-flowered member of one of his favorite shrub-steppe genera.

Throughout the course of his travels, John always solicited local knowledge. This was another trait he shared with C. H. Merriam, who declared that for a field assistant, he would "prefer to have the farmer's boy who knows the plants and animals of his own home than the highest graduate in biology of our leading university." At their new camp along Willow Creek near the small town of Lexington, Leiberg asked local settlers about the landscape ahead and received answers that contained a good deal of "nebulosity." He heard several horror stories concerning the harsh desert conditions and craggy volcanic uplifts to the south, but one man who seemed to know what he was talking about assured John that he would find plenty of grass for his horses and never go more than a dozen miles between water holes.

A number of his Willow Creek conversations turned to the subject of sheep poisoning. It was apparently common for several hundred members of a flock to die within a few hours, and the herdsmen universally blamed a particular weed. In his time there, Leiberg saw nothing to indicate that any locoweed or milk-vetch could be the culprit, and he wondered if a corrosive mineral substance in the soil might be the cause—arsenic, he knew, was a common constituent of some volcanic rocks. Toxic dangers to livestock were part of the USDA's mission, and he continued to investigate the phenomena as he pushed into the Oregon interior. Shepherds told him that incidents tended to happen during the fall, after the animals came down from their summer grazing in mountain meadows. When the sheep reached patches of alkaline soil on the plains, they browsed the vegetation greedily, and certain spots in particular canyons were known to be deadly. John concluded that the high country soils did not supply sufficient salt and that the animals were ingesting arsenic along with the alkaline salts that they gorged on in certain locations in the fall. He also decided to test his theory. "Whenever I am fortunate enough to see *personally* a sheep die with the common symptoms they are all said to exhibit, I will cut out the stomach, put it in whiskey or alcohol, and see that the department gets it."

Leiberg's instructions called for him to monitor tribal food products, so he kept an eye out for the low early-flowering biscuitroots and desert parsleys so abundant in eastern Washington. As he roamed upslope, he found "a most striking and peculiar umbellifer on the sinuous narrow lines of talus that meander in all directions off the high basaltic table lands." This was Day Valley desert parsley, which features large starchy tubers and light-purple or pinkish flowers. A few days later, he met a small encampment of Umatilla Indians who had been in the Blue Mountains digging *cous*— their Sahaptin word for another of the Columbia drainage biscuitroots. John purchased some tubers and mailed them to the department with a description.

> The roots are dried and are ready for grinding; the
> lumps of doughlike material are the roots, pounded,
> mixed with water and moulded by the [women].
> In this state, the mass is spread on low platforms
> elevated a meter or so above the ground where
> the lumps are exposed to the drying influences
> of the sun. . . . The creases on the lumps are the
> impress of the fingers of the [women] by whom
> the moulding was performed. The stuff has at this
> stage a carroty odor and is called *sap-o-lel*.

When the package of roots arrived at his office in Washington, DC, Frederick Coville found that the specimens came through in excellent condition. He and Joseph Rose identified the almost perfectly spherical tubers as Canby's

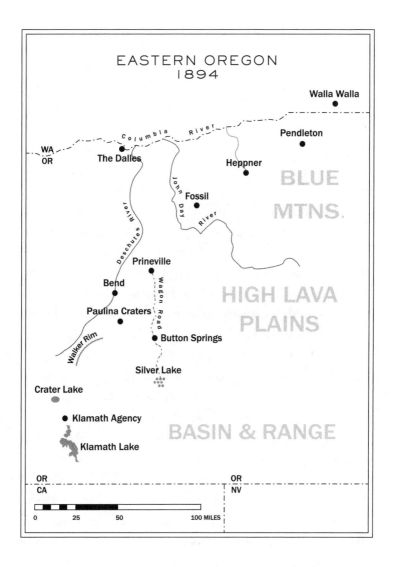

EASTERN OREGON
1894

Walla Walla

Columbia River

Pendleton

WA
OR
The Dalles

Heppner

John Day River

Fossil

BLUE
MTNS.

Deschutes River

Prineville

Bend

Paulina Craters

Wagon Road

Button Springs

HIGH LAVA
PLAINS

Walker Rim

Silver Lake

Crater Lake

Klamath Agency

Klamath Lake

BASIN & RANGE

OR
CA

OR
NV

0   25   50   100 MILES

biscuitroot and challenged John to find more specimens for the herbarium, particularly the *Lomatium cous* collected by Lewis and Clark. Leiberg had a suspicion that the term "cous" was applied to several different biscuitroot species lumped under that general heading as a generic word for root food, but the puzzle could only be solved by digging a series of plants in flower and in seed. The Umatilla party told John that he would find the plant they called *cous* growing in abundance when he crossed a low spur of the Blue Mountains on his way to Prineville, so he eagerly pushed onward. South of Heppner, in the vicinity of modern Lone Rock at close to three thousand feet of elevation, he did in fact pluck an example of the true *Lomatium cous*.

Leiberg found the road to Lone Rock surprisingly well settled, probably because the surrounding countryside harbored a superior growth of bunchgrass for grazing stock. Progress became slow and tedious as he continued south, and he came to understand why no railroads and few botanists had penetrated that part of Oregon. Rumbling through steady rain, he decided that "the country passed through should be called the Highland of Eastern Oregon." This plateau, a western extension of the Blue Mountain terrain, featured a corduroy pattern of long timberless ridges running east and west. Since the rangeland was tightly fenced, he and his helper were forced to follow a wretched washed-out road that made precipitous descents into a series of deep   canyons that punctuated the plateau. In several of the ravine bottoms, they had to unload the entire wagon and haul their gear to the top one portion at a time. In other places, the wagon sank to its axle hubs in soft mud, forcing the men to choose between digging out or unloading again.

For a plant hunter, the ongoing spring bloom proved well worth the torturous route. While laboring through the canyons, Leiberg collected two more new balsamroots, several lupines, and no less than five yellow-flowered biscuitroots. Whenever they topped a high ridge, "one could see, even miles away, thousands of acres as yellow as a rape or mustard field from the bloom of these umbellifers." When they pitched camp on Hoover Creek near the tiny hamlet of Fossil two weeks later, bad weather continued to dog them, and the resulting humidity made the gummed slips of paper in John's collection packs stick together. He began to long for the fabled desert country farther south where rain fell only in winter. Rancher after rancher swore it was the wettest spring they had ever seen, but Leiberg had heard this same story in different parts of the country for the past three years and didn't know whether to believe their memories. Stuck in camp until the roads dried up, he ruminated on the slippery, soapy nature of gumbo mud, cyclonic air movement, barometric anomalies, and the ways in which all these factors might have affected the development of the local flora. He figured that about a quarter of the hundreds of plants he had collected so far were different from the Washington species he had seen the previous summer.

At Fossil, Leiberg received word that Frederick Coville might find time to join him for a couple of weeks in July. John advised him that the stagecoach from The Dalles on the Columbia River ran south through Prineville and Klamath Falls, two towns he planned to visit along his route. Coville also forwarded a request from C. H. Merriam for John to keep an eye out for a spotted ground squirrel rumored to live in the high desert. Leiberg had not encountered any spotted creatures but did offer descriptions of three other ground squirrels as well as a species of kangaroo rat that recently had moved into the area to feast on stored grain. Local farmers were employing strychnine to reduce their numbers.

It was mid-June before Leiberg rolled into Prineville, and another week passed before he managed to dry eight bundles of plant specimens and mail them to the department. Since he had not yet heard any concrete plans from Coville in regard to meeting him along the way, John felt he had no choice but to continue south toward his intended reconnaissance of the Walker Rim region. Writing to let his boss know his plans, he concluded: "My intention is to give this tract a thorough overhauling if I find it to be as represented. Extinct craters and extensive lava flows are said to abound there." Leiberg's characterization of the area that geologists now classify as Oregon's High Lava Plains perfectly describes their origin, and he had penetrated deep into the flows when he stopped along the wagon road between Prineville and Silver Lake, just south of present-day Millican, at the end of the month.

He camped at a water hole next to a creek bed marked on the War Department map as dry, but in that wet year it maintained a steady trickle. More water ran from a fissure in a basalt face and collected in a natural cavity. He found the pool so full of tadpoles that he had to scoop them out with his shovel each morning before he could collect drinking water. He joked that some fishermen he knew would be happy to spend the summer in a place that abounded in such good bait, but even cleared of pollywogs, the water in the pool tasted as though it had been filtered through a cow stable. Neither he nor his camp hand felt any stomach twinges, so they remained there two days among an interesting new flora before continuing southeast to the oasis of Button Springs.

That stretch of road rolled through finely pulverized pumice stone that contained lake-like depressions filled with more pumice. Much of this material was as fine as sand, and relentless winds had blown it into dunes. In spite of the arid conditions, many of the hillocks were populated with groves of ponderosa pine and fine grasses. Even more unexpected was the presence of plants such as dwarf alpine-gold and Mount Hood pussytoes, both of which he associated with high, wet habitats of the Cascade Range.

At this point Leiberg had not heard from Frederick Coville for six weeks, but he still had hopes of meeting him. "We are all right in every way," he wrote, "except pretty rough and sunburned. Would now be a veritable scarecrow were we to present ourselves to the gentlemen and ladies of the department." He added that the War Department map Coville had sent him was riddled with errors, so he had to constantly rework site locations and geographic misconceptions along the way.

In the following few days, Leiberg collected in all directions from Button Springs. The surrounding lowlands appeared to be the bottom of an ancient lake that still held some shallow pools during the present wet season. Although alkaline clays soon rendered the water unpotable for humans, a healthy mix of vegetation continued to thrive, including several tough shrubs that were new to his collections. "Not much of a desert," he commented in reference to its designation as "Desert, Volcanic Ashes, and Scoria" on his faulty map. West of their campsite he trekked into the Paulina Hills to find ponderosa pines up to eight feet in diameter. Groves of mountain mahogany had colonized even the harshest of the gravelly flats, each individual tree "an elegant object with their multitude of long silky-tailed seeds." He capped off his stay at Button Springs by ascending a prominent lookout about ten miles distant. Its upper spine took the form of a cylindrical knob that reminded him of a boss on a bucket, and from his vantage point he could see how the ridge was flanked by a number of extinct craters. One of the vents had slumped into a perfect funnel shape, then had filled itself back up with an explosion of black and red cinders.

Standing on this summit, John could plainly see that all the hills for miles around were the result of volcanic action of the same formative age. Modern geologic maps agree with his assessment, describing a series of long arcs of eruptive activity that began in southeastern Oregon around ten million years ago. This procession of arcs crept steadily west, reaching Paulina and Newberry Craters one or two million years before the present. Within this raw lava field, John estimated that mountain mahogany made up about 90 percent of the vegetation, but he also found a full array of dryland shrubs, plus a host of grasses and some flowering plants more representative of Nevada's Great Basin flora than the Columbia Plateau. As his survey widened to cover more of the High Lava Plains, he documented thousands of acres of open ponderosa pine forest and extensive groves of juniper. Since the War Department map erroneously designated the entire area as bare desert, Leiberg corrected botanical misconceptions that had held sway for two generations.

John always wanted to know more about the complex role fire played in the vegetative development of western forests and rangeland. "The forest fires have not damaged the ponderosa forest outside of the Paulina main ridges very much as yet," he wrote. "But the high summits of Paulina have been swept again and again, and that forest now lies prostrate on the ground." The red cinder-laden hills left behind by such blazes appeared to be bare save for sprouts of buckbrush and manzanita.

After exploring the region around Button Springs, Leiberg made a long sweep north and then west, circling the Paulina complex to reach Farewell Bend (present-day Bend) on the Deschutes River. In late July he turned south on the stagecoach road that followed the river along the east front of the Cascades. At the road's junction with Paulina Creek, a day's journey south of Bend, he parked his wagon and set out on foot with a single pack horse for a side trip to the summit of the Paulina Craters, traveling in today's Newberry Craters National Monument. He climbed to Paulina Lake, where for once his barometric calculation agreed with the War Department map elevation of 6,335 feet—a figure that holds up well today. There the good traveling ended, and he clambered over dense tangles of downed lodgepole pine to reach the crater's rim. From his lookout, he could see that the Paulina and East Lakes formed part of an immense caldera almost twenty miles in circumference. This singular feature stood alone on the plain, with lateral foothills radiating in every direction from the giant crater. He scrambled to the summit of the ancient volcano, today's Paulina Peak, and took more barometric readings. He hoped to name the landmark after Coville, whom he assumed to be bouncing toward him somewhere on the stageroad below.

Another of Leiberg's ongoing interests was in the flora of isolated peaks such as Paulina, and he felt certain that he would find many oddities around the caldera. When the lakes' water temperature seemed warmer than expected, he pawed through red cinders to discover a number of thermal springs. He strolled along the forested western slopes of the mountain, delineating the range and elevation of each tree species. The makeup of that forest remains a fragrant mix of true firs and mountain hemlock. Plant association series developed by foresters over the past century and a half, stretching from C. H. Merriam's nascent ideas through to best modern practices, describe type habitats that include several of the shrubs and herbs Leiberg collected during his solo trek there, including two kinds of huckleberries, pinemat manzanita, and a prominent needlegrass.

During the first weeks of August, John and his cook camped at a series of ancient oases on the road south from Paulina. They cut the long-sought Walker Rim on the way to Sand Creek, clearing crunchy pumice cinders only to become mired in extensive marshes along the eastern shore of Upper Klamath Lake. They had reached yet another new geologic landscape, touching the northeastern corner of the vast Basin and Range province that stretches from Mexico's northern border across the Great Basin. Here tectonic movements along the western edge of North America led to multiple episodes of crustal extension, faulting, and bursts of volcanism during the Miocene Epoch. These created a series of roughly north–south uplifts separated by extensive valleys. The colder, wetter climate of the last Ice Age turned many of the basins into pluvial lakes, and Klamath Lake and the marsh system that surround it represent the remnants of Glacial Lake Modoc, the largest and slowest-drying of these features in Oregon.

When he crossed the Williamson River and closed on Klamath Marsh, Leiberg was following the track of the Williamson Expedition, an 1855 railroad survey team that had probed for a feasible route between the Columbia River and northern California. The expedition naturalist, Dr. John Strong Newberry, was a former colleague of Nathaniel Britton at Columbia College and one of the geologists who had examined ore samples from Leiberg's claims on the Little North Fork. The *American Geologist* had run an article about Newberry in their summer 1893 issue, and Leiberg might well have read the journal during his winter sojourn at the USDA. Both the railroad survey team leaders and the biographical memoir praised Newberry for producing a report that rose beyond a mere list of plants to a geographical study of the region—exactly the sort of practical field science to which Leiberg aspired.

As he traced the path of the 1855 rail survey, John witnessed an ancient connection between the human and natural landscape: "Passing up Klamath Marsh, we saw the Klamath Indians still living in tule huts and, most interesting, found several encampments busily engaged in making 'Wo-Kash'—the food pounded from seeds of yellow pond-lily." He took careful notes on the process and traded for samples of the various stages in preparing the *wo-kash*, which represented the same kind of dependable nutritional base that cous did for Columbia Plateau tribes. Although he did not savor the taste of the pond-lily seed flour, he did note that "the labor necessary to obtain a bushel of seed is something amazing." Like many ethnographers of that time, he felt certain that he was recording one of the last of such communal gatherings, because the women who worked the pond lilies were old, and their children were being educated and fed at the Fort Klamath boarding school.

During his brief visit to the Klamath encampment, John did not see any root cakes similar to the ones the Umatillas had shown him. He collected one tuberous biscuitroot from the pumice sands above the lake, but could not determine whether that particular species was ever used for food. He elicited bits of information about other cultural plants and assured Frederick Coville, who had remained stuck behind his desk in Washington, DC, all summer, that he would include them all in his report.

Klamath Lake marked the outermost point of his summer survey, and it was time to turn around. A good six hundred miles lay between Fort Klamath and Hope, and September was waning by the time Leiberg returned to Lake Pend Oreille. During his first week at home, he mailed a final bag of specimens to the department, bringing the total to 947 and besting the previous summer's Columbia Plateau survey by more than fifty. In his cover letter to Coville, he included a newspaper clip from the *Spokesman-Review* announcing that the farmers living in the vicinity of Nampa and Caldwell, Idaho, were alarmed over the rapid spread of the deadly Russian thistle. He expressed his concern that if the report was true, the noxious plant soon to be known as tumbleweed would thrive on the rich soil and mild climate of the Interior. "Once introduced, it will be beyond the powers of man to eradicate it. It will grow with unexampled luxuriance on the cultivated lands, and these areas will constitute permanent foci from which fresh invasions will surely come," he predicted. Leiberg's dire pronouncement offered a clear vision of tumbleweed's future arc across the steppe and rangeland that he had explored over the past two summers. He had no time to ponder further ramifications of that Russian thistle invasion, however, because his USDA contract specified that he would travel to Washington, DC, again to catalog his Oregon specimens. Within another week he had boxed his corrected maps, instruments, seed collections, and manuscript notes and departed from Hope to follow those materials east.

Carrie's response to her husband's rapid arrival and departure is not known, but she had a new career opportunity of her own. The *Medical Sentinel* of early November carried a notice announcing that Dr. Carrie Leiberg of Hope, Idaho, had been appointed to serve as a division surgeon for the Northern Pacific Railroad, adding that "this is the only instance of such distinction of a lady that we know of in the United States." Quickly picked up by other professional journals such as *Medical Fortnightly* and *Railway Surgeon*, news of Carrie's new position carried weight far beyond the Idaho Panhandle.

During the 1890s, railway companies hired physicians to attend the inevitable accidents around their tracks; over the course of the decade, passengers averaged around 3,000 injuries and 300 fatalities per annum. Those numbers paled beside the railroad industry figures, whose companies together employed close to 800,000 men in the United States. Some 26,000 workers lost time due to job-related mishaps each year, including an estimated 2,600 deaths. In a nation only three decades removed from Civil War carnage, the newly launched *Railway Surgeon* magazine saw a clear connection. "The analogy between railway injuries and those seen in military surgery is noticeable," wrote one physician in describing the nature of his duties. "Those of us who have seen a limb damaged or torn away by a cannon shot have seen as extreme injuries when a leg or arm has been crushed under the wheels of a swiftly moving train."

As lead surgeon for a district that stretched from western Montana into eastern Washington, Carrie's duties required her to keep an emergency dressing case on hand and to attend promptly to any employee or civilian injured along the rail line. She was to wire her superintendent with an assessment of each case and write reports for worker's compensation due to time lost on the job. She would carry out physicals for job applicants, make regular facility inspections within her division, and advise patients and agents as to matters of hygiene. While under contract with Northern Pacific, she apparently remained free to continue her local practice in Hope.

Mountain hemlock cone
Tsuga mertensiana

CHAPTER SEVEN

THE COEUR D'ALENES

▽▽▽▽▽▽▽▽▽▽▽▽▽▽▽▽▽▽▽▽▽▽▽▽▽▽▽▽▽▽▽▽▽▽▽▽

I n late fall of 1894, elements of political change that would greatly affect John Leiberg's life were roiling through the capital. The lingering depression was crippling Grover Cleveland's pro-business Democratic regime. As their policies failed to reverse the economic slide, several issues they opposed, including US military presence abroad, tariffs on foreign goods, farm and business subsidies, and silver coinage, all gained traction. Subjects of conservation and public land management became part of the larger debate as seminal players emerged at all levels of influence. The ambitious Republican Teddy Roosevelt, his political career temporarily stalled, took in the situation from his retreat in Dakota Territory. Young Gifford Pinchot, the son and grandson of

COEUR D'ALENE BASIN 1895

Sandpoint ●

● Hope

Pend Oreille River

Lake
Pend Oreille

Cabinet Gorge ●

Clark Fork River

▲ Packsaddle
Mtn.

N. F.

Trout ● Creek

Leiberg ●
Ranch

Rathdrum ●

Little N. F. Cd'A R.

Coeur d'Alene R.

Coeur d'Alene ●

Spokane River

Fourth of July
Pass
≡

● Prichard

▲ Sunset
Peak

Coeur d'Alene
Lake

Coeur d'Alene R.

■

S. F. Coeur d'Alene River

Mullan ●

Cataldo
Mission

Silver Valley

Coeur d'Alene
Indian
Reservation

▲ Mount Wiessner

St. Maries ●

▲ Stevens
Peak

Hangman Ck.

St. Joe River

De Smet
Mission ■

St. Maries River

Little N.F. Clearwater R.

0 5 10 15 20 25 MILES

timber barons, returned from postgraduate studies at the French National School of Forestry determined to shape a sensible forest policy in the United States. Henry Gannett, chief geographer of the US Geological Survey and one of the founding members of the National Geographic Society, had recently published his *Manual of Topographic Methods*. Gannett's rigorous approach standardized survey and mapping processes that soon would be applied to remote timberlands across the American West.

That same year, Frederick Coville began merging his Department of Agriculture plant collections with those of the Smithsonian to create the National Herbarium. His chief taxonomist, Joseph Rose, assumed the role of assistant curator, and Leiberg joined the pair for a few weeks around the turn of the year, then returned to Idaho with the aim of editing his 1894 Oregon journals for publication. Across that distance, Coville and Rose worked to identify new plants Leiberg had gathered while he peppered them with additional curiosities. "We have received a package containing two parcels of roots, apparently Indian foods, and a small package of Indian snuff marked 'Oneida, Idaho,' which appears to be in your handwriting," Coville wrote to John in March. "This I suppose we shall catalogue as coming from you. I hope you will send me on the names of the plants from which the specimens are derived."

The pace of their correspondence increased as the deadline for summer funding drew near. The US Postal Service was remarkably efficient at delivery along the cross-country train routes, but when Coville was in a hurry, he relied on the telegraph lines for speed. Shortly after Leiberg completed his manuscript, the Western Union office in Hope delivered a query from Coville: "Will you accept seven months' commission to report on botany of Coeur d'Alene Mountains? Salary as last year. Telegraph answer."

The urgency was real. Advocates for forest protection were pressuring Congress to address the status of public lands in the West, and federal agencies were sorely in need of relevant scientific information. Coville and his cohorts at the Government Land Office and the Geological Survey were developing a new set of protocols, and as soon as Leiberg accepted his latest contract, he received a thick sheaf of orders.

Your work will cover the following subjects:

1. A collections of all the species of plants in the region traversed

2. A general account of the topography and climatic conditions of the region

3. The timber resources of the country and its relation to other local industries

4. The local and aboriginal uses of native plant products, particularly food plants, and

5. An analysis of the flora of the region into its several component floras, in their relation particularly to topography and climatic conditions.

Each of the five rubrics included a supplementary list that detailed procedures down to the recommended instruments and proper method for converting individual

THE DREAMER AND THE DOCTOR

tree measurements to board feet. If these new requirements seemed daunting, they suited Leiberg's ambition to gather all possible data about the components of an ecosystem. The only question was whether he could possibly complete such a detailed assessment of so much rugged territory in a mere seven months.

Leiberg defined the Coeur d'Alene Mountains as the drainage basin for the lake of that name. He had penetrated the region from the south during his 1884 excursion out of Lewiston, and from the north and west while prospecting. Now he devised a circuitous route meant to cover the entire basin before the snow began to fly. In order to accomplish this, he would start on the southern edge and work his way north toward the areas with which he was already intimately acquainted.

John knew how to tackle dauntingly large tasks one step at a time. He asked Coville to send a thermometer, barometer, and hygrometer along with two thousand papers for drying plants. He ordered blank books for cataloging specimens and blank forms to record tree measurements. He fashioned a stout wooden tube with a cork in one end to protect the thermometer on the trail. He hired assistants with knowledge of the country and the brawn to help navigate the maze of rough wagon roads he intended to travel. He took a steamer from Hope to his Lakeside Ranch, where he refit the wagon that had served him well in eastern Oregon the previous summer. He chose a durable brace of draft horses and several dependable packhorses. When all was ready, he drove west to make his first camp at Rathdrum, where he picked up packages containing survey instruments and maps, along with another promise from Frederick Coville that he would try to join the party later in the summer.

The first day after setting out from Rathdrum, Leiberg and his crew covered almost forty miles south to the town of Rockford, Washington. Turning east, they followed Hangman Creek upstream to the Idaho state line, where John stopped to collect an unfamiliar umbellifer that he felt might be a distinctive species. Upon chewing the seeds, he detected none of the acrid or pungent taste so characteristic of the biscuitroots. As if to signal that the expedition was officially under way, he boxed up plant, root, and seeds for Joseph Rose at the Smithsonian.

In Idaho, they entered the Coeur d'Alene Indian Reservation and stopped at De Smet Mission. Here John saw Coeur d'Alene people managing large and well-cultivated ranches, and he asked about obtaining some samples of their native food products without success. "On the contrary," he wrote, "they are all well supplied with the foodstuffs of their civilized neighbors, which they produce in abundance and no doubt find much more palatable than their old wild foods."

Leiberg was correct on one count: at the time of his visit, several Coeur d'Alene families ran successful farms around De Smet, and many of them maintained close ties to the Jesuit mission. Some of these families continued to gather important cultural plants such as camas, edible valerian, and a much-valued medicinal lovage, all of which appeared among the dozen plants John collected in the vicinity. Felix Aripa, a tribal elder consulting on present-day wetland restoration around Hangman Creek feeder streams, helped to monitor the restoration of all three of those species into areas where Leiberg had seen them. Aripa described families on the reservation today who embrace modern conveniences and still retain their cultural values, continuing ancient practices such as digging roots and gathering berries. He explained that it takes timing, and time, to understand how residents utilize the place where they live. "Look," Aripa used to say. "People can speak two languages can't they?"

From De Smet, Leiberg ascended the divide separating Hangman Creek from the Saint Maries River. "The country has now begun to assume the characteristic aspect of the Coeur d'Alenes," he wrote in his daybook. Shady north slopes and deep ravines harbored a close growth of mixed conifers, a stark contrast to the parklike ponderosa pines that spread across south-facing hillsides. The tribe managed these forests by controlled seasonal burns, and beneath the open canopy of large yellow-bellied pines, Leiberg noticed the same abundant prairie lupines that were "first collected by Lewis and Clark on the banks of the Kooskoosky and apparently not very well recognized since that time."

When he topped the saddle that marked the Hangman–Saint Maries divide and looked east, Leiberg was dismayed to see the extent of recent burn scars that lay ahead. Looking back he admired a particularly expansive stand of large ponderosa pine, commenting that its survival was probably due to the fact that it lay inside the reservation. Outside those boundaries he saw a few scattered settlements and evidence of the newcomers' attempts to clear land for agriculture. "With the settlements come also the forest fires and blackened and charred stumps and trees proclaiming man's efforts to destroy as rapidly as possible the forest covering of the mountains," he wrote.

They descended along Santa Creek, a tributary of the Saint Maries that John deemed too frosty for crops but suitable for cattle fed on grass hay. Along the way, he remarked on scattered examples of old-growth western white pine. Here this species reached its greatest size anywhere in the region, and he estimated that some trees exceeded a hundred meters in height—an exaggeration to be sure, but with enough truth to make any tree lover ache for the heart of white pine country. At the end of June, after toiling through the upper reaches of the Saint Maries, they reached the divide that faced north to the Saint Joe and east to the Clearwater. John used the word "magnificent" to describe the easier traveling along the ridge where an ancient Indian trail ran between the Saint Maries and Bitterroot valleys. "Had Lewis and Clark known of this trail, what a lot of hardships they would have escaped," he noted. Among the patchwork of healthy forest, he counted eight species of coniferous trees. Most impressive were the western redcedars, which tended "to form groves of pure growth, with interlacing branches cutting off the sunlight from the ground beneath them." Heartleaf listera orchids dotted the forest duff, while tall pink streambank hollyhock decorated many of the burn scars.

They dropped down to the Saint Joe River, then continued upstream to ascend the west slope of the Bitterroot Range. After struggling through dense thickets of regenerative growth, the party reached an open ridgetop that featured subalpine fir, mountain hemlock, and whitebark pine. The horses swiftly ascended until they were blocked by huge snowdrifts that prevented any passage to the Clearwater drainage. Stymied by the snowpack ahead and a maze of fire-charred jackstraws visible on the lower Saint Joe, Leiberg decided to backtrack to the Saint Maries and follow it downstream to Coeur d'Alene Lake. Between the two rivers' confluence and the lake, they entered a slack-water delta bordered by coarse meadow sedge. It was bad country for a wagon, so they hailed a steamboat at the town of Saint Maries, walked the horses and outfit on board, and arrived in Coeur d'Alene on July 16.

There Leiberg collected his mail—including the news, which he might have anticipated, that Frederick Coville would not be able to join him that summer. John spent a couple of days poking around the outlet of the Spokane River from Coeur d'Alene Lake, but his real focus was east, where he had heard about alpine habitats and a succession of bald peaks around Mount Wiessner. To reach that area, he followed the Mullan Road east across Fourth of July Pass to the old Cataldo Mission. Parking his wagon there, he and his crew turned up Latour Creek and headed for the high country. Once again, his party struggled through second-growth conifers in the middle elevations. As soon as they gained a passable ridge, large horseflies attacked animals and men. Then, as they approached Mount Wiessner, they found that the peak was composed of masses of huge blocks of quartzite impossible to traverse with their horses. A long detour forced them across talus slides that radiated from the peak in all directions. But when they finally coaxed their animals up the final approach to the summit, Leiberg was delighted to find a *true alpine* flora, very rare in these mountains." His bounty included Sandberg's biscuitroot and Piper's golden buckwheat, plus sedums, gentians, and saxifrages that together presented a heath-like appearance. They spent the next four days collecting around the area now known as the Crystal Lake/Twin Crags Wilderness Study Area, a maze of rocky peaks and ridges that stretches from Latour Baldy and Mount Wiessner south to Saint Joe and Reed's Baldies.

After returning to Cataldo and reclaiming their wagon, they continued east to a much less appetizing view of the world. Below the confluence of the North and South Forks of the Coeur d'Alene River, they passed a shingle mill that had littered the riverbanks for miles with rejected split cedar bolts. Proceeding upstream, they entered the Silver Valley proper, home of the great mining districts and ongoing labor disputes. "The hills on either side of the valley rose steeply; the slopes and summits covered with the cleared remnants of the great forest that grew here once," lamented Leiberg. "Between the mass of dry debris that covers the ground and which is sure to be fired sooner or later and the settler's clearings, this growth stands a slim chance of ever amounting to anything." There were no plants worth collecting.

The Bitterroots still lay ahead. From their July 31 camp at Mullan, the party ascended Willow Creek, aiming for Stevens Peak. They worked their way up the drainage and around a perpendicular waterfall before striking a steep but negotiable route to the summit. The view from on top was marred somewhat by haze from smoldering Silver Valley fires, but Leiberg could still look east to the main Bitterroot Range and beyond. None of the nearby peaks, he noted, matched Stevens in height. Although its north slope consisted of a steep rocky slide down to a series of glacial tarns, the low carpet of alpine plants they had seen on Wiessner was absent along the ridges. He scrambled down a rock precipice to examine an extensive snowfield that measured thirty to forty-five feet deep but contained none of the elements of glacial stability. He delighted in the great quantities of mountain sorrel and red-stemmed saxifrage that fringed its edges but was not so thrilled about the cold that descended upon their camp that night and formed a thick rime along the crest of the northern ledge. Altogether, Leiberg's experiences that day led him to declare that "the localization of plants is one of the most striking features in these mountains and certainly points toward this region as a place where an original and widespread flora is being crowded out by an advancing one." For years to come, he would continue to ponder the way plant associations evolved in specific habitats.

After descending from Stevens Peak, the party crossed the Silver Valley to explore the ridges around Sunset Peak, which presented different features from either Wiessner or Stevens. From that summit they could look north to the gold rush towns of Prichard and Murray, which had been experiencing their booms during John's first trip west on the Northern Pacific. Now all he could see were placer diggings and fire scars that extended all the way up Prichard Creek to Thompson Pass. The vegetation that remained looked surprisingly dry, perhaps due to late-season frosts that were known to linger in the narrow valley.

The next day they descended into the North Fork. John considered this the most difficult of all the Coeur d'Alene tributaries to explore because of the density of the trees and the fact that none of the steep ridges rose high enough to offer good views of the drainage. It didn't help that downed timber clogged much of the trail. By mid-August the party had emerged from the tangle near Kingston to bundle their plant specimens and rearrange their outfit. The road to Coeur d'Alene was a good one, and they approached town to find that the cold temperatures they had experienced in the high country had also touched the valley: "Potatoes and all garden vegetables cut down past recovery."

To complete his survey, Leiberg planned to inspect the northeastern corner of the Coeur d'Alene Basin from the Montana side. He rolled back across Rathdrum Prairie, camped near his homestead on the south end of Lake Pend Oreille, then caught the steamboat to Hope. There he and his crew loaded an eastbound train with horses, supplies, instruments, and a rowboat and hopped aboard for a run up the Clark Fork River. They disembarked near present-day Perma, Montana, where the steeply rolling hills looked to Leiberg like an extension of the Columbia shrub-steppe, right down to bitterbrush and beavertail cactus. "Apparently the eastern and the western floral elements are struggling for mastery in this region," he decided. "The chances fall in favor of the eastern."

The following day, the team packed their gear and launched the boat on the Clark Fork. They pulled ashore at Horse Plains, where the river makes a wide sweep southward, and a break in the mountains on the north side creates a large rolling plain. The dryland flora there was completely parched, but Leiberg saw that the "springs which break out in hundreds of localities along the river banks, especially on the north side, prove that there is an enormous underflow from some place back in the mountains." He soon identified additional signs of glacial action in the area, including great benches of gravel and vast heaps of boulders. The features he described were all remnants of Ice Age floods, which deposited several hundred feet of gravel across the Clark Fork Valley floor and combed level flood terraces along either side of the river. The rolling ridges on the Horse Plains were in fact huge ripple marks left by the deluge, while the boulders that caught his eye had floated on ice rafts that melted and dropped their cargo across the plain. To this day, pockets of ice and water trapped within these conglomerate features continue to emerge from banks in the form of copious springs along that section of the Clark Fork.

From Plains the party floated west, portaging the long run of rapids at Thompson Falls. Leiberg noted that the country was growing wetter, allowing a typical Coeur d'Alene flora to flourish. By the time they reached Trout Creek, the fire damage that was so prevalent in these forests reappeared, with an estimated 50 percent of the cover recently destroyed. A number of homesteaders were making a go along this stretch of the river, with saw and shingle mills operating amid the smoke. After portaging a traditional fishing site at Noxon Rapids, the plant collectors loaded their dory on a train bound for Lake Pend Oreille in order to avoid more dangerous water at Cabinet Gorge.

From the gorge, Leiberg and his crew ascended the steep slope to Green Monarch Ridge. They traced the divide between the Clark Fork and Coeur d'Alene Rivers, working through John's home turf above Lake Pend Oreille and the Little North Fork. On a single long day they skirted the east flank of Packsaddle Mountain, then held steady until they touched the Coeur d'Alene's North Fork just before dark.

"The summit of the ridge was difficult in places owing to the presence of burned timber," John commented, "but an accurate knowledge of the country here enabled us to travel rapidly." Another day's run landed them back at Cataldo Mission, where they pitched their tent in the same meadow they had utilized less than three weeks before. It was the first week of September by then, and an early snowstorm had dusted Stevens Peak and the surrounding ridges— exactly the conditions Leiberg had been hoping for. "Being desirous of ascertaining the conditions prevailing on the summit of the high peaks in the Coeur d'Alenes during a severe rain or snow storm," he wrote, "I determined to make an ascent of Wiessners Peak."

With the barometer falling, his party set out first thing the next morning along the same Latour Creek route they had taken in July. That evening they made a dry camp less than two miles below the summit. The following day, with the weather still holding, they moved to one of the glacial lakes tucked into the foot of a rocky precipice in the hope that the cliffs would provide shelter from the storm that was blowing in.

And blow it did. On the morning of September 7, the men heard the patter of rain on their tent, and as the hours wore on, dense clouds descended. By noon the wind was howling at gale force—John's cue to clamber up to the high ridge to experience the full force of the storm.

> There was one continual crashing of trees in the forest below me on the southern slope as hundreds of them were falling. On the summit trees were torn up from the ground, taken high up in the

air and hurled into the chasms below. It was
impossible to stand erect, and it was necessary to
lie down on the ground and grasp a short sapling,
which did not offer much resistance to the wind.

The clouds themselves seemed to pulsate up and down, and
Leiberg noticed that when they settled "a mist condensed on
the trees and shrubs and caused the water to run off them
in rivulets."

The next morning the sky cleared just long enough for
the party to escape from the high country before another
storm dumped six feet of snow. From Cataldo they headed
back into the Little North Fork drainage, and two days
later they were exploring the same Bare Knob Meadows
(now Honeysuckle Campground in the Panhandle National
Forest) that John had passed many times while prospecting in the vicinity. With that final bit of the survey completed, they followed the Leiberg-Athol Trail across Chilco
Saddle to Lakeside Ranch. After tending to his animals, he
loaded his gear aboard the familiar steamer and rode north
to Hope, where on October 2 he closed the book on his 1895
field season.

Leiberg's "General Report on a Botanical Survey of the Coeur
d'Alene Mountains in Idaho during the Summer of 1895"
appeared as a publication of the US National Herbarium in
1897. Frederick Coville wrote a concise introduction, explaining that the author's long and varied local experience made
the monograph much more than an "ordinary investigation."

John began by explaining how he had shaped the tangled route of his itinerary to fit the territory. His section on topography speculated about the formative geology of the region, from Precambrian basement rock to the creation of different peaks such as Wiessner and Packsaddle. He traced each major stream through its intermediate lakes to the Columbia. The climate section made up ten pages of the eighty-five-page report; here John defined an area that is now recognized as a narrow strip of interior rain forest by following pressure systems from the Pacific up and over the Cascades before ushering them in and out of the Coeur d'Alene Basin: "The heat carried by the wind is so great that not only does it produce marked effects on the Rocky Mountain region, but it even extends in a lesser degree as far east as the Missouri River in North Dakota."

Leiberg's mining chapter summarized the history of exploration and industry in the basin and reflected his special affection for "cupriferous silver lodes," which he deemed to be uncommon, little explored, and promising for the production of silver, antimony, and lead. As far as agriculture was concerned, he believed that only the fertile river bottoms qualified as viable farmland. In these lowlands, he recommended that dams and diversions be constructed to control the water flow, and that existing wetland vegetation be converted to more profitable hay crops such as timothy grass. Cattle grazing might be practical in the ponderosa pine parklands but had proven worthless everywhere else—the quick burst of grass that came from intentionally burning dense white pine stands constituted a terrible waste.

Because Leiberg's contact with native peoples was limited to his brief passage across the Coeur d'Alene

Reservation, his knowledge of cultural plant use did not extend much beyond camas, which he said was fast disappearing from the lower portion of the Saint Maries and the Saint Joe as farmers drained marshy areas to plant crops. He had tasted some traditional earth-baked lichen cakes and noted that the tribes utilized several kinds of huckleberries, two different raspberries, and serviceberries. Even with these additions, his list of tribal food plants barely scratched the surface of the resources that he passed during the course of his journey.

John next addressed water supply, emphasizing how the streams of the Coeur d'Alene powered early sawmills and ore concentrators, ferried logs to the mills, washed gravel in search of gold, and filled ditches to irrigate crops. This flow was key, and especially vulnerable, to the mineral reduction processes of the Silver Valley. "After it is used, the water is of course returned to the channel. It is then heavily charged with the siliceous slimes derived from the crushed gangue of the ore, and more or less of the metallic elements which the concentrating machinery failed to save, such as the sulfides of lead, iron, antimony, zinc, and arsenic in various combinations," he wrote. "The color of the slime-laden water is a dirty gray, and the particles held in suspension are deposited along its course. After passing through these establishments, the water is unfit for either drinking or irrigation purposes." This indictment of Silver Valley water quality rang true for decades after Leiberg's time and has proved most troublesome to remedy.

John devoted more than half of his report to various aspects of the timber resources of the Coeur d'Alenes. Logging rights on public land had become a pressing political issue, and Frederick Coville encouraged Leiberg to "make just as thorough and far-reaching a report on the timber land question, both general and specific, as you have the time and material for. It is especially desirable, as you suggest, that the system of timber management you describe shall be practical." When the usually reserved Coville received a preliminary draft in December, he "read it with the greatest interest" and was especially vocal in response: "I wish to congratulate you on producing so good an account of your summer's work, particularly with reference to the timber question." It is no wonder that the chief botanist was impressed. In this section, Leiberg poured out detailed descriptions for each of the fourteen different coniferous species he had observed and delineated their plant associations within his forest zones.

The last twenty pages of the report fell under the heading "Forest Destruction," and it was here that John's voice rose to its most passionate pitch. "The Coeur d'Alene forests are in the process of rapid and total extinction," he declared. He traced how the region had arrived at this juncture within the space of a mere thirty-five years. The completion of the Mullan Road through its heartland had brought a steady stream of immigrants, and fire was their way of clearing land. Construction of the Northern Pacific Railroad along the Clark Fork River and Lake Pend Oreille had decimated that corridor—when Leiberg traveled the route in 1884, he had witnessed continuous lines of fire from the slash piles along the newly laid track. The gold and silver strikes of that decade brought hundreds of prospectors who routinely set fire to the dense growth of timber and shrubs that interfered with their search for mineral-bearing outcrops. On his first trip to the Idaho Territory, he had passed through mile upon mile of primeval forest in the Coeur d'Alenes. Eleven years later, in 1895, along many of the same routes he found that "there was not a single foot that the fire and ax had not run through, and the larger quantity had been uselessly and totally destroyed."

Leiberg's account of the damaged watersheds that surrounded the Silver Valley, coupled with the doghair stands that sprung back on soils devoid of protective duff, foreshadowed the devastation of wildfires that would continue to sweep the region. Even in the face of such destruction, he still believed in the regenerative powers of the forest and presented sound reasons for protecting the remaining mature growth. From the essential role that forest cover played in soil and water conservation to the practical necessity for forest products, he made a case for thoughtful management. His arguments led naturally to a final section titled "A New System of Forest Protection." Here John pleaded for the establishment of forest districts overseen by commissioners with the legal authority to exert some measure of control. The commissioners would discourage agricultural settlements in unsuitable areas, and they would enforce a system of annual licenses for mineral exploration, wood cutting, charcoal burning, and logging that would prevent long-term deprivations.

The villains that Leiberg denigrated in his report made up only a small percentage of the region's population, and he felt reasonably certain that the majority of residents would support such a conservative, practical licensing method. In the Little North Fork, after all, he and his peers had successfully employed similar measures of moderation.

"Timber and fuel are needed to develop the West," John wrote. "The people must have them. For want of a proper system of licenses easily obtained, they resort to all manner of trespass. The strong hand of the government, without delay, fear, or favor, is urgently needed to put in effective force regulations that shall thoroughly protect the forests of the West and restrain the waste that now runs rampant throughout their entire extent." These were arguments that he would repeat and expand as he carried out more far-flung forest surveys and wrote more voluminous reports over the next several years.

Crater lake collomia
Collomia mazama

CHAPTER EIGHT

BASIN AND RANGE

▽▽▽▽▽▽▽▽▽▽▽▽▽▽▽▽▽▽▽▽▽▽▽▽▽▽▽▽▽▽▽▽▽▽▽▽▽

F or years John Leiberg had been dreaming of publishing a flora of the Intermountain West that would truly reflect its majesty. "Every working botanist in this region feels the need of such a work," he wrote. "Our western plants will never be satisfactorily arranged unless done by botanists living here and having an intimate acquaintance with the *field botany* of the region." He knew such a task would require considerable labor and hoped to enlist Charles Piper, a young botany instructor at Washington State Agricultural College in Pullman, as a cohort. When Piper replied that Portland's Thomas Jefferson Howell was already well along with a similar project for the entire Pacific Northwest, Leiberg stepped back from his idea, but he did maintain an enduring correspondence with Piper, who was also director of the state college's growing herbarium.

In the course of many letters, the pair discussed subjects ranging from the minute dissection of plant parts to the possibility of publishing David Douglas's neglected Northwest journals. Leiberg often encouraged the professor to pursue unresolved botanical mysteries, such as defining a particular buttercup Douglas had recorded at the base of alpine snowfields in 1826 but that Leiberg had only seen in low to middle elevations. He regaled Piper with a treatise on the importance of the Olympic Mountains in his singular theory concerning plant evolution, and tied himself in knots trying to separate the varying characteristics of the lodgepole pine across the breadth of its extensive range. With special passion, John made a case for the urgent need to blanket the Intermountain West with baseline botanical surveys. "Sheep and cattle are rapidly destroying the native plants, and by the time private explorations reach these regions, the flora will have been totally exterminated," he wrote. When Piper suggested that Leiberg share his expertise with a botany class at the Agricultural College, John answered with an honest evaluation of his own qualifications. "I note your remarks in the matter of teaching," he wrote. "It was very thoughtful and I *greatly appreciate* it. My training has not been such as to fit me for a teacher, and I would not be at all successful in this direction. I prefer fieldwork, either economical or purely scientific."

The correspondents discussed more down-to-earth issues as well. Piper wrote a regular garden column for a Spokane newspaper, which John read faithfully. The Leibergs had set out a large number of apple, pear, peach, and plum trees at their ranch, and several of the trees had become infested with green aphids. They hoped to take the offensive against those pests when spring rolled around, and John wondered if the professor could recommend a serviceable sprayer.

There were more pressing matters than aphids on Leiberg's mind as New Year's Day 1896 approached. Frederick Coville had recently written to say that he had not been able to secure expenses for John to travel to DC that winter to work on plant specimens as they had planned. Coville would do his best to fund another field survey for the coming summer, but that depended on appropriations from the legislature. How John Leiberg wished he could give those legislators a piece of his mind, and not just about funding the surveys. He wanted to collar them to pay attention to the dangers besetting public lands in the West. The existing laws were totally inadequate, he fumed, and were too weakly enforced. Timber companies were exploiting loopholes to amass land. Contractors for railroad ties were trespassing on public sections and cutting trees with impunity. Lazy, worthless firebugs were setting blazes with no thought of the magnificent forests that had been growing for centuries. The waste and destruction made his blood boil.

John had many more opinions on the subject, which he shared with Coville in a series of garrulous letters that anyone who has been cabin-bound during a long Idaho winter can appreciate. Continuing a theme from his Coeur d'Alene report, he extolled a licensing system that would bring in enough revenue to offset the costs of protecting these irreplaceable forests. If implementation of such a method depended only on executive order, he felt it would come to pass. But left up to Congress, he feared, "the matter seemed utterly hopeless."

In other communications, Leiberg refined his system of plant associations as it applied to the Coeur d'Alenes— no easy matter in that region of wildly diverse coniferous growth. He toted up all the drayage costs for his first three expeditions to show how frugal he was in the field. He proposed an eight-month expedition that would continue his exploration of eastern Oregon and asked Coville about the chance of it being funded for the coming season: "Not necessarily an official statement, simply your personal opinion in the matter. It would be a favor I would much appreciate." A full month passed before Frederick Coville had any news to relate, and then all he could do was praise Leiberg's licensing and enforcement solution for public lands forest protection, update him on the political tangle that had stalled Congress from making any headway on the problem, and relay the cold fact that his summer contract remained in limbo.

By return mail, Coville received nineteen pages of closely written script that exposed the full range of Leiberg's mental turmoil. In one sentence John thanked his boss for "efforts to introduce [him] to the notice of public men interested in the problem of forest protection," such as Gifford Pinchot and Henry Gannett; in the next, he expounded on the organic links between the region's geological history and the conditions of its present-day flora: "we must know the one to understand the other." That in turn led John to fret about the fate of his ambitious Oregon expedition. What if it was delayed? How could anyone possibly understand the subtle variations among the dryland species without seeing them at their natural peak in March and April?

If his contract failed to materialize, Leiberg told Coville that he wasn't sure what he would do during the coming summer. Probably prospect around the Little North Fork and peck on his claims a bit. Try to spend time in the garden with his pumpkins and squash, and make sure that he properly exterminated the aphids on his fruit trees. He might travel from Sandpoint west to Priest River to search for the wild cranberry that supposedly grew there. In summary, if there was no work available with the Department of Agriculture, he trusted that he and Coville could remain on good terms. "I will not cease to hold in very grateful and vivid remembrance the many acts of courtesy and kindly generous treatment I have been the recipient of at your hands," he concluded.

While her husband fretted about his work situation, Carrie Leiberg received an urgent call from a patient whom she identified as "Mrs. J." The doctor arrived at the house in question to find an unconscious woman—extremities cold and pulseless; lips, tongue, and face without color. A quick examination revealed profuse uterine bleeding. The doctor found a soft mass protruding from the woman's vaginal opening "which, when quickly removed, proved to be a very much decomposed placenta." Carrie soon got the bleeding under control and attempted to revive her patient. Mrs. J. rallied but remained in a weak condition, and since the placenta appeared to be complete, no further examination was attempted.

By the following day, the patient had recovered sufficiently to relate her story. About a month previous, upon discovering that she was pregnant, Mrs. J. had taken the train to another city and found a doctor who arranged for her to have an abortion. Uncertain about the credentials of the provider, Carrie appended a question mark after the title of doctor. In any case, Mrs. J. told her that the result was a stillborn male child, about six inches long. The provider assured the woman that she could return home, secure in the likelihood that "the jolting of the train would bring the afterbirth." That did not happen, and the woman had suffered from two strong episodes of bleeding before a third convinced her to call Dr. Leiberg.

Carrie calculated that Mrs. J. had carried her placenta for more than three weeks before she expelled it. As a follow-up treatment the doctor applied "the usual remedies," which included doses of ergot. This common grain fungus has been used medicinally since ancient times because contact with the club-shaped fungal bodies makes smooth muscles contract. In this case, it promoted uterine spasms, which Carrie hoped would help expel any remaining small clots or loose tissue.

The ergot treatment scotched the bleeding almost completely. Over the next week, Mrs. J. regained some strength and began to show color in her lips. Then a sudden sharp pain and renewed hemorrhage brought Carrie back to the scene. Within a few minutes of her arrival, the woman gave birth to a tiny stillborn fetus, this time with the entire placenta attached. After the delivery, Mrs. J. rebounded quickly and was soon restored to health.

Carrie determined that the second fetus was in its eighth or ninth week of gestation and must have been conceived during the third or fourth month of the original pregnancy. She thought it was most unusual that "the death and expulsion of the first embryo did not interfere materially with the vitality of the second," and she felt reasonably certain that if she had not treated the woman with several small doses of ergot, the second embryo would have completed its full term. Her sober summation of the case in a medical journal, titled "A Double Pregnancy," illustrated the realities she faced as a physician.

Spring 1896 brought a simpler problem to the Leiberg household. An Idaho senator was searching for photographs illustrating the resources of his home state for a presentation to the National Geographic Society. John happened to be away from home, so Carrie assembled the best scenic photographs that they had on hand and mailed them to Washington, DC, with an apology that there were so few. The senator had also asked for pictures of buildings and industrial establishments; when John returned, he promised to make inquiries and forward any that he succeeded in locating.

On the subject of photography, Leiberg greatly regretted not having taken a camera on any of his excursions for the department and had been looking at advertisements and pondering the model that would be most portable and give the best results. He had made a decision and put in an order when a telegram arrived announcing that the commission for his Oregon plant survey had in fact come through.

This was followed by a familiar promise from Coville that he would join John at some point during the summer.

In April, Leiberg assembled his outfit in Spokane. The kit included a wagon, 1,500 plant-drying blotters, an Eastman Kodak camera that took five-by-seven-inch photographs, and a US Army–issue sharpshooter shovel. He and his assistant, a Mr. Hunter, loaded the gear into a boxcar and then boarded a passenger train to Ontario, Oregon, where the Malheur River meets the Snake. There they purchased a team of four horses to pull the wagon and set off into the Snake River Plain. This trip marked the earliest date that John had been able to witness spring in the shrub-steppe, and he noticed the way emerging flowers hugged close to the shelter afforded by well-spaced shrubs such as bud sage. Cultivated plants did not fare quite as well, as late frosts were ruining the blossoming fruit of hopeful orchardists.

Leiberg and Hunter moved up the Malheur River to camp at the Rhinehart Buttes near Vale where, as usual, local geology captured John's interest. The buttes were composed of conglomerates that had precipitated from thermal springs, similar to places Leiberg had seen on his previous Oregon journey. The difference here was that many active springs remained in evidence, with water temperatures ranging from 120 to 180 degrees Fahrenheit. John observed that while some deposited limey carbonate, others left iron sulfides as their residue. From one particularly hot pool, he collected a green slime that contained a familiar freshwater alga. He marveled at the species' ability to endure such scalding water and realized that he was observing a primordial life process in action.

EASTERN OREGON
1896

At his next mail pickup, Leiberg received news from
Frederick Coville that the National Academy of Sciences
had formed a group called the National Forest Commission.
Five years earlier, Congress had passed the Forest Reserve
Act, which granted the president power to protect valu-
able forest lands by withdrawing them from public use.
Benjamin Harrison had designated ten million acres in
Wyoming, western Oregon, and the Southwest. Now his
successor, Grover Cleveland, was considering adding more

reserves and was asking the commission to recommend areas for inclusion. Its most powerful members included Bernhard Fernow, Charles Sargent, and Gifford Pinchot. Fernow was a German-trained forester who had been head of the USDA's Forestry Division for the past decade, and who struggled to apply European silvicultural methods to the diverse American provinces. Sargent was a Harvard professor who had helped identify some of Leiberg's early Idaho plant collections, but his real passion was for trees, and his 1884 *Report on the Forests of North America* gained him chairmanship of the panel. Gifford Pinchot was appointed secretary and put in charge of a committee to develop a management policy for the reserves.

Pinchot immediately set out to gather as much information as possible. When he visited the Agriculture Department, Frederick Coville shared Leiberg's report on the Coeur d'Alenes, which provided a summary of conditions in the Intermountain West and held just the sort of detailed ecological and economic data that Pinchot hoped to gather for all western timberlands. But that was a project for the future. For the present, the commission needed to assess the areas that held potential as reserves, and Pinchot wanted to visit them all. The Bitterroot region of western Montana and northern Idaho was his first priority, and he was hoping to hire someone trained in forestry to accompany him. "You will at once recognize the importance of the affair," Coville wrote Leiberg. "While I should hesitate for any reason to ask you to leave the plains of southeastern Oregon, the importance of the subject suggests to me that you might to good advantage undertake to pilot Mr. Pinchot into the Bitterroots." Leiberg's reply assured Coville that with two or three days' notice he could meet Pinchot at Spokane or Hope, but first he needed assurance that the gentleman could stay upright on a horse and sleep outside beside a campfire: "This will be no picnic excursion," he cautioned. John need not have worried. Pinchot loved nothing more than packing through rugged country, and he had already worn out plenty of guides during previous whirlwind trips through the Southwest.

Raw energy leaped from each page of John's response to Coville's invitation. This was an opportunity to show someone in power "the effects of tie and lumber cutting where method and care are unknown quantities, where the summer fire runs unchecked, where all efforts of man are put forth to destroy." Leiberg outlined two possible routes, one that started in the Coeur d'Alene basin and one confined to the Clearwater drainage. Both were economical excursions that included day-by-day itineraries. "Mr. Pinchot will not have time within the four weeks to cover any more territory," he admonished Coville. "And in *no* case can he more than obtain a general idea of the Clearwater and Salmon River basins unless he spend at least one full season there."

Leiberg was collecting south of Vale by this time, and he returned to his base camp on May 25 to learn that a recent Forest Commission meeting had resulted in a change of plans, and his services would not be needed. "It is evident that they contemplate a more detailed examination of the mountains hereafter," Coville informed John. "I have given them the benefit of your various reports and letters, and they will know about you when they reach the point of continuing their work." By sharing Leiberg's copious correspondence and thoughtful writings, Coville hoped to familiarize Gifford Pinchot with the scope of John's abilities.

Leiberg's notes on northern Idaho would certainly have been relevant to Pinchot when he did venture West that summer, packing through the Bitterroots to peer into the Clearwater drainage. For five months Pinchot toured potential reserves by train and wagon; on foot and horseback. Sometimes he traveled alone, at others he joined a group of commissioners who were traveling by rail. John Muir, the mountaineer and outspoken conservationist, came along for much of the journey and swept Pinchot away with his outdoor charisma. The pair ascended the Oregon Cascades to Crater Lake, then probed the southern Sierras.

Relations among commission members remained generally cordial, but chairman Charles Sargent and Pinchot differed on several fronts. Sargent believed that the reserve lands should be taken out of circulation and treated as preserves. Pinchot felt that the forests should be open to access and utilized for the benefit of the country. In Pinchot's opinion, Sargent the botanist saw the forest as a collection of individual trees and failed to realize "that forestry is not botany, but something vastly different." Pinchot the forester saw an ecosystem whose components needed to be studied and managed in a way to insure perpetual reproduction of the trees. For enforcing regulations on the reserves, Pinchot pictured a civilian corps of forest rangers, while Sargent favored the US Army. "His autocratic habit of mind," wrote Pinchot, "included an inability to understand that out in the woods, mere orders do not go." The two men had plenty of time to discuss their differences while they visited no less than eight western states. By the time they returned to Washington, DC, Pinchot had gained an overview of the possible reserves, and no one realized better than he the challenges of devising a workable management plan.

Meanwhile, Leiberg and Hunter crept up the Malheur River to Harper's Ranch, whose owner had offered them a place to camp. They next cut south along Cottonwood Canyon to access the Barren Valley, a dry lake bed full of soft adobe-like mud that almost swallowed their heavy wagon. They were able to cover enough of the country east of Steens Mountain to determine that all the surrounding ranges were interconnected, not isolated as shown on the US military map they carried. John thought the divide between the Owyhee and Malheur drainages, with its long slopes and great enclosed plateaus, was the most magnificent grazing region he had seen in the West. Three or four large cattle operations shared the entire range, which allowed the plant collectors to roam freely with all the water, wood, and grass that they could want, unimpeded by a single fence.

About two-thirds of the acreage in eastern Oregon's Malheur County today rests under the jurisdiction of the Bureau of Land Management. Leiberg's plant collections, habitat observations, and interactions with local ranchers from this trip comprise a snapshot of open range grazing land near the beginning of white settlement. During his time along the Owyhee-Malheur divide, he saw silver sagebrush as the most abundant shrub, and a biscuitroot new to him blanketed the slopes in the millions. He sent samples of that and several other new umbellifers to Joseph Rose for determination, directing his friend's attention especially to one with a forked root that thrived in the adobe mud of the Barren Valley. He found it "sweet and more pleasant to the taste than those of the common species, and though growing in muddy soil is not poisonous." To prove the point, he ate a quantity and suffered no ill effects. For good measure, he tossed a clump of its native adobe clay into the mail sack with the tuber.

Because post offices and banks were few and far between in the areas where Leiberg traveled for his summer surveys, he arranged to pick up and drop off his mail at designated stops along the route. Carrie customarily cashed John's stipends from the Department of Agriculture, then forwarded the cash he needed for food and supplies in the field. When the first two monthly checks from the department did not arrive in time, she wrote to Frederick Coville that her husband "is particularly conscious to compass a large amount of work this season, and so wants everything to move with clockwork regularity. In order to do that 'the sinews of war' must be ready when needed."

Even though her artful application of Cicero's "endless money forms the sinews of war" quote must have made someone in the department office smile, the payments were still not forthcoming, so a few weeks later Carrie sent a curt telegram to Coville: "The check for July for John B. Leiberg field agent has not yet arrived. It is needed in the field. Please wire me regarding it." This time, Coville promptly sent a personal letter assuring her that he would address the matter.

Leiberg, for his part, seemed not at all perturbed by his lack of funds. As was his habit, he talked to everyone he met along the way and received an invitation from a rancher named Devine to camp at the edge of the Alvord Desert—a salt flat on the bed of another desiccated Pleistocene lake in the Basin and Range province. The ridge of Steens Mountain formed an imposing uplift to the west, reaching an altitude of 9,600 feet. At Devine Ranch, John learned that Frederick Coville had come west and was traveling with C. H. Merriam's mammal-collecting crew in the Harney Basin, just on the other side of the Steens. After a series of comic miscommunications, Coville and Leiberg finally rendezvoused at the tiny settlement of Shirk just off the mountain's southwest flank. From there they set out across the broken terrain, making for Klamath Lake.

Following a series of rugged wagon roads through the accessible valleys, the pair zigzagged from Beatys Butte to Guano Ranch. They slipped south into Nevada, then back north through the Coleman Valley. After gaining that next rim, they crossed the Warner Valley into mountains of a much larger scale. The basin beyond the Warner Range led them around the edge of huge, water-filled Goose Lake, which straddled the California border and hosted the army post of Fort Bidwell, where they were able to resupply. Their pace picked up as they reentered Oregon and scoured new terrain between Lakeview and Drew's Gap. On one long day they scaled the nearly eight-thousand-foot summit of Cougar Peak in search of alpine plants. After crossing the Quartz Valley, the road paralleled the Sprague River, which allowed them to make their first straightforward east-to-west progress of the journey. When they cut the Williamson River at Chiloquin Bridge, they were rolling in Leiberg's 1894 wagon tracks.

The men spent three late-August days at Fort Klamath and the Klamath Indian Agency, where they met Joe Kirk, the agency interpreter, and White Cindy, a Klamath woman who lived by the lakeshore. Frederick Coville questioned them about cultural plants, then expanded his interviews to include other informants, both white and tribal, from around the agency. He wrestled with the pronunciations of their native tongue and soon had Klamath names for many of the local trees and grasses. Klamath people explained the difference between elegant mariposa lily and death camas, and showed him how they prepared the native lambsquarters that grew around the lake. The single biscuitroot in the area was little used by the Klamaths, but Modoc people gathered it with great enthusiasm around nearby Tule Lake.

The Klamaths did favor *wo-kash*, the yellow pond-lily. Coville watched people gather considerable quantities of its seeds in the shallow waters of Klamath Marsh, then roast them on coals until the seedcoats cracked like parched corn. Whereas in 1894 Leiberg had thought he was witnessing the last throes of a cultural tradition, Coville wrote that *wo-kash* "is such a favorite food with the tribe that its use is likely never to be wholly given up." Coville proved to be right, and his persistence in collecting usage and language for almost ninety different cultural plants made his subsequent monograph a model of early ethnobotany. Leiberg was a contributor and may well have introduced Coville to the Klamath informants; the experience seemed to broaden John's opinion of traditional plant use. "Your list is much larger than I thought would be the case. It should be a most valuable addition to our knowledge of the aboriginal tribes," he told Coville. "If a botanist could spend a year, at least, at each of the agencies west of the Missouri, what a vast fund of interesting information could be obtained."

From Klamath Agency, the two collectors trekked upslope to Crater Lake, where Frederick Coville fell in love with the Cascades. The country's chief botanist would continue to visit these mountains for years to come, and he climbed several of the range's iconic peaks with the Portland chapter of the Mountaineers Club. But none of his subsequent excursions yielded any plants finer than the endemic currant and collomia he and Leiberg found on this first trip. The collomia in particular, with its deep-blue flowers and almost luminescent light-blue stamens, occupied Coville's mind for months to come.

After they descended from Crater Lake to the Deschutes River, Coville boarded a stagecoach bound north for The Dalles to catch a train back to Washington, DC. Leiberg directed his wagon into the High Lava Plains again, crossing the John Day country via Mitchell and Fossil on a slightly different track than he had taken in 1894. He dropped Mr. Hunter at the rail station in Pendleton, ferried his bedraggled outfit across the Snake, and followed the Palouse Hills north through Colfax to Spokane. As soon as he arrived at Hope in late September, he collapsed into bed with a churning stomach bug. John never got sick in the wild and blamed his illness on "the terribly filthy water" he had made the mistake of drinking while passing through the settlements of Pendleton and Walla Walla.

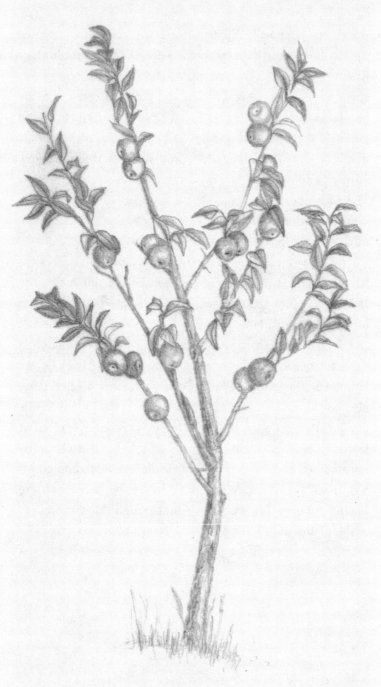

Apple tree
Malus pumila

▽▽▽▽▽▽▽▽▽▽▽▽▽▽▽▽▽▽▽▽▽▽▽▽▽▽▽▽▽▽▽▽▽▽▽

CHAPTER NINE

SOLITAIRE

▽▽▽▽▽▽▽▽▽▽▽▽▽▽▽▽▽▽▽▽▽▽▽▽▽▽▽▽▽▽▽▽▽▽▽

L eiberg had important news to absorb while he recovered from his stomach upset. At the beginning of August, Government Land Office surveyor Oscar Sonnenkalb had arrived at Idaho's Township 53 North. Sonnenkalb's rod-and-chain survey would lay out section lines across Rathdrum Prairie, east to the Chilco Saddle, and north to include the Leibergs' peninsula at the south end of Lake Pend Oreille. His results would determine which parcels of land belonged to the Northern Pacific Railroad and which were available for homesteading. John and Carrie were about to learn the status of the property that they had protected so carefully for a decade.

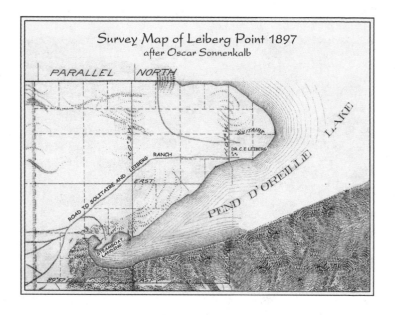

Survey Map of Leiberg Point 1897
after Oscar Sonnenkalb

Sonnenkalb was a German surveyor who had gained experience in the Snake River Plain of southern Idaho. After trying a few contracts in the forested regions of the Panhandle, he discarded his "home country" crew for local men "who had grown up from childhood with the ax in their hand—Swedes, Norwegians, Scotchmen, some trappers and voyageurs—those were the boys who could do the work." These ax men established a course among stands of valuable western white pine along Lewellen Creek, then made for the peninsula "over gently rolling land, through heavy fir and tamarack timber and dense high undergrowth." Sonnenkalb found the route "mostly covered with burnt, fallen timber, making the execution of the surveying work exceptionally difficult." Thickets of hawthorn and willow that had sprouted from the charred earth did not make the task any easier.

As his crew toiled from south to north, marking off a grid of forty- and eighty-acre lots, they crossed a braid of wagon roads that ran across Rathdrum Prairie; one of these he labeled on his map as the "road to Solitaire and Leiberg Ranch." This single track wound to the peninsula's end through a sandy loam that Sonnenkalb gauged would be well suited for agriculture. On a protected bench a bit past the steamboat landing, he noted that "Dr. C. E. Leiberg has made fine improvements, with the view of establishing a health resort and hospital on the promontory at the point." Sonnenkalb's meticulous map set the resort's name, Solitaire, in a curve of letters that covered two lots. An adjoining pair of lots included a cluster of four structures tucked into the property's southwest corner. Over a mile of fencing enclosed thirty-five acres of cultivated land, a twenty-five-acre orchard, and a ten-acre meadow for grazing livestock.

Although the Solitaire resort never came to fruition, Carrie obviously had an ambitious project in mind. She may have harbored the idea since her winter at the Chicago Polyclinic, hoping to serve local women as well as patients from afar. Or perhaps she had larger dreams: across the state line in Spokane, Dr. Mary Latham had established her own women's hospital within the same year, calling it the Lidgerwood Sanitarium. The paths of the two doctors often seemed to mirror each other—Latham had planted an extensive orchard in north Spokane—and it would have made sense to partner an urban health center with an isolated retreat like Solitaire.

No matter what Carrie intended, Sonnenkalb's survey proved that the four lots were in Section 2 of Township 53 N. Since the Northern Pacific owned odd-numbered sections, the Leibergs would not have to purchase the land but could file a homestead patent. The couple now owned a nest egg that would become, exactly as John had predicted, a very valuable piece of property.

After recovering from the rigors of his summer journey, Leiberg spent most of that fall bantering with Frederick Coville about their ongoing projects. They fussed over the names of new plants collected on their swing through southern Oregon, especially the blue collomia from Crater Lake. Coville was preparing a presentation about the trip for the National Geographic Society and asked Leiberg to create a map of Oregon forest types to accompany it. John took offense at edits Coville suggested for the geological section of the Coeur d'Alene report, then considered resigning unless the department agreed to pay his travel expenses to DC.

At one point, the chief botanist mailed Leiberg the popular book *In the Heart of the Bitter-Root Mountains*, a true adventure tale about a group of young hunters on a winter expedition that ended in disaster. John's response explained in great detail how the party, led by a Mr. Carlin, revealed themselves to be a bunch of "self-willed obstinate tenderfeet." This was especially true of Carlin, who was well known to locals "as an utterly worthless cigarette-smoking dude." Remembering that Coville had expressed a desire to explore the western slopes of the Bitterroots, Leiberg suggested that he avoid the trails taken by the Carlin party, then outlined an alternate route that would provide good traveling and magnificent scenery, with a promise of arriving at the divide in good spirits. To prove that established residents could handle a little weather, he forwarded a newspaper photograph that showed twenty-five feet of snow at a mining operation on Sunset Peak. Then, close on the heels of Coville's final editing comments for the Coeur d'Alene report, John announced his formal resignation.

By this time, the presidential election pitting Democrat William Jennings Bryan against Republican William McKinley was entering its final weeks. Bryan's campaign was buoyed by the support of the Populist Party, which shared wide appeal among Idaho farmers and workers who mistrusted big banks and corporate monopolies. When the large mining companies of the Silver Valley backed Bryan's proposal to allow unlimited coinage of silver, conventional political logic, at least as it was understood back East, was flipped on its head. But western voters had their own particular issues. That November, Bryan carried Idaho by a large margin, while McKinley prevailed nationally in a victory that most eastern politicos saw as stabilizing.

Within a matter of weeks after the election, Frederick Coville addressed Leiberg's resignation by offering him a permanent appointment as Special Field Botanist at the US Department of Agriculture. The salary would be $150 a month, including funds for another winter in the nation's capital. When terms of the commission arrived at Hope on November 28, Carrie dispatched a prompt answer on the stationery from her office, the letterhead stamped in attractive purple ink. She informed Coville that John was away at their Lakeside Ranch, and the lake had been unnavigable for days due to horrid weather. She would relay the news to her husband as soon as the storms abated.

By mid-December, John was on his way to the District of Columbia, while Carrie continued in her role as railroad physician in Hope. Late on the night after Christmas, she responded to a call from Dr. Loop, a colleague four years out of Baltimore Medical College who also served as a surgeon for the Northern Pacific. Their patient, a mother of two young children, was nearing the end of her third pregnancy. On the evening in question, the woman and her children had been alone at home when she stood up from her chair and began to bleed so profusely that she fainted.

Luckily her husband, a railroad man, soon arrived from his shift at the depot and sent for young Dr. Loop, who in turn called for Dr. Leiberg, who "found the patient in a state of profound collapse, due to a sudden and terrific uterine hemorrhage." The woman's clothing was saturated with blood, and there was an immense pool on the floor. A quick exam revealed her pupils to be widely dilated, her extremities cold and covered with clammy perspiration, her pulse very weak, and her heart rate dangerously high at 130 beats per minute. Carrie determined that the patient was carrying a large child that needed to be turned before there could be any chance for a safe delivery. She and Loop stanched the bleeding, but the woman was in no condition for them to chance a forced labor or a cesarean section. They let her relax for a while, applying hypodermics of brandy and strychnine to build her strength. Every hour through the night, they fortified her with a tablespoon of Horlick's Malted Milk dissolved in hot water.

Over the course of those treatments, the patient's pulse gradually became slower and stronger, but when morning broke there were still no contractions. Three days later, another round of bleeding began, just as painless and profuse as before. "As we had remained constantly in attendance, expecting precisely such an occurrence, we were prepared to meet this, and controlled it promptly and effectually," wrote Carrie. They changed the packing every six hours until the following morning, New Year's Eve. By that time, the woman's pulse had settled at a weak but regular ninety beats per minute. The doctors decided that their patient was as ready to give birth as she would ever be, and began dosing her with Fluid Extract of Ergot at the rate of five or six drops every twenty minutes. Carrie managed to turn the baby by external manipulation, and at one in the afternoon, the patient finally went into labor.

At four, the child was wedged far enough into the birth canal to stop its mother's bleeding, and the doctors removed their absorbent bandages. An hour later a "blue baby" was born that weighed almost eleven pounds. "Continuous effort resuscitated it for a short time, but its death occurred about three hours later," Carrie recorded. The mother herself remained deathly white, yawned continuously, and suffered from great thirst, nausea, and light-headedness—"a chain of symptoms well calculated to cause great anxiety."

At that point, Dr. Leiberg had to make sure the placenta was passed. With calculated probing, she carefully separated the placenta from the uterine walls, beginning at the outer margin and proceeding incrementally, "firmly pressing [her] fingers against the denuded uterine tissue to prevent as much loss of blood as possible." The procedure took about twenty minutes and resulted in less hemorrhage than she and Loop expected. They had prepared for a transfusion but decided it wasn't necessary. The patient rallied, her uterus began to contract firmly, and the doctors began to feel the worst was over.

It wasn't. Two hours later the patient experienced a violent seizure accompanied by all the symptoms of cardiac arrest. Her heartbeat doubled, and Carrie recorded the same dilated pupils and clammy extremities she had witnessed initially—altogether another "profound collapse." She and Loop elevated the foot of the bed, applied dry heat to the body, administered strychnine and nitroglycerine, and watched the symptoms gradually subside. Four hours later, the woman endured another seizure of shorter span. "The dawn of the new year found her just alive, that was all."

The doctors decided that the patient needed nourishment. They employed more Horlick's Malted Milk at the rate of a few drops offered every hour, and later believed that the Horlick's had prevented death by exhaustion. The woman completed her convalescence without another setback and was rapidly regaining strength when Carrie penned an article about the case for Portland's *Medical Sentinel* a few weeks later, in February 1897.

That same month, outgoing President Grover Cleveland followed the recommendation of the National Forest Council and signed an executive order, known as the Washington's Birthday Proclamation, that set aside thirty-three thousand square miles for thirteen new forest reserves, including two in northern Idaho. With that single stroke of his pen, Cleveland more than doubled the size of federally controlled timberlands and ignited a firestorm of controversy. Unfortunately, the Forest Commission had not been able to present the president with a new management policy before the announcement. Therefore, under the existing law, his proclamation closed the reserves to all commerce and settlement; in fact, to public entry of any sort. The new reserves were all located between the Rockies and the Pacific, and western legislators were outraged that they had not been consulted. Mining and timber companies considered this move a direct economic threat, and many homesteaders viewed it as an affront to their patent rights. John Leiberg, who was sorting plants at the National Herbarium, immediately wrote a letter expressing his opposition to the act as written and delivered it across the hall to Frederick Coville, making sure to include two extra copies so that his boss could relay an Idaho perspective to Gifford Pinchot of the Forest Commission and to Henry Gannett, Chief Geographer at the US Geological Survey.

Leiberg did not mince words. "The proclamation is inopportune and places everything that has been done for the protection of the western forest areas *in most imminent danger of being lost*," he began. While previous forest reserves had been set aside in regions with no appreciable mineral resources, these new designations surrounded profitable deposits in both the Rocky Mountains and the Cascade Range. By neglecting to make provisions for mining and other commercial interests before the reserves were created, the commission had exposed the system to the full broadside of those industries' political power. "It won't be long before the West will make itself heard," Leiberg predicted.

While John waded into the battle over forest management, Carrie focused her energy on spring orchard plantings. She set a crew of men to work and contacted a Willamette

Valley nursery for seedlings. "I have seen the trees my friend ordered, and if you beat them they will be *dandies*," Carrie wrote, advising the nurserymen to send their stock "well boxed, as they get rough treatment out this way." That said, she hoped the order could be on its way very soon, because she wanted to supervise the planting before she traveled east later in the month.

In early April, John wrapped up his winter work at the herbarium in DC and headed west. Carrie started her own journey east, and they met at the Mississippi River. On April 15, a clerk in St. Croix County, Wisconsin, just across the river from St. Paul, issued a marriage license to John B. and Carrie E. Leiberg. They selected a Methodist-Episcopal service for their vows, which were witnessed by the vicar and someone from the office. Neither Leiberg left any clue as to the motivation for a ceremony that had been delayed for more than a decade. Perhaps John decided that if he was going to engage in a public struggle for the soul of the western forest lands, his personal life might come under scrutiny. Perhaps Carrie wanted to make sure that if anything happened to John she would have a legal claim to their homestead lots. Perhaps they both felt the need to protect themselves from complications rising from their previous marriages, or they were thinking of Bernard's status. Whatever their motivation, change was in the air for the Leibergs.

For the past decade, John had steadily filed new mineral claims while continuing to make the annual investment of $100 per claim required to proof his existing ones. Now it appeared that he might be able to reap some benefit from his relentless work. He told Elizabeth Britton: "Confidentially, there is a very good prospect that with this year we will begin to realize upon some of our mining properties, in which case I will have unlimited means and abundance of time to carry on my botanical studies so far as I please."

For the present, Leiberg's botanical studies concentrated on the camas blooming near Lake Pend Oreille and on an intriguing balsamroot that a Northern Pacific engineer brought him from Montana. Along with several other plants that he knew Coville would find desirable, he mailed a pair of folded bark baskets that Kalispel people used for holding huckleberries and similar soft fruits. He was also busy planning for his summer work in the Priest River country, the site of one of the new forest reserves designated in Grover Cleveland's proclamation. A shipment of supplies had already arrived in Hope: five sacks of plant driers, plus postage franks, vouchers, blank notebooks, and envelopes. He would require all this gear and more, as his assigned tasks included "a brief account to the principal kinds and amount of its timber; the relation of the reserve to adjacent or included settlements, agricultural land, or mineral land; the desirability and feasibility of increasing or decreasing the present limits of the reserve; the nature and amount of any depredations now being committed or likely to be committed; and recommendations relative to its administration in furtherance of the present laws."

In early May, even the lowest hills remained white with snow, and John reckoned it would be late June before any serious survey activity could begin in the high country. He did make a preliminary foray around the eastern edge of the proposed reserve and determined that its boundaries should be expanded east toward Bonners Ferry and south to include the upper Pack River drainage. As to the western ridge of mountains that ran up the Washington State side, there would be a lot to learn when snowmelt finally allowed access. Along the way, he heard rumors about various schemes designed to pillage extensive amounts of timber prior to the finalization of the new forest reserve regulations. As always, he was deeply concerned at the extent of uncontrolled burning. On the stretch of the Great Northern route between Sandpoint and Bonners Ferry, he counted nine fires over a distance of thirty-four miles along the railbed. Some had been started by settlers clearing land, others by locomotive sparks, and it did not bode well for the summer. "It is evident the law against fires in the forests has no terror for the people out here yet," he wrote Coville. "The country is full of smoke from fires in the valleys."

Leiberg was back in Hope on May 7, in time to read a newspaper headline reporting that the Senate had voted to overturn Cleveland's February 22 proclamation. "If correctly reported, this marks the beginning of the total destruction of the forest reserve system," John wrote to Coville. He thought the resentment in the western states so strong that one crack would bring down the whole concept. He strongly disagreed with the existing law: "The reserve system is too much like a 'keep off the grass' order to command either respect or obedience out here," he wrote. Now he worried that it had engendered a feeling of hostility against *all* government involvement in public lands.

John still believed that a plan for the management of forest lands could be worked out along the lines of the proposal he had put forth in his Coeur d'Alene report. He envisioned a system that would charge fair licensing fees to prospectors, miners, lumbermen, and stockmen. Resident managers who knew the area would vigorously enforce regulations and monitor conditions. In his opinion, many westerners supported the need for regulations on matters such as homesteading, burning restrictions, and commerce on public lands. At the same time, any call for government control brought back memories of federal troops rounding up activists during the Bunker Hill strikes. Leiberg remained firmly convinced that "no successful laws and regulations in the matter will ever be made until they are fashioned by men that are fully conversant with the temper and habits of western people, and with the financial and industrial questions involved." He told Coville that Congress needed to take action as soon as possible in order to get a volatile situation under control.

Over the next month, Congress continued to debate the fate of the forest reserves and eventually reached a compromise. Instead of a total annulment, they imposed a nine-month delay on the establishment of any new reserves. They reversed the prior law so as to allow public access, including prospecting. They defined the purposes of the reserves as watershed protection, forest protection, and timber supply. They charged the Interior Department with oversight and appropriated funds for a survey. On June 4, President McKinley signed the Forest Management Act of 1897 into law.

While waiting to learn the future of the forest reserves and his summer survey work, Leiberg occupied himself with photographing timber stands near Lake Pend Oreille. With an eye toward documenting conditions in western forests, he sent the department pictures of burned areas around the Panhandle. Coville asked for more shots of horses, healthy trees, and larger landscapes to provide context. Leiberg was plotting a series of photographs of every species of conifer in the Northwest when a transformative note from Coville arrived. "My arrangement with Mr. Gannett has been to have you transferred to the Interior Department on the rolls of the Geological Survey for the summer, beginning July 1."

Henry Gannett's orders called for Leiberg to make a month-long assessment of the proposed Priest River Reserve, then depart for the Bitterroot Forest Reserve and survey there until the end of the field season. When John expressed reservations about the scope of his duties with the Geological Survey, Coville had a ready answer. "Mr. Gannett is willing to have you do such botanical work as you can," he assured Leiberg. "In addition to the preparation of your report for him, I presume that you can get two or three specimens of everything that the country contains."

Coville, who had edited Leiberg's previous reports, tried to send him a clear message that he should stay on task. "The only words of advice I have for you relative to your work with the Survey," Coville concluded, "is to make them the very best report you can produce and make it practical. In writing, be as brief and concise as is consistent with a clear presentation." In other words, John would do well to harness his prose within the specified parameters. Whether Leiberg would be able to follow this advice was another matter.

Small cranberry
Vaccinium oxycoccos

CHAPTER TEN

FROM THE PRIEST
TO THE BITTERROOT

▽▽▽▽▽▽▽▽▽▽▽▽▽▽▽▽▽▽▽▽▽▽▽▽▽▽▽▽▽▽▽▽▽

T he war is on," Gifford Pinchot wrote of the controversy over management of western public lands in
1897. The creation of thirteen new forest reserves
brought to the fore many perplexing conflicts that remain
unresolved today—including state sovereignty, wilderness
preservation, multiple use, and commercial development.
Pinchot felt that much of the public opposition would dis-
solve when people realized that the new law provided free
entry for all citizens and that the natural resources were
going to be put to use for their benefit. Soon after the bill
passed Congress, he took a job as Confidential Forest Agent
for the USGS, with orders to examine the reserves, report

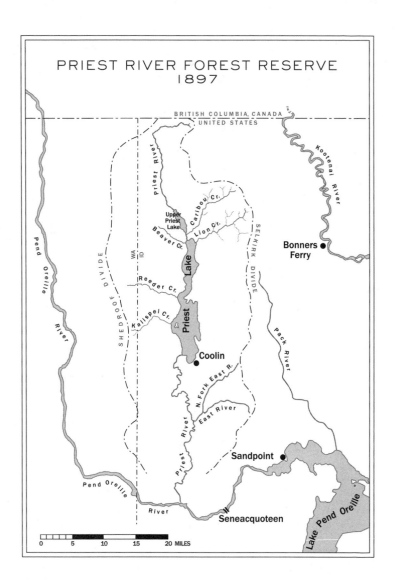

PRIEST RIVER FOREST RESERVE
1897

BRITISH COLUMBIA, CANADA
UNITED STATES

Kootenai River

Pend Oreille River

Priest River

Upper Priest Lake

Caribou Cr.

Lion Cr.

Beaver Cr.

SELKIRK DIVIDE

Bonners Ferry

SHEDROOF DIVIDE

WA ID

Priest Lake

Reeder Cr.

Kalispel Cr.

Coolin

Pack River

N. Fork East R.

East River

Priest River

Sandpoint

Pend Oreille River

Seneacquoteen

Lake Pend Oreille

0   5   10   15   20 MILES

on their conditions, and prepare a plan for a forestry service to oversee them. But before any policies could be put in place, millions of acres needed to be surveyed and classified. He quickly formed a working partnership with chief geographer Henry Gannett, who was responsible for mapping the land and inventorying the forest stands in the new reserves.

Gannett, who had earned the nickname of "Quad" for his standardized topographic maps, dispatched a crew to each of the designated reserves to establish benchmarks, then lay township and range lines along the proposed boundaries. From this information, cartographers began to develop base maps. At the same time resource surveyors worked to determine the extent of forest assets as well as to identify agricultural lands and prospective mineral properties. The men performing these duties required an expert knowledge of forestry, and Gifford Pinchot was happy to provide Gannett with some likely names, including Pinchot's friend Henry Graves, who handled the Black Hills Reserve in Dakota Territory. H. B. Ayers, a respected geologist and timber inspector for the Northern Pacific Railroad, was assigned first to western Montana's Flathead Reserve, then the Washington Cascades Reserve. While Leiberg may have lacked the formal training of these men, he made up for it in field experience. He also strongly agreed with Gifford Pinchot's brand of practical forestry.

Under its original boundaries, Priest River stood as the smallest of the new reserves, encompassing around 650,000 acres. The Priest harbored some of the most desirable timber anywhere in the region, especially western white pine. At that time, the only appreciable number of logs taken from the proposed reserve had been cut from the lower portion of the river to supply ties for the railroads. Recently, however, Great Lakes eastern white pine companies, seeking replacement stands for their own depleted stocks, had begun sending cruisers into the area. Pinchot and Leiberg were in agreement that selling timber should be one of the purposes for the forest reserves, and their stated goal was to manage the resources within each reserve in a sustainable manner.

At the end of June, Leiberg clipped a newspaper report that one of the USGS topographers was in Spokane outfitting for Priest River. With his usual close eye on the weather gauge, John surmised that an approaching stretch of summer storms would slow the newcomer's progress, and he chafed about the delay before he could get into the field himself. He finally began his own work in the first week of July by following the Pend Oreille River downstream from Sandpoint to Seneocquateen, the ancient tribal crossing just below that river's outlet from the lake. He laid out a botanical notebook very much like the ones he had kept in previous summers and proceeded to collect species of shooting star, violet, and saxifrage. He pondered the possible cultivation of an interesting chokecherry and scraped a scalepod from a wet granite ledge before following Priest River to the southern tip of Priest Lake and its sole post office at Coolin. For the next week, he shadowed Henry Gannett's mapping crew along the west slopes of the Selkirk Range, an uplift that rises steeply from the east shore of Priest Lake into a north–south ridge that encompasses several peaks over seven thousand feet in elevation.

Meanwhile, Gifford Pinchot departed DC to take a firsthand look at "the most valuable body of timber in the interior of the continent." He and his brother took a train west, picked up a favorite guide in the Montana Rockies, and headed for Priest River. At Coolin, the trio secured a rowboat, then over the next six days covered the length of Priest and Upper Priest Lakes, interviewing local people along the way. On his final day there, Pinchot ran up the modest summit of Coolin Mountain, then went fishing for his farewell meal. After supper, John Leiberg dropped by, and the agent boiled down their encounter in his field diary: "Met Leiberg."

The two men would have found much to talk about that evening, from their admiration for western white pine to the best camera to carry in the wilderness. They would have agreed on many of the policies Pinchot hoped to implement in the forests, and on specific issues in the Priest River complex. Leiberg was formulating a plan that would consolidate all of Idaho's public lands into one parcel bounded by Priest Lake's eastern shore and the Selkirk Crest. Pinchot eventually turned that concept into reality, and today the federal Forest Service controls blocks to the west of the lake, while Idaho state lands lie on the east side. The two men also shared a preoccupation with fire, and many of Pinchot's later writings about burns on western forest reserves echoed Leiberg's language, such as this assessment of the Priest River situation: "There is probably not a body of one thousand acres on the whole reserve which has not been more or less seriously injured by fire."

After his brief parlay with Pinchot, Leiberg worked the lake's west shore to Reeder Creek, taking documentary photographs along the way. He collected tiger lilies and rein orchids before he found the wild cranberry, savored for its tart fruit, that he had heard so much about. John identified this species as the same one that grew on the Pacific Coast and pondered the widely separated ranges of several similar plants that thrived west of the Cascades, then reappeared in isolated areas within the Idaho Panhandle and southeastern British Columbia. He next cut across the channel below Upper Priest Lake to explore Caribou Creek, named for a woodland caribou subspecies known as the Selkirk herd, which dwindled away to effective extinction in the year 2018. He made his way down the lake's east side into a large stand of larch and white pine on the lower Priest River, picking up along the way another pair of rein orchids and a grapefern that serve as indicator plants for rich habitat. His survey ended back at the junction of the Priest and Pend Oreille Rivers four weeks after he began.

Leiberg was aware that more legwork was needed to better understand the drainage. "In a region so difficult of traverse as the Priest River Reserve," he wrote in his report, "it is not to be expected that every small subdivision has been examined in detail in the brief time allotted to the work, nor that the average [timber] estimate is absolutely exact. A general summary of the conditions is all that has been attempted." Within these limitations, he provided a surprisingly thorough account of the basin, building on a host of sharp geographical observations.

He delineated the geologic forces that shaped the basin, with the "sinuous crest" of the Selkirks (which he called the Priest River Range) formed from granitic rocks: "It has been deeply sculptured and eroded by glacial action, creating deep canyons and wearing the crest in many localities to a mere narrow margin between the great precipices on either side." Anyone who has hiked east from Priest Lake aiming for one of the distinctive knobs along the Selkirk

Crest can see the precision of that description. In contrast, the range that enclosed Priest Lake on the west side was much less rugged, presenting longer, more rounded slopes and troughs between the lateral ridges—clear indications of a different and older geologic origin. These two north–south ranges, separated by no more than twenty miles at the base of Priest Lake and converging near the Canadian border, captured weather systems to funnel an unusual amount of annual precipitation into the basin.

Although lacking the modern concept of a lobe from a continental ice sheet licking down to shape Priest Lake, Leiberg did speculate that a mountain glacier had plowed out of the higher Selkirks to fill the basin with ice. He observed how lower Priest River had cut through a significant moraine, partially draining a Pleistocene lake and leaving behind extensive wetlands. When he surmised that "these flats and bogs are important conservators and regulators of the water supply of this basin," he was expressing a key tenet of wetland value long before it entered modern ecology textbooks. He also recognized the lacustrine silts deposited atop glacial subsoils on the gentler western slopes of the reserve and described how the long-term succession of beaver dams in the days before commercial trapping had helped to create a tapestry of marshy flats and meadows covered with deep fertile mold.

These constituents supported timber stands of astonishing productivity, and Leiberg tallied sixteen species of trees, eleven of which were cone bearers. Seven of these conifers he considered to be commercially valuable. In his estimation, over 90 percent of the high-grade timber came from just two species: western white pine, which the locals called silver pine, and tamarack or western larch. In his haste, he missed a corridor of old-growth cedar and western hemlock that still extends from Upper Priest Lake north almost to the Canadian border. But in his day, those species were not considered prime timber, and he was not far off when he wrote that the pine and tamarack he saw around Priest "surpassed in density any other area of similar composition in the West."

Adhering to Henry Gannett's instructions, Leiberg tabulated the marketable timber within the reserve. In one of the many tables included in his report, he recorded western white pines up to five feet in diameter, 375 years of age, and 120 feet clear to the first branch. He found comparably sized larch as old as 420 years and cedars that had lived for eight centuries. He estimated that the standing merchantable timber from all of his designated zones would approach five billion board feet. Following his own and Pinchot's definition of sustainable use, Leiberg defined that figure as "the amount that may be safely cut without impairment of the strength of the forest." In order to efficiently tap the resource, he thought that weirs would need to be constructed on major creeks to transport logs from the slopes. The level of Priest Lake should be raised by a terminal dam in order to yard the timber during autumn's low water. Sawmills would be needed within the drainage, and markets for their products would have to be developed back East. And somebody, somehow, would have to put an end to the senseless burning that marred every level of the basin before this invaluable forest was destroyed.

Leiberg's Priest River report made no mention of lightning strikes as a factor in these burns, but by examining ring scars on old stumps, he did recognize the presence of prehistoric fires in the basin, and he documented a very large wildfire that had swept more than half of the reserve in the early 1700s. He also described a new regime that had begun with the arrival of gold seekers moving north from California in the 1860s. Since then, fires had crept into the reserve from mining operations around its boundaries, beginning with the Metaline districts of the Washington side and extending to activities on the Kootenai and Pend Oreille Rivers. During his visits to the reserve, he saw prospectors, hunters, and trappers light fires indiscriminately. He watched supervisors of the Coolin wagon road pile up slash and set it aflame with no regard for containment. On a smaller scale, large logging companies were circumventing restrictions by hiring squatters to stake homestead claims. The squatters would burn open spaces and build rough cabins to prove up their applications, then sell the land to the logging company and depart forever. More serious homesteaders, encouraged by railroad fliers that promised bountiful crop returns on free land, used fire to clear openings for fields. In all but a few low-lying areas, late and early frosts ruined their crops every single year until they too abandoned their claims.

Leiberg faithfully documented these human activities with his camera. After disappointing results from the convenient film equipment he had carried on his Oregon expedition, this summer he went to the trouble of packing an older box camera and glass plates. His efforts were rewarded with clear images, many of which appeared in his final report above captions providing concise comments on the scenes:

"Destruction of a Mixed Forest, Priest River Forest Reserve."

"Burnt White Pine Forest Priest River Forest Reserve: Destruction Total."

"Fire Started by Road Supervisor in July 1897 in the White-Pine Timber One Mile Below the Junction of the East Fork and Priest River."

"Squatter's Claim in White-Pine Timber, Showing Usual Improvements on This Class of Claims."

Beyond this devastation, Leiberg catalogued stages of plant succession and forest recovery after fires swept through. He gauged the vulnerability of emerging stands and emphasized the difficulty of breaking the cycle of wild-fire once it began. He also stressed how the loss of forest cover hastened snow runoff, causing detrimental effects downstream. He further noted how hot wildfires often incin-erated the humus, effectively sterilizing fragile glacial soils and retarding by decades and perhaps centuries the forest's resilience to the natural fire regime.

Although he complained bitterly about the destructive actions of a few humans, Leiberg remained sympathetic to the region's homesteaders and recommended redrawing the reserve's boundaries so as to exclude most of the via-ble agricultural areas. While commercial mining had not yet reached the rugged portions of the Upper Priest when he made his survey, John knew that "a great many quartz claims have been located in three mineral-bearing zones. It is well within the range of possibility that profitable discoveries will eventually be made in this direction." Over the next few decades, several commercial mines did operate with varying degrees of success.

After completing his Priest River survey in mid-August, Leiberg returned to Lake Pend Oreille, where he remained for barely a week before tackling an even more ambitious task. Of the thirteen forest reserves set aside by President Cleveland, the Bitterroot was the largest. At that early stage, it encompassed over four million acres of territory on both sides of the Continental Divide, with 80 percent of its expanse in Idaho and the rest in Montana. John planned to begin on that smaller western portion, so he headed for his former winter haunt of Hamilton, where Gannett's mapping team had established their headquarters. From there they could access three well-known tribal trails—Lolo to the north, Lost Horse in the middle, and Nez Perce Pass to the south—that remained the range's major cross-routes, just as they had been when Lewis and Clark made their journeys almost a century before.

Traveling on horseback, Leiberg climbed to Lost Horse Pass. He ran the ridge that marks the state boundary, collecting alpine plants along the way, then dropped over to the Idaho side to briefly explore Bear Creek in the Selway drainage. At Nez Perce Pass he approached the Clearwater-Salmon divide, which bordered another huge forest reserve that was under the charge of a separate USGS team. It was rugged country and daunting work, especially as fall weather descended on the mountains.

On September 30, after six more weeks in the field, Leiberg came down from the hills to set up camp near the town of Darby in the Bitterroot Valley. There he fired off a frustration-filled letter to Frederick Coville. "My summer has been pretty trying," he wrote, adding that he didn't think he would sign up for another detail with the Geological Survey. "The scope of country assigned to me has been altogether too large for so rough and difficult a region as the Priest River and Bitterroot." Henry Gannett was prodding him to dash over to the Salmon River Mountains before the weather deteriorated, which, John wrote, "I cannot do. The five horses I brought into the field are completely used up, one dead, having travelled fully a thousand miles over a mountain country." Worse yet, he hadn't been able to collect many plants, "owing to the necessity for hustling to get over the large area expected to be covered."

But what a country it was, awesome and humbling in its complexity. In the Bitterroots, none of the associated plant habitat types that Leiberg had formulated in other forests seemed to apply. He found his favored white pine zone to be entirely absent. Subalpine larch dominated long stretches of timberline where he was used to seeing whitebark pine. Lodgepole pine grew in three distinctly different forms depending on aspect, and he hadn't seen any mountain hemlock at all. "I have heretofore imagined we could construct zonal limitations for our trees," he confessed. "I have asked the Lord to forgive me for this presumption."

He paused a week later near Hamilton to pen some further observations. Since Coville was always curious about cultural plants, John promised to send him samples of a certain yellow-green lichen that was used for a dye. Aware that Coville was also studying aspects of wild bighorn versus domestic sheep grazing in the Cascade Range, Leiberg aired his support of a proposal to introduce Angora goats into the Bitterroots. He thought it would be well worth the investment to see if they could survive competition with native goats and deer, and he explained how a new generation of forest rangers could easily protect the introductions from poachers because the goats would always be visible on the Bitterroots' precipitous granite walls. He dared to hope that in the long run, Angora pelts might replace those of the fast-disappearing Bering Sea fur seals.

Although he only spent a brief time on the Clearwater side of the divide, he had seen some intriguing fauna and urged C. H. Merriam to send a crew to search for new rodents. More significantly, John had been outraged at the wasteful practices he had witnessed among a few local hunters there. At a salt lick on the Clearwater, he had seen eleven elk shot and left to rot, while in a nearby drainage one bear hunter laid out forty deer for bait. Leiberg was not opposed to hunting by any means, for he knew that wild game was often the only resource that separated many farmers and homesteaders from starvation. But he believed that killing for mere pleasure was ruthless and should be squelched.

In the forests he had toured, ponderosa pine comprised by far the most productive timber species, but Leiberg counted subalpine larch as a new favorite. "Short, stout, and elegant, light feathery foliage springs from the alpine heights of indescribably rocky craggy peaks and ridges. It seems like a relic from a long since past." He liked the way this larch flourished atop the hard, naked granite of the high country, sprawling across hundreds of acres where no shrub and scarcely any small herbacious plants ever ventured.

Within the basins below those alpine zones, wherever he had traveled that season, "it [was] the same story—fire and ruin." Leiberg contrasted the very small number of mindless "firebugs" against the "overriding will of the balance of the people" and declared that "if the government ever expects to bring order out of this lawless disregard, it will have to handle the evil with something else than a velvet hand." John believed that the glass plates he was packing home from the Bitterroots would provide visual evidence to back up his claims.

Although Leiberg did not show quite the flare of his cohort H. B. Ayers, who posed one homesteader playing the fiddle on his burned-over tract, John's photographs still make for evocative viewing. One shot of grazing land in the Bitterroot Valley, enhanced by delicate hand-coloring, looks past fine riparian habitat to rolling hills. Vistas of aristocratic, well-spaced stands of yellow pine carry the characteristic fire scars of a regular low-impact burn cycle, and each caption includes estimates of board feet per acre in timber yield. Doghair stands of lodgepole pine look ready for another all-consuming conflagration. Alpine ridgetops dive into smoky valleys below, and bold cliffs line "sluice box" canyons on the Montana side of the divide.

Leiberg's lens captured human elements of the high country as well. A squatter's cabin stands in the midst of a logged-over tract with no cultivated land in sight; a gravel flat has been cleared of brush but looks marginal for growing food or forage. Teepees range across the alpine meadows of Nez Perce Pass, with groups of horses hobbled beneath wind-topped snags. "There were a lot of Snakes, Flatheads, and Nez Perce out on a hunt along the pass, lying in wait on deer trails," John wrote Coville, and he soon mailed two packets of Flathead tribal medicine that he had obtained at the encampment. In another photograph, a large yellow pine rises above a decimated stand of younger growth. The pine carries a distinct scar at the height of a man, hinting that the old tree once had a section of bark stripped away for the sweet scrapings of its cambium layer.

Despite all that he accomplished during his six-week stint in the Bitterroots, Leiberg remained dissatisfied "This summer has demonstrated that plant collection is *entirely* incompatible with the examination of forested lands for the Geological Survey," he told Coville. "Either I have been too minute in my examinations or Mr. Gannett does not understand the difficulties and amount of time required to cross-ride a region of this character. Have thoroughly made up my mind that I will not accept any further details for such work." This was typical end-of-season bluster for Leiberg, and when he closed the letter by stating that summer was the only practical time to explore the Clearwater and Salmon River basins, it was clear he meant to return to the Bitterroot Reserve.

The next day, he sent a package to the botany department that included a new umbellifer for Mr. Rose. In an appended note, he added that as soon as he checked in on his family in Hope, he looked forward to joining his two compatriots for their winter sessions in the herbarium. Leiberg was scheduled to arrive in Washington, DC, by the first week of November, but several days passed before Frederick Coville received a letter explaining his failure to appear. "It is owning to sickness in the family," John wrote. "My little boy, in school in Spokane, is laying sick down there with diphtheria. His mother is in attendance, and I don't like to go away until convalescence sets in." No other explanation was necessary, because both men knew that diphtheria could be fatal.

This bacterial disease is now known to be spread by airborne droplets, but in those days, poor sanitation took most of the blame. Classic symptoms included a gradually worsening sore throat that bloomed into a visible grayish mucous patch. Often the lymph nodes swelled to produce the "bull neck" referenced in many contemporary accounts. If the mucous patch expanded to block the airways, the resulting cough sounded like the bark of a sea lion—a signal indicator of diphtheria. Many doctors resorted to a tracheotomy to facilitate breathing, which introduced a whole new set of complications.

During the 1880s and '90s, several breakthroughs had been made in the understanding and treatment of the disease. Scientists had isolated a specific bacteria as the cause of infection, and a new intubation device reduced the number of tracheotomies performed. Vaccine inoculations successfully tested on guinea pigs led to experiments on human subjects, and by 1894, a serum produced from horse blood was being offered to the public in New York City. In the rural West, however, it would be years before any of these measures tamped the aura of fear that surrounded the disease and its complications, which included hearing loss, decreased kidney function, heart failure, and paralysis. Around the same time that Bernard was suffering from the affliction, the *Spokane Daily Chronicle* ran a series of articles railing against the persistence of the disease; one story, headlined "Stamp It Out," contained interviews with citizens who bemoaned its prevalence and called on the health department to quarantine more patients.

It was under those circumstances that Leiberg informed Coville that it might be a while before he could be expected in DC. "Whilst I do not apprehend a fatal termination and cannot do anything to hasten recovery yet for the mother's sake, whose heart is bound up in the boy, I do not like to leave until I hear that he is beyond danger." John did not mention whether he had made the trip to Spokane to visit Bernard, but within days he was pressing on with his usual variety of work. He offered to send some huckleberry and serviceberry seeds to Charles Sargent, who was experimenting with commercial berry cultivars. Then he turned to the completion of his homestead application.

He noted the legal description of his four lots according to Oscar Sonnenkalb's Government Land Office survey, then stated that he had settled there more than a decade before. He explained his investment of time and effort in the property over those years, and estimated the worth of the place to be $4,500. Two local witnesses vouched for the fact that he had already established his residence on the peninsula by the time they arrived to settle their own farms and that Leiberg had resided on the site with his family ever since. They agreed that even when his work had kept him away from his homestead for some weeks at a time, his family usually stayed on. One of the witnesses, twenty-four-year-old Robert A. Lewellen, was part of the family that lent their name to a feeder creek along the Leiberg-Athol Trail and probably had a long association with the Leibergs.

The most recent of John and Carrie's stated improvements lay in their orchard, where over two thousand fruit trees were in the ground. Over the summer, two professors from the Agricultural College in Moscow, Idaho, had visited the Leiberg ranch as part of an inspection tour. A local newspaper noted that "Leiberg is a government botanist and was absent on business at the time the scientific gentlemen from Moscow arrived." The professors were impressed by the plantings at Lakeside and were convinced that Lake Pend Oreille was "destined to be one of the greatest fruit-producing regions in the world. The rich south hillsides are adapted to fruit raising, and already several parties are realizing a good income from that source, even though the orchards and vineyards are small."

After completing his homestead application, Leiberg's focus soon turned to finalizing the required report from his previous season's fieldwork, then to plans for further exploration. The coming year promised to lead him back into the wilds of the Clearwater drainage and the isolated backcountry he had longed to penetrate since his initial horseback ride of 1884.

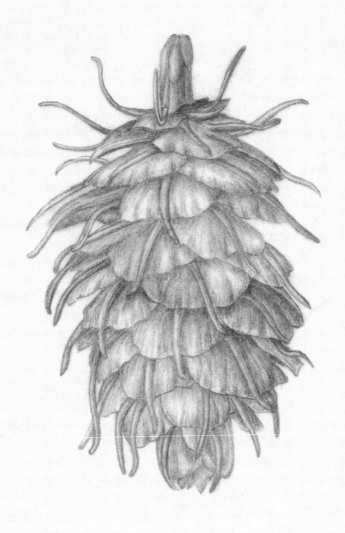

Subalpine larch cone
Larix lyallii

∇∇∇∇∇∇∇∇∇∇∇∇∇∇∇∇∇∇∇∇∇∇∇∇∇∇∇∇∇∇∇∇∇∇∇∇

CHAPTER ELEVEN

FURTHER

∇∇∇∇∇∇∇∇∇∇∇∇∇∇∇∇∇∇∇∇∇∇∇∇∇∇∇∇∇∇∇∇∇∇∇∇

Late in 1897, as Bernard Leiberg recovered from his bout with diphtheria, his parents decided that it would be best for the twelve-year-old to return to Hope rather than continue to attend school in Spokane. Sometime in the following year, Carrie purchased a new edition of Charles Sajous's *Annual and Analytic Cyclopedia of Practical Medicine* and inscribed her name neatly in the top corner of the front endpaper. This multi-volume physician's manual summarized the latest accepted methods of treatment for all kinds of situations that general practitioners might encounter, from diagrams showing how best to set displacement fractures to the most recent literature on hemophilia. The entry on diphtheria in Carrie's edition

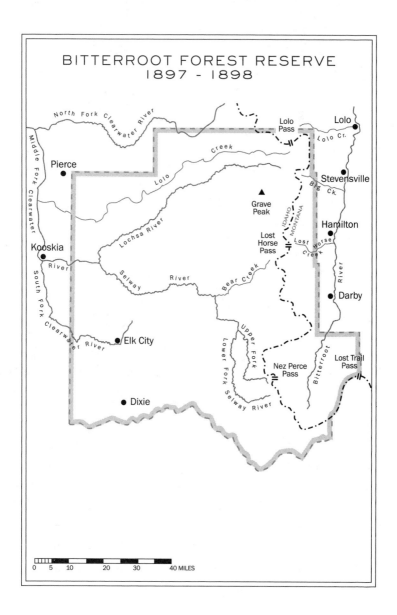

BITTERROOT FOREST RESERVE
1897 - 1898

North Fork Clearwater River

Middle Fork Clearwater

Lolo Creek

Lolo Pass

Lolo

Lolo Cr.

Pierce

Stevensville

Big Ck.

Grave Peak

IDAHO
MONTANA

Hamilton

Lochsa River

Lost Horse Pass

Lost Horse Creek

Kooskia

River

Selway

River

Bear Creek

River

Darby

South Fork Clearwater River

Elk City

Upper Fork

Lower Fork Selway River

Nez Perce Pass

Bitterroot

Lost Trail Pass

Dixie

0   5   10   20   30   40 MILES

188

ran more than sixty pages, examining all aspects of the disease, and would have reminded her of everything she experienced during Bernard's convalescence in Spokane.

Meanwhile, John Leiberg was immersed in compiling the information from his surveys in the Priest River Reserve and the Montana portion of the Bitterroot Reserve. His resulting reports discussed forest resources on both a geographic and a practical economic scale. He had always demonstrated an ability to write clear prose, but now the protocols of forest mensuration—specific measurements that translated into expected yields of board feet on the stump—allowed him to communicate in the language of numbers. The tables and charts that emerged from his work provided baseline information for users ranging from early forest technicians on the ground to congressional aides who wrote the next wave of legislation. In addition to hard facts of resource extraction, John included his personal ideas covering a wide range of subjects. While some of his propositions sound far-fetched today—no one considers introducing Angora goats into the Bitterroots a good idea—others demonstrate his perceptiveness.

One theory that appeared in his report, stirred by long hours of riding high country ridgelines, was that the Bitterroot Valley must have held a considerable lake at the end of the last glacial epoch. Building on observations that he had been making for years, Leiberg visualized the valley as an arm of a much larger lake that subsumed the junction of the Bitterroot and Clark Fork Rivers and followed the course of the Clark Fork all the way to its terminus in Lake Pend Oreille. It would be twelve more years before geologist Joseph T. Pardee shook his discipline with a refinement of

Leiberg's general description, postulating the existence of Glacial Lake Missoula. Another two decades passed before J Harlen Bretz pointed to that outsized lake as the source of the violent flood features that Leiberg had noted across the Inland Northwest, from ripple marks at Horse Plains on the Clark Fork to boulders scattered across the Ephrata Fan in the Columbia Basin. John even identified the location and source of Glacial Lake Missoula's impoundment: "The existence of the lake was probably due to a block of the valley trough of Clarks Fork by ice masses sliding into it from the adjacent mountains." His speculation lacked only the awareness of a continental ice sheet with advancing lobes to jibe perfectly with Pardee, Bretz, and today's universally accepted Ice Age flood story.

Thanks to Henry Gannett's support and some highly skilled Geological Survey cartographers, Leiberg's reports for the Priest River and Bitterroot Reserves featured a series of artfully rendered foldout maps of forest habitats and conditions. Priest River came first, with one figure depicting the principal timber species in delicate shades of green and ochre surrounding blue lake water. A second, titled "Forest Density," smudged healthy green woodlands and yellow pockets of farmland against the brown of "Burnt Areas, Mainly Restocking." The result, which resembles a healthy leaf infected with a pervasive fungus, emphasized Leiberg's mantra that human-caused fires would have to be controlled if the timber resources were ever to realize their monetary value. The maps must have impressed Gannett, because he authorized several more for the final version of the Bitterroot report. Timber species were displayed in a collage of ranges and topography that allowed Leiberg to trace subalpine larch in exquisite detail. A figure titled "Extent of Burned Areas within the Last 35 Years" provided an overview of conflagrations that had crept up most of the major canyons from the Bitterroot Valley toward the Montana-Idaho line.

With those two reports completed, Leiberg penned a thoughtful article for the February 1898 journal of the American Forestry Association. In this piece he described how the development of mining in the western states required a dependable supply of sawn lumber for reinforcing underground shafts and for structures on the surface. By that measure, fires set by prospectors were retarding the development of the very industry they intended to enhance. A greater awareness of the value of the forests was essential to the long-term health of both the mining and the timber industries.

John's 1898 field season as a surveyor in the Forest Reserves began almost as soon as his *Forestry* article went to press. The Forest Management Act of 1897 had suspended the establishment of western reserves for nine months, and as that deadline approached, the USGS very much wanted to complete their land assessments. While the northern reserves remained snowbound, Gannett assigned John Leiberg to undertake a three-reserve survey in southern California, covering the San Bernadino, San Gabriel, and San Jacinto Mountains (areas encompassed today within the Angeles and San Bernardino National Forests). Although this was far from Leiberg's home turf, the department needed an experienced field surveyor who could perform a careful assessment of the forests and produce a professional report that satisfied their political needs.

Leiberg completed the fieldwork between March and May. He traced the habitats of six different native pines, including three that were new to him. Open stands of yellow and sugar pines provided the most serviceable timber resource, but he climbed to ninety-five hundred feet to photograph windblown stands of limber and lodgepole pines. He also calculated that the bewildering mix of local oaks might add to the overall value of the timber resources. He witnessed the torch-like periodic burn rates of chaparral brush and documented several hundred head of burros ranging across the slopes and through the larger canyons of the San Gabriel. Today, California silviculturists have taken Leiberg's stand information and board foot estimates, adjusted them for the smaller kerf size of modern band saws and the fact that loggers now trim limbs farther up the crown, and created historical context for the forests they are trying to manage.

While John was working in the San Bernardino Mountains that spring, the Spanish-American War broke out. It was over by the summer solstice, a brief episode that must have seemed far away from the dry mountain valleys of southern California. But the war served to resurrect the political career of Teddy Roosevelt, an ally of Gifford Pinchot. On the first of July, encouraged by Roosevelt and other friends, Pinchot accepted a position as Chief of the Forestry Division in the Department of Agriculture. He came on board only after attaining the Secretary of Agriculture's promise of a free hand. With that assurance, Pinchot continued his efforts to create a consistent management strategy for the system of forest reserves.

During the same week that Pinchot assumed his new leadership role, Leiberg headed back to the Bitterroot Reserve to tackle the Clearwater drainage on the Idaho side of the divide. Over the course of the next three months, he was able to define the canyon system of the six major arteries of the Clearwater: the Lochsa and Selway Rivers, Lolo Creek, and the river's three named forks. This sextet constituted "by far the most noteworthy and striking feature in the topography of the Clearwater basins. Its windings and ramifications are very great . . . measuring more than five thousand miles in aggregate length." His explorations of those serpentine drainages helped to put a face on the remote Clearwater. Due to a lack of climatic records from the area, he relied on information from local trappers and hunters, whose winter work carried them deep into the backcountry. They described long ridges that trapped weather systems to create belts of heavy precipitation, mostly in the form of snow. They also advised Leiberg to use Grave Peak as a hub in navigating the Lochsa-Selway complex. Roaming the ridges, he speculated about the geology that formed them and about the specialized plants he found there.

One of those totem species was Pacific dogwood, revered by many as the most beautiful flowering tree in the Pacific Northwest. "This shrub is of rare occurrence in the Bitterroot Reserve, being confined in its range to the bottom lands and stream banks of the central and lower portions of the Middle Fork and the Selway valleys," he wrote. "That the species should occur in the basins of the Clearwater drainage is remarkable. Its home in this latitude is in the Cascades and, so far as known, it does not grow at any intermediate station." His description of dogwood range, habitat, and elevation limits remains valid, and the eastern extension of its coastal range matched the pattern of plants like the wild cranberry and red-flowering currant that he had noted around Priest Lake the previous year. Together these showy species led Leiberg to expand his notion of an interior wet belt, which he had recognized in the Coeur d'Alene and Priest River basins, an idea not codified by science until the 1950s. Well over a hundred coastal disjunct plants and shrubs have been documented since that time, and more recently, botanists have focused on coastal mosses and lichens that occur in havens such as the Aquarius Research Natural Area in the Clearwater National Forest. During his forays around the Panhandle, Leiberg collected several bryophytes that slot neatly onto the list.

Utilizing data from his earlier Clearwater journey and oral accounts from all manner of people who moved through the reserve, John delved deeply into the fire history of the region. He circled thousand-year-old cedar groves in Moose and Bear Creek Canyons, and pondered how those trees had survived in a place where burns were so prevalent. He tracked the spread of flames away from three ancient tribal trails that traversed the basin and spoke with travelers about the accidental spread of signal fires along ridgetops. One older Nez Perce man explained that regular intentional burns insured the healthy growth of game browse and desirable berries. Over the course of the summer, John counted enough tree rings and fire scars to produce a graph of acreage burned beginning in 1719. The diagram showed prehistoric spikes in fire activity that leaped higher with the arrival of miners after the first gold strikes of the mid-1800s. He lamented that "for many years the Lochsa Basin has

THE DREAMER AND THE DOCTOR

been a favorite field with prospectors hunting 'lost mines,' concerning which all sorts of wild and fabulous tales are extant. The timber has suffered enormously from fires that have been set to facilitate the search." He struggled to walk through matchstick thickets on former burns now composed of 80 percent lodgepole pine, and he photographed hillsides where the aftereffects of wildfires had resulted in a complete erosion of the soil, leaving dismal prospects for reforestation. But Leiberg was heartened to see that the frequency and extent of fires had decreased dramatically over the last few years, with both public and corporate sentiment turning decidedly against firebugs.

By the time John emerged from the Clearwater and returned to Lake Pend Oreille that fall, Bernard was back in school at Hope. Leiberg's commission included another winter in Washington, DC, and Frederick Coville was already making plans for a comparative study of the summer's gleanings from Lolo Pass, the lower Lochsa, and the Clearwater. "When you come we will try to get hold of the Lewis and Clark plants for your amusement and mine during the winter," he wrote. "I think we can get a large amount of information out of them." Despite that enticement, John remained in Hope with Carrie long enough to cast their ballots in the November midterm elections of 1898.

Of the five states in the United States that allowed women to vote at the time, four lay in the northern Rockies. Idaho's male voters had passed women's suffrage only two years before by an astonishing two-to-one margin. As Idaho women awaited their first opportunity to vote, the state's newspapers noted a calmer, less antagonistic atmosphere than usual and wondered how many females would actually go to the polls. It turned out that their numbers fell just short of the men, and Superintendent of Public Instruction became the first statewide office to be held by a woman. In addition, three female candidates were elected to the Idaho House of Representatives.

After making his annual trek to Washington, DC, Leiberg completed the California and Clearwater assessments and found time to peruse the Lewis and Clark plant collections with Frederick Coville. Then John organized his thoughts about fire and conservation for Idaho forests north of the Salmon River. Incorporating aspects of his research from the Coeur d'Alene Mountains, the Kootenai River north of Bonners Ferry, and other areas that lay outside the designated forest reserves, his paper appeared in that year's *Geological Survey* report.

Under the guidance of his DC cohorts, Leiberg completed one more publication. C. H. Merriam and Henry Gannett both sat on the editorial board of *National Geographic Magazine*, which was quickly becoming known for challenging features concerning American wildlife and forests. The magazine's fifth issue included a piece by Gannett on the redwood forests of the Pacific Coast, mapped and illustrated in the publication's early style. This was followed by a lengthier article by John B. Leiberg titled "Is Climatic Aridity Impending on the Pacific Slope? The Testimony of the Forest."

Leiberg began his piece by stating that "a steadily progressing aridity is slowly replacing former, more humid climatic conditions" from the west slope of the Rocky Mountains to the Pacific. He had noted this phenomenon in all plant communities from desert to alpine and had documented changes in forest structure wherever he traveled. The abundance of petrified wood in the Columbia Basin proved to him that the area had once been extensively forested. He described how three species of juniper slowly encroached and then dominated previously diverse forests in the Basin and Range region of eastern Oregon. In mountainous areas that received more precipitation, he found that smaller-sized tree associations were slowly gaining an edge over larger species. His carefully structured argument left no doubt that he and the *National Geographic* editors hoped to present forests as living systems that experienced dynamic change. There was much to learn about the process and much to think about going forward.

Despite this productive season of publications, neither Leiberg nor Coville was satisfied with John's paltry botanical collections from the Clearwater. The amount of information demanded by Gannett's forestry forms, combined with the rigors of mountain travel, had left little time for pressing plants. Coville argued that during the upcoming field season the Geological Survey should pay more attention to the flora, and at least give their field agents a chance to collect herbarium specimens. Thanks to Coville, Leiberg's 1899 assignment included the instruction to sample any herbaceous plants that he might encounter while carrying out his other duties.

Gannett next dispatched John to the Ashland and Cascade Range Forest Reserves of southern Oregon. These reserves took in large portions of the Siskiyou Mountains south of Ashland, the Rogue and Umpqua River drainages on the west slope of the Cascades, and parts of the upper Klamath Basin on the east side. Leiberg began his journey from Ashland, collecting a globe gilia and two trilliums as he ascended the Siskiyou slopes in early June. He reached the summit of Big Red Mountain and snipped alpine laurel at the top of Siskiyou Peak, then dipped south of the California state line to probe Sterling Mountain.

After returning to Ashland, Leiberg made his way north to Medford and followed the Rogue River Valley, visiting sawmills along the way to study tree rings so he could tabulate stand ages on a local level. He explored the Rogue to its junction with the Applegate River, where he picked up crown brodiaea, a lily he held in high regard. The Applegate was named after a family of well-known early settlers, one of whom had guided Frederick Coville on a mountain excursion through the region in 1897. The same R. I. Applegate may have led Leiberg farther upstream on the Rogue, crossing a divide to catch a corner of the Umpqua drainage that was included in one of Gannett's quadrangles. On this run, Leiberg paused at Abbott Butte to unlock a treasure trove of new plants that included Sitka mistmaiden, an alpine favorite he had collected on Stevens Peak in the Coeur d'Alenes.

From Abbott Butte, Leiberg tailed off the east slope of the Cascades to Diamond Lake, then turned southeast to revisit Crater and Klamath Lakes. Along the way, he assessed the fire resistance of each tree species he encountered. He had been tracking the common tribal practice of peeling ponderosa pine bark for sweet cambium and noticed that "along the eastern margin of Klamath marsh they are found by the thousands." As he the moved through the area, he realized that the cambium scars made the normally fire-resistant pines much more vulnerable to low-intensity burns.

East of the Klamath wetlands, Leiberg ascended the Sprague River to the marshes around its confluence with the Sycan. Nearby, he saw "a remarkable and striking example of surface denudation," the result of a very hot fire that had stripped the soil of its nutritive complexity. The thick brush and doghair tree stands that grew back were certain to provide explosive fuel for the next fire to come, and John wondered whether this discouragingly short cycle could ever be broken.

From the Sycan he returned to the Klamath River and bore southeast, where near the town of Keno he found his first rosy gilia. He crossed the California state line again to Copco in the Iron Gate country, then twisted back via Fish Lake and Mount McLoughlin, a signature Cascade volcano that served him as both a landmark and a haven for plants.

All along this Oregon journey, on both sides of the Cascade Divide, Leiberg continued to contemplate members of the parsley family. He was back at the Klamath Indian Agency in early October when he sent one related plant to Joseph Rose at the National Herbarium. "Do you recollect the strange looking marsh umbellifer collected by me and Coville at Crater Lake in 1896?" he inquired. He had visited its habitat "at the base of the last rise to Crater Lake, on springy ground" twice that fall in search of viable seed and finally thought he had found some. But the plant did not fit with any of the lovages, angelicas, or biscuitroots of his experience. "Are we dealing with a new genus?" he asked his taxonomic friend. In fact he was dealing with the uncommon western cowbane, a robust member of the family that can grow as tall as a man. It still belongs in a genus all its own.

By the time Leiberg returned to Lake Pend Oreille in November, Carrie had moved from Hope to Lakeside Ranch, and Bernard attended a small community school just off the old Leiberg-Athol Trail. For the first time in several years, John did not immediately dash off for the nation's capital. The family wintered quietly on the peninsula until it was time for him to take on his next assignment, assessing the huge Sierra Forest Reserve in northern California.

He spent the 1900 field season, from Independence Day through late October, in the watersheds of the Feather, Yuba, and North Fork American Rivers, which are now divided among the Plumas, Sierra, and Tahoe National Forests. Once more he did yeoman work, producing a broad-based overview that foresters have assimilated into their latest models. He delineated how gold-bearing deposits had attracted extensive logging higher into the Sierra forests than they had in the Cascades. He also documented that since the onset of the first 1849 Gold Rush, vast stretches of the high country habitat had been overgrazed by sheep. Herders habitually set fires to regenerate greenery for their animals, which eventually left many small patches where "the grass and weeds have been so thoroughly eaten out that even the sheep have abandoned them." After a few years, these small meadows sprouted with thousands of red fir seedlings, rendering the ground impossible for a man to walk through and extremely vulnerable to the next cycle of fire.

When Leiberg completed his California survey that fall, he echoed the same complaint that he had voiced following his sojourn in the Bitterroots. "I had such a large area of country to cover and the time was so short that there was no time to spare for the collection of seeds," he wrote to Coville, but remained characteristically optimistic. "It may be different another season."

Barren strawberry
Waldsteinia idahoensis

CHAPTER TWELVE

SILVER AGAINST GOLD

I n late June 1900, just as Leiberg was leaving for the Sierra
Reserve, the Republican Party of Kootenai County, Idaho,
held their nominating convention. They filled a slate for
the November county elections, then selected a dozen dele-
gates to attend the upcoming state convention in Boise. One
of the nominees for that larger gathering was Dr. Carrie
Leiberg of Athol. A *Coeur d'Alene Press* article noted that Dr.
Leiberg, "the only lady delegate, was also honored by being
made one of the candidates for the legislature": she would
be running for a seat in the state House of Representatives.
From a modern perspective, it is possible to conclude that
the *Press*'s "Kootenai in the Lead" headline was meant to
trumpet the ongoing movement of women seeking office.

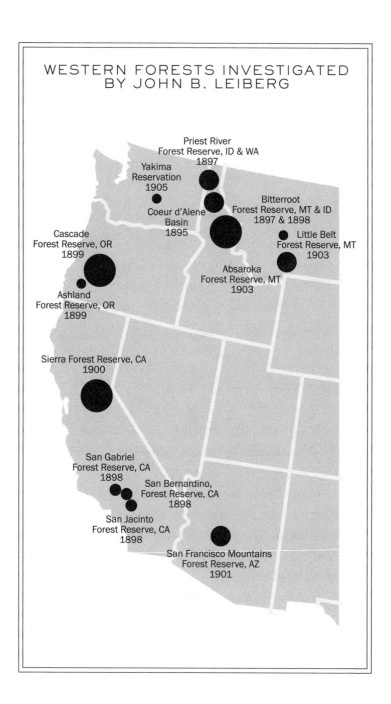

WESTERN FORESTS INVESTIGATED
BY JOHN B. LEIBERG

Priest River
Forest Reserve, ID & WA
1897

Yakima
Reservation
1905

Coeur d'Alene
Basin
1895

Bitterroot
Forest Reserve, MT & ID
1897 & 1898

Little Belt
Forest Reserve, MT
1903

Cascade
Forest Reserve, OR
1899

Absaroka
Forest Reserve, MT
1903

Ashland
Forest Reserve, OR
1899

Sierra Forest Reserve, CA
1900

San Gabriel
Forest Reserve, CA
1898

San Bernardino,
Forest Reserve, CA
1898

San Jacinto
Forest Reserve, CA
1898

San Francisco Mountains
Forest Reserve, AZ
1901

The main issue in the Idaho Panhandle for the 1900 election echoed the national furor over whether to replace the traditional gold standard with a bimetal system that would allow the free coinage of silver. The central role of silver in the state economy, complicated by union struggles against big mining corporations, created a divisive tangle among voters. While newspapers in other parts of the country ranted about international tariffs or how to handle territories overrun during the Spanish-American War, the five suffrage states focused on bills that targeted alcohol and gambling because many women saw control of these evils as essential to family health.

Traditional political affiliations split into multiple contentious factions. The Prohibitionist and Socialist Parties, though small in number, held fast to their single issues. Silver Republicans, who could not abide the gold standard that President McKinley intended to retain if reelected, broke away to hold their own convention. Democrats favored bimetallism. The Populists had emerged from the labor movement and wanted nothing to do with gold or big business. In order to have a better chance at gaining seats, these latter three parties joined together as the "silver party" or Fusionist ticket. Their platform agreed on free silver but little else; one splinter group, the Middle of the Road Populists, decided to run their own candidates. Meanwhile, the goldbug Republicans stood firm in their support of protective tariffs and retention of the Spanish territories of Cuba, Puerto Rico, and the Philippines. They nominated a new vice presidential candidate to run with McKinley in the person of recent war hero Theodore Roosevelt.

Surprisingly, all of these diverse blocks had supported Idaho's suffrage referendum in 1896, and each of the three major parties elected women as state representatives in 1898. The Democrat and Republican women represented districts in southern Idaho, a long distance geographically and politically from the Panhandle. But the new Populist, thirty-year-old Mary Wright, hailed from the town of Rathdrum. Wright quickly proved to be such a talented organizer that Populist members chose her as their caucus leader, and she dove into negotiations with the Republicans and Fusionists to devise an effective leadership. Over the course of the next state house session, Wright and her colleagues passed an anti-gambling bill—a significant victory for the women's movement.

Since the position of state representative was then viewed as a temporary public service rather than a stepping-stone to further political ambitions, neither Wright nor her two southern Idaho counterparts stood for reelection in 1900. Many voters would have encouraged other women to step into their places, and Dr. Carrie Leiberg, a professional and a resident of the same county as Wright, must have seemed like a natural choice. Dr. Mary Latham, who had long been politically active in Spokane even though Washington State women did not have the right to vote, could also have influenced Carrie's decision to place her own name on the ballot. It came as no surprise that she ran as a Republican, because many prominent suffragettes, including Susan B. Anthony, grew out of the abolitionist movement and had always stood with the party of Abraham Lincoln.

Dr. Leiberg ran a low-key campaign. Over the summer and early fall, newspapers noted when she lunched with a garden club in Sandpoint or transacted business with the board of equalization in Rathdrum but did not mention that she was on the ballot. When the votes were counted in November, it was clear that local sentiment had drifted the other way. Although her Republican Party's presidential candidate, William McKinley, won by a handy margin, Kootenai County's Fusionist ticket swept the state senate position plus all three house seats. The margin against Carrie Leiberg was 1,843 to 1,350, and she received about fifty votes fewer than each of her defeated male Republican cohorts. Although a woman was reelected as school superintendent, no other female representative won statewide office in 1900. Their count in the Idaho house for the next two decades totaled only a handful of seats, and another half-century passed before women began to appear regularly on the floor of the state senate. Carrie's timing, like that of many aspiring politicians, turned out to be one election cycle too late.

As far as is known, she made no comment for publication regarding either the motivation for her run or disappointment over her loss, and after November she resumed the rhythm of her former life. Fourteen-year-old Bernard continued to attend the school near Lakeside Ranch, and when John arrived home following his Sierra survey, he almost immediately received his next assignment. Coville, Gannett, and Pinchot were fretting about the situation in Arizona's San Francisco Mountains. Located north of Flagstaff—the majority of the original reserve is presently contained within the Coconino National Forest, but also touches parts of the Kaibab, Prescott, Tonto, and Apache National Forests—the San Franciscos represented sacred ground for early conservationists. C. H. Merriam had developed his early notions of plant associations and elevation zones there, and Gifford Pinchot had rambled through the range with John Muir. Before the decade was out, a young Aldo Leopold would accept his initial posting as a forest assistant in the Apache. In 1900, however, the San Franciscos were a battleground. Dynamite bombs had been tossed at the house of one agent by locals who blamed the government for everything from restrictive forest reserve policies to a persistent drought. The sheep ranchers were up in arms over grazing restrictions, and a pervasive water rights dispute loomed over the region. "I think you will appreciate the very great desirability of completing the investigations of the San Francisco Mountains Reserve," Coville wrote to Pinchot. Soon after the turn of the new year, the USGS assigned Leiberg to take his investigative skills to Arizona. It was far from his home range, but no one could make a more concise and thorough measure of a forested landscape.

Since John's commission did not begin until June, he spent the spring of 1901 on Lake Pend Oreille. He and Carrie sowed thousands of apple seeds to obtain grafting stock, including a good number of the popular Tolman Sweet variety. He planted six bulbs of a sweet wild onion that he had collected in the Sierras and watched them sprout and put up scapes. He mused with Coville about the peculiar odor of Idaho gooseberry and sent some samples of biscuitroots and yampah for the herbarium's cultural plant collection. He also favored the herbarium with information about folk remedies he had heard about, suggesting medicinal benefits that might be extracted from the roots of winged dock, devil's club, and clustered frasera, an outsized member of the gentian family. He noted that lodgepole pine sap, touted as a cure for all ills, was selling for $250 a barrel in the Sacramento Valley but felt certain that a pungent oil distilled from the foliage of western redcedar might prove even more effective.

Memories of odd smells and scenes from his previous expeditions did not prevent Leiberg's mind from wandering toward the future. Both he and Carrie were weary of Pend Oreille winters, and Frederick Coville had recently provided a personal recommendation to a Brazilian rubber company that was looking for a botanist, assuring them that John would be a good hire. The job did not come through, and when Leiberg heard a rumor that all Geological Survey forest reserve assessments were about to be suspended, he inquired about a position with the Department of Agriculture's newly established forestry service in the Philippines. Those richly wooded Pacific islands were now a protectorate of the United States, and he may have recalled the magic of wandering through tropical forests while traveling with his father. The possibility of exploring the Philippine flora was an added enticement, and he again asked Coville to put in a word for him.

During his train ride south to Arizona that June, John wrote Elizabeth Britton and reiterated his desire to return to his botanical roots. He was excited about seeing a totally new flora in the dry mountain forests and hoped to find time to collect a few undescribed plants. He assured his friend that "doubtless some new mosses will turn up" and that she would be the first to see any difficult or unusual species.

After his arrival in Flagstaff, John roamed among the tightly defined vegetation zones of the San Francisco

Mountains until September, orienting his movements around the twelve-thousand-foot beacon of San Francisco Peak. On the lower slopes, he saw alligator junipers of impressive girth, including one with a diameter of thirty-nine inches one foot from the ground. He wrapped his measuring tape around new species of oaks, marveled at the vigorous restocking abilities of quaking aspen, and calculated the timber value of a variety of firs and pines. It would take a pair of additional cruisers another summer to methodically examine all the sections on the huge reserve, but John was able to describe the basic features of the San Francisco Mountains in a report that satisfied the immediate needs of Pinchot and Gannett.

Leiberg emphasized that careful thought would be required to successfully manage the sensitive reserve. Local lumbermen relied on ponderosa pine as their most productive resource, but John expressed concern about the species' overall health: "The yellow pine forest in the reserve is, broadly speaking, a forest long since past its prime and now in a state of decadence. Owing to climatic conditions which are slowly approaching aridity, the yellow pine is here gradually diminishing in reproductive vigor." He identified a lack of cone production and small number of male and female flowers as two symptoms for this weakness. The cone crop remained mysterious to him, but he described watching flowers wilt in the face of hot dry winds blowing from the Colorado Desert—proof, for him, that elements of climatic change were in the air.

He found that overgrazing and fires further hampered timber production. Large sheep herds loosened the soil, then pulverized it to dust, and the animals' voracious eating habits were ruinous to any young recovering forest. As in other locations he had visited, herdsmen sometimes attempted to stimulate new green growth by setting fire to their grazing grounds. Leiberg attributed other burns to simple carelessness, but those factors paled next to the great number of blazes caused by summer lightning strikes, which occurred more frequently on the San Francisco than on any reserve he had yet visited. The complexity of both the origin and the dynamics of these forest blazes called for further study.

John agreed with farmers who complained that timber companies were not leaving behind enough seed trees after their logging operations, but he disputed local claims that such practices, combined with frequent fires, had altered the patterns of spring runoff from mountain slopes. "The real surface regulator of run-off in this reserve is the ground cover of tufted or sward-forming grasses which hold the soil in place," he wrote. "Overgrazing is the real problem here." Originally more than fifty species of grass had populated the reserve, but that number had been greatly reduced except in places lacking sufficient water for livestock.

When Leiberg finished writing up his Arizona data in Washington, DC, that winter, he had authored a dozen papers based on his forest reserves fieldwork. Combined with documents prepared by his colleagues, these broad-based assessments of western public lands provided a valuable tool for a new generation of professional foresters who were being trained at the three existing academic programs that offered the discipline: Cornell University, the Biltmore Forest School, and the Yale School of Forestry. The last and youngest of this trio, recently endowed by the Pinchot family, had hired Gifford Pinchot's friend Henry Graves from the Division of Forestry as director. Graves was charged with weaving ideas that included "best practices" and "field experience" into the fabric of Yale's curriculum. These concepts were welcome in the administration of Theodore Roosevelt, who had just ascended to the presidency in the wake of William McKinley's assassination. In his first message to Congress, the famous outdoorsman Roosevelt made clear his support for the causes of conservation and practical use: "The fundamental idea of forestry is the perpetuation of forests by use . . . The preservation of our forests is an imperative business necessity."

In this atmosphere, the published reports on western forest reserves garnered broad public attention. The *Washington Times* ran two lengthy articles about Leiberg's report on the Sierra Reserve. An examination of the same report made the front page of a Greenville, South Carolina, paper. An assessment of his Arizona work appeared in Pennsylvania's *Allentown Morning Call*, while Oregon's *Hood River Glacier* admired the report's splendid photographs and colored maps of the storied San Francisco Range. Arizona publications, including newspapers in Williams and Prescott, followed suit. All of these articles applauded Leiberg's concerns about fire and overgrazing, sometimes as banner headlines, and all hoped that the federal government would take steps to protect one of the nation's most valuable resources.

At this point in his career, John Leiberg was ready to focus on the health of a single forest. He had built up a store of goodwill within several agencies, and over the winter of 1901 to 1902, administrators arranged to place him in a job that fit his abilities. That spring found him settling into a new office in the town of Stuart (now Kooskia), on Idaho's Clearwater River, where the rich flora and moist mountain ridges would be his to explore with the care they deserved. "The long drawn out 'agony' is over, and I have received my commission as a forest supervisor of the General Land Office," he wrote. "By the heading on this sheet of paper you will see that I got here finally, thanks to all my good, kind, and generous friends in Washington."

The Clearwater should have been the perfect landing spot for Leiberg. He was forty-nine years old and remained fit enough for the rigors of an outdoor life. He had a position of some authority in a place where he was familiar with the local people and their economic needs, and he had ideas about how both they and the forest could survive.

Yet after only five months on the Clearwater, John began quarreling with his superiors about expenses. He had accepted the Land Office's salary offer of $1,800 a year but felt that they should reimburse his travel costs. The department did not want to grant their forest supervisor any stipend at all, advising that he should draw such funds from his salary. That was exactly the problem, retorted Leiberg. He knew that previous managers had experienced the difficulties of traveling the backcountry and the costs of supplying their own horses and outfits, and then reverted to staying at headquarters for the duration of their commission. "The Bitterroot Reserve, with its few and difficult trails, its rugged mountains and deep and well nigh inaccessible canyons, consumes horse flesh and camp equipment like a rapidly revolving grindstone abrades the iron pressed against it," John argued. He could not abide to sit in his office and let assistant rangers do the field work. He needed a travel budget that would allow him to get far out in the mountains. When the GLO refused to budge, Leiberg sent a letter of resignation.

"Even the best and most prudent of men sometimes are cornered, and perforce are obliged to choose between the horns of a dilemma, either of which is sharp pointed enough to leave behind painful and lasting stings," he wrote. John clearly viewed himself among that group of honorable cornered men, and perhaps even took pleasure in constructing his sharp-pointed metaphor. But unlike his previous disputes with Frederick Coville over travel expenses, this time no one smoothed his temper. Leiberg's resignation was accepted, and he later admitted that "the relinquishment of the position I had striven so hard to obtain was an act more repugnant to my feelings and desires than anything else I ever did." He feared that he had squandered his solid reputation in Washington and would pay dearly for his sudden departure from the Clearwater. "I have no doubt my standing with the department has been lowered, quite likely whatever merit I may have gained during the past ten years service is wholly wiped out," he told Coville. "I expected it would be so, but all the same I don't deserve it."

Back at Lakeside Ranch, John seemed at ease with his decision. "Am no longer at Stuart, having resigned the position of Forest Supervisor in September. The expenses of the position were wholly beyond the salary attached, and I dropped the place," he told Charles Piper before moving on to their usual botanical discussions. Piper had collected a plant known as Idaho barren strawberry on a trek up the Clearwater the previous summer. The barren strawberry was another of the interior rain forest plants that piqued Leiberg's curiosity, yet he had never seen it in all his travels through the drainage. "Some of our western plants are remarkably local," he told Piper. As an example, John recalled the waterlily he had plucked from a pond near the Granite train depot fifteen years before. "Did you ever hear of it?" he asked hopefully. At the time he made his initial collection, he thought the lily must be common in all the pothole ponds across Rathdrum Prairie, but he had never seen it anywhere else. Indeed, Leiberg's waterlily remains a scarce and little-understood plant in the Idaho flora, both his first great triumph and a lingering puzzle. From the grandest to the most minute scale, life was full of such mysteries. One could never tell exactly where they came from, or how far they might lead.

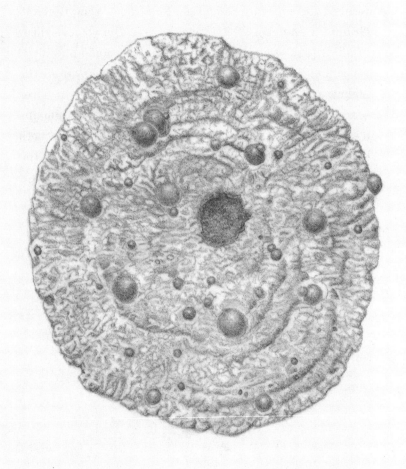

Leaf lichen
Strigula smaragdula

CHAPTER THIRTEEN

THE WORLD AWAITS

▽▽▽▽▽▽▽▽▽▽▽▽▽▽▽▽▽▽▽▽▽▽▽▽▽▽▽▽▽▽▽▽▽▽▽▽▽

J ohn Leiberg began the year 1903 convinced that his time as a government field researcher had come to an end, and he leaped at the chance to help Charles Piper and Frederick Coville write a flora of the Intermountain regions of Idaho, Washington, and Oregon. In one of his typically long letters, John predicted that such a collaborative project, if properly framed, would be of great value to students of botany and to the public at large. He thought that the efforts of collectors on the dry side of the Cascades had been "a mere skinning of the easily accessible places" and dreamed of returning to sites that he had not properly explored. These included the ancient geologic ribs of the Blue Mountains, Steens Mountain and the dry

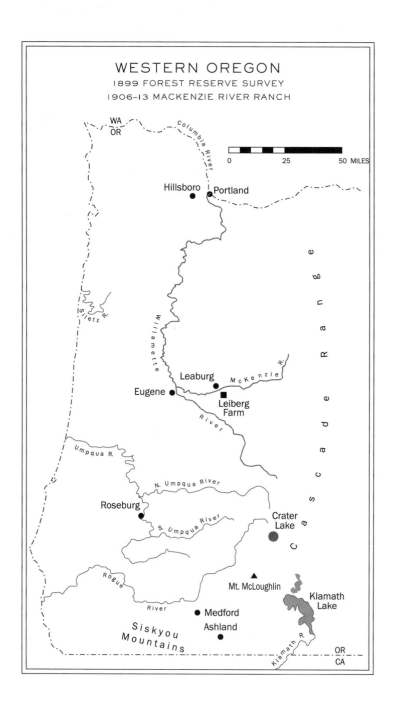

WESTERN OREGON
1899 FOREST RESERVE SURVEY
1906–13 MACKENZIE RIVER RANCH

WA
OR

Columbia River

0   25   50 MILES

Hillsboro   Portland

Siletz R.

Willamette

Leaburg   McKenzie R.

Eugene   Leiberg
Farm

River

Cascade Range

Umpqua R.

N. Umpqua River

Roseburg

S. Umpqua River

Crater
Lake

Rogue

Mt. McLoughlin

Klamath
Lake

River   Medford
Ashland

Siskyou
Mountains

Klamath R.

OR
CA

lake beds around the Alvord Desert, the Snake River lava fields, and the scoured coulees of eastern Washington. All of them teemed with undescribed species.

On a philosophical note, he admitted that he and Piper sometimes disagreed about the details of taxonomy and plant evolution. This to John only illustrated "how different men may view the same objects, and what different opinions they may acquire in consequence." Their disputes were usually in good spirit, and Leiberg believed that they could still work together. For the present, he knew that Piper would be returning to the Clearwater country, and John wanted to steer him toward a yellow penstemon he had noted south of Lost Horse Pass and an unusual silene that flourished along a narrow granite ridge in the upper reaches of Lolo Creek.

Then, before he had a chance to work any further on Piper's botanical proposal, Leiberg discovered that he had not ruined his reputation among government foresters after all. Frederick Coville told him that a position in the Philippines would undoubtedly open up in the near future and that perhaps John should pick up an elementary Spanish textbook. First, however, Henry Gannett offered Leiberg another season as a special agent, assessing forest reserves east of the Continental Divide. John spent June of 1903 in the Little Belt Mountains of central Montana, then roamed the Absaroka and Beartooth Ranges from July through September. Once again, he climbed legendary peaks in the wake of Gannett, Muir, Pinchot, and Roosevelt. Along the way, he collected several interesting mosses from the Judith Basin and Yellowstone National Park that eventually found their way to the New York Botanical Garden for determination. He also discovered that the forest reserves remained in the public eye: while laying over in Livingston, Montana, a newspaper column identified John as a member of the US Geological Survey in town on important business.

Leiberg returned home that fall to find eighteen-year-old Bernard living on Market Street in Spokane, while Carrie practiced at least part-time in the city. Over the Christmas holidays he applied to the Bureau of Insular Affairs for work in the Philippine Forestry Division. His cover note stated that he would be ready to embark for the islands as soon as he completed his reports on the Little Belt and Absaroka Forest Reserves. He also pointed out that the Bureau would have to waive their maximum age restriction for foreign agents—he had just turned fifty in October.

Early that summer John sailed alone to Nueva Cadenas, in the Philippine state of Arubos Camarines on the Island of Luzon. Replying to a letter from Joseph Rose at the National Herbarium, Leiberg explained: "Have been over here since July 5 doing forestry work, if clerical work on forestry subjects can be so considered." He said he was dissatisfied with both the local people and his job, and he complained that he had not found the time to collect any plants at all. But he did tell Rose that the tropical warmth seemed to agree with his constitution, and over the course of the following winter he apparently found new ways to enjoy the island life. When he resigned his post in March 1905, he indicated that he would be willing to return, and the chief of Philippine Forestry scrawled a note below his overqualified clerk's termination notice: "Service satisfactory. Application for reinstatement would be favorably considered."

The year 1905 proved to be a watershed for conservation in the United States. Under President Roosevelt, who had just been elected for his first full term, Congress transferred the forest reserves to the Department of Agriculture and created the framework of National Forests that we know today. Gifford Pinchot, as expected, was named as their initial chief. He quickly set to work assigning professional foresters to manage the tapestry of landscapes that had been described by men like John Leiberg. The system remained a work in progress, entangled with shifting jurisdictions across the West, and Leiberg continued to do fieldwork. That August, Pinchot dispatched John to Yakima where, according to newspaper accounts, "before opening the Yakima Indian Reservation to settlement, the president will create a forest reserve, embracing the best timber land in the reservation. To determine just what lands shall be reserved, J. B. Leiberg of the Forest Service has been sent to make a personal inspection of all the timber lands."

Although no formal report resulted from this misguided attempt to transfer treaty-bound Yakama tribal lands into the National Forest system, another party remained interested in the inspector's movements. An October 1905 note from a Minnesota congressman to the Secretary of the War Department stated: "One of my constituents is anxious to obtain the present address of Mr. *John Bernard Leiberg*, a government employee. . . . If you will kindly send it to me you will confer favor on him and on me." The secretary's prompt reply informed the congressman that Mr. Leiberg could be found at the Heath Block, Monroe Street, Spokane, Washington. At the time Carrie was operating a family practice out of the Mohawk Building in downtown Spokane, and Bernard was completing an apprenticeship at the Excelsior Carriage and Gas Machinery shop.

That December, almost fifteen hundred miles east of Spokane in Mankato, Minnesota, the estate of James E. Marvin was working its way through probate. Carrie Leiberg's first husband had passed away over the summer, leaving behind properties estimated to be worth between $75,000 and $100,000. While Marvin's will distributed most of his holdings to relatives in Minneapolis and Blue Earth County, the sum of $1,500 was earmarked for his former wife, Caroline E. Marvin. When Carrie and Bernard learned of the dispersal, they hired a lawyer to sue for a larger share. A Minneapolis newspaper described the litigation: "At the time of the granting of the divorce, Mrs. Marvin says her infant child, Bernard, was ill, and rather than assume the responsibility and expense of raising it, Marvin told his wife that if she would take the boy and raise him, he would leave the child half of his property when he died. This was merely a verbal agreement." Apparently the twenty-year-old compact carried some weight with the judge, because at the probate hearing in Minneapolis, Carrie and Bernard were awarded an additional $3,000 as long as they renounced any further claims to the Marvin estate. For anyone who assumed that because of their shared name, Bernard was John Bernard Leiberg's natural son, these events cast a new light on their relationship. They also apparently triggered an identity switch for the young man, who from that time forward assumed the name of Bernard Marvin.

In January of 1906, only a few weeks after Carrie negotiated her settlement with the Marvin estate, she and John signed a much more significant financial deal when they accepted a $5,000 down payment from a startup transit company toward the purchase of Lakeside Ranch. The buyers planned to begin construction of a million-dollar electric trolley line from Spokane to the steamboat landing as soon as the snow was off the ground. With a balance due on the purchase of $41,000, it was clear that John and Carrie, who had been a part of the Lake Pend Oreille scene for the past two decades, were pulling up stakes.

Before the couple departed, the promoter of the electric line republished Leiberg's 1897 *Science* article about Lake Pend Oreille petroglyphs in the *Spokesman-Review*. It included a more recent photograph of John standing beside the famous bear paw prints, which he had painted white to make them more visible in the newspaper. Carrie Leiberg may have taken this portrait, which shows that the square-shouldered young buck with the steely gaze of the 1891 Coeur d'Alene photo had gently aged. John still sports an Open Road–style slouch hat and watch fob, but nothing looks as crisp as it did in the studio, and he has shed his suit coat. His khaki shirt is gently rumpled, and his vest hangs unbuttoned. Hands clasped behind his back accentuate a bulging waistline, and bright sun lightens his mustache and eyebrows, imparting a somewhat sleepy look.

This older John Leiberg was still ready to move, and the sale of the ranch, combined with any profit he may have gained from his quartz claims, set the family in motion toward the next stage of their lives. Bernard completed his gasworks apprenticeship and, no doubt aided by the Marvin estate settlement, pursued an engineering degree from the University of California at Berkeley. John and Carrie followed the Columbia River downstream, then cut south through Oregon's Willamette Valley in search of a place with warmer winters. They purchased land along the McKenzie

River about twenty miles east of Eugene. The nearest town shared the name, but not the spelling, of its two newest landowners, and John's next correspondence bore the confusing location of "Leaburg, Oregon."

Their property on the McKenzie consisted of several adjoining rundown farms, which they hoped to bring back into production within a year. Fields bordered the river on both sides so that, as John told Frederick Coville, they had "plenty of chances for playing Izaak Walton." Fishing must have proved too passive a recreation, because before long Leiberg appeared in the office of a nearby newspaper to talk about developing the area's lumber trade. He told a reporter that he planned to build a "mission bungalow" on his twelve-hundred-acre ranch. The dimensions of the house were stunning: a footprint of one hundred twenty-three by sixty-four feet, with a main hall seventy-eight feet long. Several large fireplaces would be mostly ornamental, because he was working on a steam plant to provide heat. He foresaw the possibility of a railroad spur up the valley, and he needed only to install a private ferry system across the river to make his new home easily accessible.

No matter how large a bungalow he intended to build, Leiberg clearly did not consider the McKenzie River farm as a final stop. Soon after his arrival, he accepted a brief Department of Agriculture commission in Alaska, fulfilling a long-held desire to botanize around Haines and Juneau. Upon his return, he queried Joseph Rose at the National Herbarium about plant-collecting forays in the Philippines. For some time, he and Carrie had been preparing for a trip to the Pacific Islands. "If my wife can stand the climate, it is improbable that we will ever return to the US except for brief visits. We will collect, of course," he told Rose. "We will be prepared to make collections far more complete and in better shape than has ever before been."

Four months later, in the spring of 1907, John and Carrie were still packing for their Philippine trip. "Our stay and extent of work out there will depend wholly upon the effect of the climate on my wife. For my part, I find the tropic heat and humidity far more agreeable than chilliness, snow, and frost, and I think she will find it the same," John wrote. They would be residing at a little village on San Miguel Bay, a beautiful spot well positioned for botanical exploration.

Before they could leave, however, Carrie balked. "It has come to our knowledge that an epidemia of some sort of malignant fever has been ravaging Luzon for several months past," John wrote. "Mrs. L. thinks it inadvisable to venture over there now, so we will wait a while." They would remain on their McKenzie River farm for the time being, and if matters on the islands continued to look unhealthy, they might stay there permanently—"all depending on how Mrs. L. views it." To Carrie, their land on the McKenzie—a beautiful run of "fertile beaver dam and river bottomland" below Mount Nebo on the west slope of the Cascades—constituted a fine spot to settle down.

John spent the following winter arranging his plant collections to turn over to the University of Oregon. Using the plant catalogs from his Washington and Oregon expeditions, he created an orderly summation of his life with flora that extended back to his Midwest railroad days. His gift to the university of over fifteen thousand specimen sheets provided a fitting cap for a far-reaching career.

But John remained restless. In the summer of 1908, Elizabeth Britton received a letter from her former faithful correspondent, who in seven years of silence had not forgotten how to wax poetic. "Many and diverse changes have occurred since then," he told her in reference to the gap in communication. "With us the changes of time have brought fair weather and we are sailing in our little boat of ease and peace contentedly to the final haven." He wanted to delve into the immense opportunities for research in the Philippines before he reached that haven. "I and my wife will go over there this coming fall to spend one or many years in a delightful little nook I came across in southern Luzon. Our purpose, or rather my purpose, in going there is chiefly to obtain mosses, hepatics, and lichens to study the microscopic flora and fauna of the estuaries and tidal swamps." John knew that Robert Statham Williams, his former peer in Rocky Mountain flora and now a colleague of Britton's at the New York Botanical Garden, had made a collecting trip to the Philippines within the past few years, and wondered if he had published anything about the mosses there. Beyond that, John updated his former mentor on the McKenzie River news and asked her to give his salutations to Mr. Britton.

John and Carrie did embark on a round-the-world cruise that took up most of 1909. Moss specimens arrived at the New York Botanical Garden from Honolulu that March, then from the Philippine Islands of Polillo and Luzon between April and July. In August the couple boarded a steamer in Hong Kong bound for the Mediterranean through the Suez Canal. In Europe they toured John's Swedish homeland on their way to London and the plant mecca of Kew Gardens.

By December they had crossed the Atlantic to Chesapeake Bay and made their way to the National Herbarium, where John discussed blueberries with Frederick Coville as they rambled through the collections.

After the turn of the year, he wrote Elizabeth Britton that he had uncovered some remarkable specimens of leaf lichens in the Philippines. These cryptogams, also known as epiphyllous or foliicolous lichens, utilize leaves as their substrate for growth, and their fruiting bodies look like minute pimples on the hosts. John had been told that the dots were too small for scientific men to bother with, but he believed that if researchers could find fossil imprints of early leaf lichen ancestors, perhaps they could unravel stages of floral development worldwide. Britton was delighted with Leiberg's return to her world. "You have added greatly to my pleasure in life and given me a new tropical interest," she wrote. She had cataloged many leaf lichens on high mountain plants during her Caribbean fieldwork and would start collecting them in earnest now. In the meantime, she hoped that John would stop by the garden and look at her specimens before returning home. "If you make us a little visit, Mr. Williams and I will do all we can to help you," she promised, but John's poor health prevented the Leibergs from detouring through New York.

Back in Oregon, he wrote an explanation of his illness for the *American Journal of Clinical Medicine*, titled "Diabetes Mellitus: A Personal Experience—Do Intestinal Parasites Sometimes Cause It?" He began his account by admitting to his status as a layman in the field but felt he was qualified to write about the subject not only because his wife was a physician and he was afflicted with the disease, but also because he spent much of his time in "microscopical work with high powers and did not make loose and unsubstantiable statements in matters relating thereto."

In the fall of 1908, Leiberg related, he had experienced all the familiar stages of diabetes mellitus (also known as type 2 diabetes): pale and frequent urinations, thirst, emaciation, headache, vertigo, and dimness of vision. He and his wife tracked specific gravity, volume, and sugar concentration in his urine and experimented with standard treatments of the day, including alkalies and codeine. Thinking that a change of climate and diet might improve his deteriorating condition, the couple sailed for the far Pacific in spring 1909. By the time they landed in Japan, his symptoms had disappeared, and during a stay of four months in the Philippines, traveling on foot through wild country and camping often in wet weather, he saw no recurrence of the diabetes.

On the return voyage, all the familiar stages reappeared, but this time the alkalies and codeine had no effect. When he arrived back at his Oregon home, he "could scarcely walk without reeling from side to side." It was then that he and his wife began to look into his situation in earnest, reviewing the other medicines he had taken during the past year in an attempt to understand what might have caused the disease to disappear while he was in the eastern Pacific. "And on doing so we solved the mystery," he declared.

Leiberg had worked in the tropics before and knew that *Ascaris* roundworms were prevalent there. On past trips, he had dosed himself with a potent mixture of santonin and calomel—the first a natural remedy prepared from the buds of certain sage species, the latter a paste of mecurous chloride used as a cure-all by many naturalists for over a century. On his latest trip to the Philippines, he had relied on a commercial medicine known as Barron's Worm-Remover that contained additional ingredients. His strong health while in the islands made him wonder if his diabetic symptoms might have been caused by an intestinal parasite.

After Carrie provided John with a dose of saline laxative, he pulled out his trusty microscope. His fecal samples contained "millions of cysts varying from 0.01 to 0.2 microns in diameter, and most of those contained daughter cysts filled with coccidia-like bodies." (Coccidia are small, single-cell parasites best known for causing diarrhea in dogs.) The Barron's Worm-Remover was brought back into play: nine granules each night followed by two more in the morning. The parasites were expelled, and within a week his symptoms had vanished.

Leiberg remained uncertain about what conclusions should be drawn from his pathology. He did not intend to imply that all cases of diabetes were of parasitic origin, but his experience offered a simple test and treatment for those that were. He theorized that the source of his infection might have been raw honey, which he had eaten in California before the onset of his first diabetic episode and again during his visit to Sweden before his second attack.

Following the appearance of Leiberg's article, several physicians wrote letters to the medical journal that testified to their own use of santonins for treatment of diabetes but disagreed about their effectiveness. Some supported the intestinal parasite claim, while others insisted that it was off track. One Texas doctor detailed years of research that in part corroborated Leiberg's conclusions, but emphasized that his own "pathological findings were in the islands of Langerhans in the pancreas and not in the kidneys" as others had insisted. This happened in the same year that English physiologist Edward Albert Sharpey-Schafer's studies of the pancreas led him to describe and name insulin, which he indeed traced to the islets of Langerhans. That discovery made a huge difference in the treatment and management of diabetes, but a century later many aspects of the disease remain mysterious, and several recent investigations have focused once again on gut flora.

The medical journal included a few words from Dr. Carrie Leiberg in order to clarify the treatment the couple had developed. She wrote that her husband's best results were obtained when he took half a grain of codeine three times a day for five days. Then he would observe a midday fast, wait an hour, and take a full dose of the worm remover. The following day, she would provide him with a generous dose of the saline laxative. "It is wonderful to see the change in Mr. Leiberg since his recovery from what we both feared was a fatal affliction," she concluded. "He is now robust, strong, has a fine appetite, and is in perfect health."

With the tropics behind them and John's diabetes under control, the Leibergs returned to the construction of their McKenzie River bungalow. Over the summer of 1910, they contracted a Eugene company to work on the residence. The following year, displeased with the quality of work on the project, Carrie sued the contractor for negligent construction. A jury ruled for Dr. Leiberg but only awarded her $200 of the $1,500 she originally sought. The court ordered the contractor to pay all legal fees, so both parties must have left the court with a sour taste in their mouths. By the time the litigation was settled, however, a more pressing issue occupied Carrie Leiberg's mind.

Early in 1911, Bernard Marvin, as he now called himself, took a draftsman job in the town of Hillsboro, just west of Portland. He was twenty-five years old, had attended Berkeley, and impressed most of those who met him over that spring and summer as a man of exemplary habits. In mid-September, he was engaged in drawing a detailed map of Washington County, Oregon. He kept his drafting tools and some extra clothes at the office. He dropped his watch off at a local jeweler for repair and posted a letter to his mother. Then he simply went missing.

Someone recalled seeing Marvin on the street at 11:00 p.m. the previous Sunday—the young man seemed to be something of a night owl—but when he failed to show up for work that week, friends began to fear for his safety. Police searched the banks of the Willamette River and scoured a sewer trench near the Southern Pacific depot to no avail. His coworkers said that Marvin had complained about headaches prior to his disappearance and wondered if there might be a connection. Two full weeks passed before Bernard knocked on the Leibergs' door, a good 150 miles from Hillsboro. Unkempt and unshaven, he met his mother's relieved greeting with the cool gaze of a stranger.

"I am a logger," he said. "My name is George Lewis and I am going to a sawmill where I am going to work."

Carrie insisted to her visitor that he was not George Lewis, but her son, Bernard. The man insisted that he was Lewis. Carrie questioned him about other matters and quickly learned that her son's memory reached back only a few days in time. When she pressed him for past details, their exchange grew heated, and George Lewis ran away. Carrie and John (described in most articles as Bernard Marvin's stepfather) set out to find Bernard and convince him to get help. After a few days, police officers caught up with Marvin, still calling himself George Lewis, marking tallies at a nearby sawmill. He swore he had never been to college but could not remember any events beyond a few months past. Carrie talked him into meeting her at a Eugene hotel and brought a colleague to examine him. The doctor could find nothing specifically wrong, but declared that Carrie was definitely the young man's mother and theorized that it must be a case of either dual personality or lapsed memory due to a blow on the head. Carrie leaned toward the latter diagnosis.

Several reporters compared Marvin's predicament to an amnesia case in Seattle that had been featured in many West Coast newspapers over the previous summer. Now it was Bernard's turn in the spotlight, and a Portland newsman traveled to Eugene to get the story. He felt that George Lewis/Bernard Marvin was "a victim of dual personality," but "the dual man" refused to give a full interview. He stated only that he was suspicious of the woman who kept calling herself his mother, that he was pretty sure his parents were dead, and that even though he could not recall any part of his past, he considered the whole affair a matter of mistaken identity.

Carrie went to Hillsboro to personally investigate rumors that Bernard had been involved in a late-night dustup two weeks before he disappeared. When that proved to be a false lead, she hired a Portland psychologist to evaluate Bernard's mental condition. This was not the first time that her son had displayed odd behavior, according to Carrie. Bernard had weighed only three pounds at birth, and he was always a weak child. He did not walk until age five and showed himself throughout childhood to be "peculiar and extremely sensitive." The boy was smart, but even though he made top grades in his studies at Berkeley, Carrie could tell from his letters that he lacked self-possession and personal confidence. After he left the university, she had gotten him a railroad job in Montana, where he had saved his money carefully; at one point she was sure he had over a thousand dollars in the bank. But the man who knocked on her door as George Lewis was penniless.

Reporters interviewed other people who were not so sympathetic toward Bernard Marvin. While living in California, he had passed bad checks in Oakland and fled to Reno, where he despondently turned himself in to the police. Marvin had arrived in Hillsboro so broke that he asked the sheriff if he could spend the night in the jail. The sheriff had referred Bernard to the drafting firm for work, where he had taken money without authorization, and he had also fallen behind on his lodging payments. Letters found in Bernard's room revealed that he had been courting a fourteen-year-old Siletz girl. She had recently rejected his offer of marriage, which may have left him depressed again. Authorities had tracked his movements to the girl's aunt's home on the Siletz River Indian Reserve before he had headed south to the McKenzie River.

The man who insisted he was George Lewis finally gave an extended interview on November 10. "Someday, the real Bernard Marvin will hear of all this fuss that is being stirred up here about dual personalities and lost memories, and there will be an awful row," he declared. He had taken a liking to Eugene and thought of settling there. "Of course it is impossible now. I am a marked man after all this, and people turn around and point me out on the street," he continued. He wanted to look for employment more challenging than working with his hands. "I am going to get into something that takes some headwork, and that has some future in it"—newspaper reporting, or criminal investigation, or perhaps bacteriological research. "I have given a good deal of study to bacteriology and am very much interested in it. Of course, I have been handicapped by not having access to a good microscope. If I had ever had access to a well-equipped laboratory, I could have done something along that line." This was a strange statement, given that John Leiberg had always possessed a good microscope and maintained a home laboratory while Bernard was growing up.

As the interview continued, Marvin regaled reporters with his command of classical literature and the exploits of Xenophon. A headline in the next day's *Morning Oregonian* read "Logger's Learning Runs Deep." His split between head- and handwork became more evident when a reporter followed him to work at the Booth-Kelly Lumber Company outside Eugene, where the "Dual Man" was putting in full shifts as a tally counter. The job required him to keep track of the size and length of each plank as it was loaded on a train car while simultaneously adding up the total number. Veteran tallymen around the yard were impressed that Marvin could hold both columns in his memory: "When the loading of the car is completed he can tell immediately the number of board feet in its cargo, having carried the totals forward mentally." Such mensuration bore an uncanny resemblance to the stumpage and projected board footage charts that Leiberg had calculated during Bernard's high school years. The mystery of what was going on in the young man's head remained unsolved.

Ginkgo leaf
Ginkgo biloba

CHAPTER FOURTEEN

THE DOCTOR CALLS

t is impossible to know how Bernard's ongoing drama affected John Leiberg's personal life, but the troubles did not stanch his correspondence. On New Year's Day 1912, he offered his salutations to Elizabeth Britton, who was on the way to Cuba for fieldwork. He wished he could join her, he wrote, because the tropics agreed particularly well with both him and his wife. During their sojourn in the Pacific, Carrie had developed an interest in corals and shells, while of course John would never get enough of lichens and mosses. "It is our intention as soon as we can close up our property interest in the US to go live for two years or more in the Torres Strait region, the southern portions of the Philippines, New Guinea, and Borneo."

On a more mundane level, John continued to consult with Frederick Coville about leaf mold, the colors of lupine blossoms, and the way honeybees worked among the many varieties of Northwest huckleberries. He considered depositing his collection of mosses, hepatics, and lichens in the National Herbarium, a fitting destination for many years of dedicated work. And for no apparent reason, he began to harbor termites in his home laboratory. He found that the colonies took well to captivity as long as he kept them supplied with wet decaying wood and did not mix the original groups. "The study of these parasites is a genuine 'lustspiel' all through," he wrote, drawing on a German term for a showy entertainment. Soon he had thousands of individuals crawling through tubs of fetid logs, and he came to appreciate these "most remarkable organisms. The more one studies them, the greater grows one's wonder."

Examining the tiny creatures under the microscope, Leiberg discovered that the digestive system of each adult termite harbored thousands of protozoa that included flagellates, spirochetes, and ciliates—"a menagerie more extensive and remarkable than man ever got together." Many of these organisms were as transparent as glass, so that John could observe their inner workings. While previous researchers of termite digestion had watched their subjects quickly expire, Leiberg concocted a fluid that kept them alive for up to thirty-six hours. This allowed him to compile life histories of several different microscopic forms. His drawings and illustrations filled more than twenty pages, including a sketch of one ciliate's pharyngeal tube that resembled a small volcanic cone. He measured its opening at less than 0.3 micron in diameter and determined that none of the other organisms swimming in the termite's gut could enter the tube except for its specific food. "I have studied these as they never have been studied before," he boasted.

Leiberg believed that his finds were well worth publishing, and after receiving some mild encouragement from Frederick Coville, he expressed his pent-up desire for recognition: "I have never heretofore particularly esteemed any special credit for discovering new things; but these researches have cost an incredible amount of labor of the painstaking sort, and whatever credit belongs to such things I would, in this case, like to claim." There was more. Early in the spring of 1913, he chanced upon a slide of gut protozoa that were busily replicating. Under a magnification power of one thousand, he had the pleasure of watching every phase of division in scores of individuals, a *lustspiel* that continued far into the night. As might be expected, the division of such protozoa looked very different to Leiberg than it had to previous researchers. "Do you know, Mr. Coville," he mused. "I believe every worker in protozoology should first study botany. I know that in my case the powers of observation have become immensely acute and comprehensive for the very minute forms through my work in botany."

Thoughts of minute life forms transported Leiberg to the transformative nature of dirt. It seemed to him that current science had little knowledge of the behavior of American soils. He expounded on leaf mold and the underlying stratum of mineral contents, the oxides and sulfates that liberate chemical compounds in unpredictable ways. He and Carrie farmed a meadow on the McKenzie River that yielded seven tons of red clover hay per acre but would not grow peas worth a darn. In his opinion, this could only be ascribed to the qualities of the native rocks and their constituent minerals. The soil and the sun together created the colors in his favorite flowers, from the rainbow variety in lupines to the odd pink-blossomed strawberries he had seen on certain hillsides. He believed that such color changes came down to variations in the intensity of light and atmospheric disturbances, because "solar energy, when *broken up and refracted by the cell lens*, is life and evolution in all its phases." In a contemplative mood, he continued: "Except, that is, for self-conscious life, which is a derivative from some more profound font than a mere sidereal sun."

With that metaphysical thought, Leiberg closed his letter to Frederick Coville, signing with the usual flourish of his full name. Then, filled with the excitement of the moment, he added a postscript on the subject of spontaneous generation, which he believed might be possible through just the right balance of light refraction and pressure "so as to start the interrelations of atoms which we call life." The best way to observe that process in action would be for a careful researcher to carry their microscope into the "universal solvent" of the ocean, where the underpinnings of all life originated. "No one," declared Leiberg. "No one knows what goes on in the sea."

John's train of thought here might seem improbable even for him, but it did anticipate a pair of creation theories. Depictions of nascent life on Earth now begin with microbial mats bobbing in warm-water lagoons. Equally prescient was Leiberg's intuition that refracted light might stir evolutionary change in single cells. British botanist Robert Brown had described the stuttered random movements of moss pollen grains almost a century before, and Leiberg surely would have noticed this Brownian motion during the course of his endless sessions squinting through his microscope. He might also have read Albert Einstein's 1905 paper describing the chaos of fast-moving single molecules that produced Brown's effect. Science today still has not reconciled the powers of biochemistry with particle physics, but Leiberg could feel that the connection must be there. He possessed an uncanny ability to visualize different life forms in their natural environment, then to journey through their vastly different universes. Subjects that piqued his interest might be as ephemeral as subtomic particles, or as visceral as a serpent's strike.

Two weeks after Leiberg set forth his theory concerning the liquid origins of life, several southern Oregon newspapers ran a most unusual obituary that told the story of Civil War veteran Luther King, who had passed away at the old soldier's home on the coast. Rattlesnake King, as he was known, had earned his nickname when he went out to pick huckleberries on a summer afternoon in 1875 and was bitten by a rattlesnake. He immediately returned to his camp to slash across the fang marks and suck out the poison, and the wound healed nicely. Over the next twenty years, King almost forgot about the incident. "Then on the last day of July, 1895, he felt a peculiar irritation on the instep of the bitten leg, and the next morning the irritated spot was a running sore, rotten to the bone." For the entire month of August, he lay in a kind of coma, hardly eating or drinking, so that most of his friends thought he was dying. Yet on the first day of September he stood up, called for something to eat, and soon felt like himself again.

Luther King's strange pattern of itch, suppuration, coma, and recovery was repeated every August for the next eighteen years. Over that time his leg became pocked with eighteen ugly scars, causing him to believe that the serpentine characteristics were part of his being. "I'm just like a snake in August," he told one friend. "I shed my skin then. I eat nothing and I sleep nearly all the time. And I'm poison like a rattlesnake. I believe that if I should bite you in August, you would die." Until the year he passed away, Luther held out hope that when his scars reached the number of the original snake's rattles, his body would finally be healed.

Rattlesnake King's story jogged the memory of John Leiberg, who responded to the obituary with a letter to the editor of the *Roseburg Register*. As a youth, Leiberg wrote, he had spent two years with his father chasing pirates through the channel between Taiwan and the Philippines. In villages among the scattered islands, they often encountered people suffering from the same kind of recurrent suppurating snakebites that King described. The villagers said that wounds of this nature were "caused by the bites of a snake called, using the literal English translation, 'Great Corkscrew Dragon.'" During Leiberg's visit to the Philippines three years previously, he had met a Portuguese surgeon who declared he had witnessed this phenomenon several times in the Chinese hinterlands, and Dutch physicians at Batavia told him that it was a common occurrence among the Japanese.

These unlikely recollections of the Great Corkscrew Dragon marked John Leiberg's final written words to appear in the public arena. The great artesian well of words, which had flowed so freely for decades, suddenly ran dry. A mid-October notice in the *Eugene Morning Register* revealed that John B. Leiberg had been admitted to the local hospital and was reported to be seriously ill. He passed away there on October 28, 1913, three weeks past his sixtieth birthday. The death notice praised Leiberg as "one of the most able botanists in the nation today," and pointed out that "though he retired from active service some years ago, he continued his work with unabated activity and devoted his entire time to research."

Ten days later, Carrie wrote to a woman who had recently mailed a book to John.

Dear Miss Harrison

The disease, diabetes, from which Mr. Leiberg has suffered for several years, took a turn for the worse about Oct 1. Gangrene set in on the finger of one hand. He went to the hospital in Eugene but got rapidly worse, the gangrene having invaded the whole hand and arm. Everything that medical science could do for him was done, but to no avail. He died Oct 28 conscious to the last and with an abiding faith in individual existence beyond the grave.

Carrie informed Miss Harrison that her book, *The Two Crusades*, had arrived about the time John's serious symptoms began, and she did not know whether he had read it. She had found an envelope addressed to Miss Harrison atop John's desk, but no letter. "Evidently he had started to write to you but got no further than addressing the envelope," she concluded.

Carrie waited another two weeks before informing Frederick Coville of her husband's death: "I am writing tonight to a number of Mr. Leiberg's friends to inform them that he departed this life October 28. He always felt a warm friendship for you, also Mr. Gannett. I do not know his address and would be glad to have you tell him that [John] has gone." In closing the letter to her husband's close associate and friend, Carrie added: "He was a good man. No higher praise can be given anyone." Months later, under Coville's guidance, she arranged to transfer John's ten thousand moss and lichen specimens to the National Herbarium. The Smithsonian Annual Report of 1914 deemed them "a notable collection of cryptogams."

Much more time passed before word reached Elizabeth Britton about John's passing. "It is a great shock to us to learn of the death of your husband, and it seems strange that almost a year has gone by without our hearing of it," a perplexed Britton wrote to Carrie the following fall. The last time Britton had corresponded with John, he had expressed a great enthusiasm for epiphyllous lichens. "You know we were always good friends and kept up a more or less intermittent correspondence," she wrote, wishing she could know more about what happened. "Will you tell me about him if you feel that you can do so?" she asked. "Do let me have a line from you and accept our sympathy and condolences." If Carrie made any reply to Britton's plea, it has been lost.

After her husband's death, Carrie remained on the McKenzie River farm, where consoling friends visited her during the weeks following the funeral. When she filed John's will in probate court, the local paper described the inventory of his belongings as the remains of "a man who communed with nature on the banks of the wild McKenzie." The farm and house were listed in Carrie's name, and he left behind only a hundred and fifty dollars' worth of personal property. His effects consisted of a microscope valued at twenty dollars, a photo-microscopic unit that he had employed for his termite studies, fifteen scientific books printed in German, a hundred magazines and pamphlets, a ten-dollar watch, and fifty dollars' worth of clothing. His will contained no mention of Bernard (who still thought he was George Lewis), but it did acknowledge his two children with his first wife, Mattie. To thirty-four-year-old Godfrey and thirty-year-old Cassiel, Leiberg bequeathed the sum of five dollars each.

That same fall, Carrie Leiberg posted an odd query to the Portland *Oregonian*. "I am exceedingly anxious to send a letter to the manager of the Barnum & Bailey Circus Company. You will do me a great favor if you can tell me how to address it so that it will reach him." The paper published Carrie's question along with the location of the circus's winter quarters at Baraboo, Wisconsin. Her search was probably connected to a recent clue concerning her son Bernard's whereabouts, because over the past three years, he had wandered far from his mother's protection.

Then, in January of 1915, newspapers from Boise to Los Angeles suddenly picked up his story again: "Bernard Marvin, whose strange case of dual personality puzzled physicians and held the attention of the Pacific Coast for weeks in 1911, has been restored to his former self after four years of lapsed memory." Marvin, it turned out, had awakened one morning believing himself to be a young draftsman working on a map of an Oregon county. Upon noticing that the scenery around him did not look familiar, he reached for his breast-pocket notebook, wondering why he had not included a profile of the surrounding horizon on his map. The notebook was not there. When he asked a passerby where he was, he learned that he was in San Luis Obispo, California. A glance at a newspaper informed him of the large gap in his temporal reality. In the next instant, Bernard remembered exactly who he was, including the fact that his mother was a doctor in Leaburg, Oregon. Upon receiving a telegram, Carrie rode the train south from Eugene to help her son reassemble his interrupted life.

The outline of Bernard's story mirrored that of a well-publicized 1887 incident in which a Rhode Island minister disappeared from his parish without a trace. Several months later he regained his senses in Pennsylvania, where he had established a new life. That case defined a psychological syndrome of brain fugue, amnesia, and recuperation, which today falls under the umbrella of dissociative identity disorder. One reporter following Bernard Marvin's story assured readers that the former "dual man" was "now recovered, and his normal self again. He plans to resume his work as a civil engineer within a few weeks." Of course Carrie knew that untangling her son's confusion could never be that simple, and she convinced him to return to the McKenzie River and live with her for the time being.

As World War I slowly drew the United States into its vortex, Carrie Leiberg maintained her medical license and received regular visits from friends and peers. She found time to improve the grounds around the farm, hiring a carpenter to erect a woodshed and tending to a productive garden. In October of 1916, she brought several boxes of late-fruiting strawberries into Eugene to display at the First National Bank, where patrons thought they tasted as good as any early-summer berries. Three months after that achievement, she sold her entire place, totaling more than twelve hundred acres, to a wheat farmer from eastern Oregon. The price was said to be around $50,000 for what may have been the largest tract owned by a single individual in the McKenzie Valley. The Leiberg parcel was noted for its "magnificent mansion built on a most picturesque site, selected by the former owner to enhance the style of architecture of the mountain home." As the transaction wound its way to closing, Carrie donated John's zoological and botanical library to the University of Oregon to complement his extensive herbarium.

That same month, Godfrey and Cassiel Leiberg filed a lawsuit against the sale of the ranch in Lane County Court. It was not a pretty case. The brothers asserted that their mother, Mattie, married John Leiberg in Iowa in 1877, and that after they were born, Carrie Marvin became intimate with their father. In 1883 the family moved to Idaho to escape her seductive ways, but Carrie Marvin followed them to Lewiston until "finally Leiberg deserted his family and went away with her, and she lived with their father in illicit relations until his death on the McKenzie River ranch."

At the time John Leiberg left his family, he had allegedly promised Mattie that he would pay for the education of his sons, but "on account of the opposition and influence exercised over him by Carrie Marvin," no funds were ever forthcoming. In regard to the deeds that Carrie held for the McKenzie River property, the brothers declared that Leiberg's mental faculties were so impaired by age and sickness that Carrie had been able to convince him to sign all the properties over to her. In light of these actions, Godfrey and Cassiel brought a claim on all the McKenzie River holdings, as well as a 320-acre ranch in Umatilla County, Oregon, that was also deeded to Carrie. The total value of the estate was rumored to approach $300,000.

It took another year and a change of court venue before a Portland judge handed down a decision exonerating Carrie Leiberg on all counts. Their 1897 Wisconsin marriage certificate proved that she and John had been legally wed. The judge found that the couple's properties had been accumulated originally through Carrie's efforts, so there was no question of coercion. Finally, the court declared that John Leiberg's mind had remained sound up to the moment of his death and that his final wishes had been fairly represented in his documented will. Godfrey and Cassiel, along with their mother, Mattie, did not readily accept the verdict, and before the year was out, they ran ads in Portland papers seeking information about land that John B. Leiberg might have owned in the Philippines. Those queries came to nothing.

Carrie Leiberg emerged from the quagmire as a woman of considerable means. She began splitting her time between Oregon and California, keeping up her medical license in both states for a while. In 1918, she worked part-time for the Multnomah Hospital in Portland before moving permanently to the San Francisco Bay Area, where her sister Hillary lived. Little is known about Bernard's life during this time, but as World War I wound down, he enlisted with the Army and shipped overseas. In post-war Germany he served as an engineer aboard trains that transferred citizens amidst the chaos of hastily redrawn national boundaries. He arrived back in Oakland with a German woman named Thekla Salomon; they were married in February of 1921 and soon moved in with Carrie.

Around 1922, Dr. Leiberg purchased a grand house in Oakland formerly owned by lumber baron Asa White. Her extended family often dropped by to visit. One grandniece who spent considerable time at the house as a youngster recalled that Carrie remained interested in gardening, always putting up vegetables for the pantry, and would fry doughnuts as a treat for visitors. She kept a parrot that intimidated little girls, and pursued her hobby of furniture-making in a converted shed behind the main house.

To the grandniece, Bernard seemed a little odd. Some people said that her uncle was lazy, and she usually saw him polishing gemstones in a room dedicated to his seashell and rock collections. According to a stream of newspaper reports, however, there was much more to Bernard's life. After he returned from Germany, he volunteered as the American Legion's director of job procurement for World War I veterans. A photograph showed him seated at a desk in a crisp suit filling out a job application for a forlorn "Buddy." Bernard continued to serve on the executive committee of the legion post while Thekla began a long run in the society pages, regularly appearing in the news of various social and charitable clubs. She hosted several events at Carrie's grand house on Seventeenth Avenue, including a formal whist party for two hundred and a fundraiser for the League of Women Voters.

Thekla and Bernard also liked to travel. In 1927 they took a three-week driving tour of the California Gold Country, rolling through some of the same foothills John had trod during his Sierra Forest Reserve survey. Two years later, they ventured north to Idaho and called on some of the early settlers Bernard had known around Lake Pend Oreille. The locals had heard all about their former neighbor's famous memory loss, but when he and Thekla spent a day in Hope, childhood recollections held sway. "Bernard was looked upon as a prodigy when small," one friend recalled. "At the age of six years he knew the Latin names of all the flora collected by his father, and could read the Latin doctor books."

By 1934, Bernard was working for the Pacific Gas and Electric Company. That summer, while he investigated the crash of a small plane into a company powerline, Thekla accompanied Carrie to Eugene, where they visited a series of the doctor's former acquaintances and looked in on her former McKenzie River farm. A widow for more than two decades, Carrie had turned eighty-two that spring. When she passed away three years later in March 1937, her remains were shipped by train to Eugene to be buried beside John in the Masonic Cemetery. Her death received little public notice. The *Journal for the American Medical Association* ran two short lines, and the Woman's Medical College in Chicago (which by that time had been incorporated into Northwestern University) printed only the briefest of mentions: "March 2. Mrs. Carrie E. Leiberg Deceased." No newspaper in Oakland, Eugene, or northern Idaho published an obituary, but a sentiment from one of her husband's letters could have served the purpose. Carrie, he wrote, was "untrammeled by narrow creeds or dogmas, full of nought but kindness, good-will, and sympathy for every living thing." Given the chance, many of her patients could have remembered the times she attended an accident on the tracks, or traveled through a stormy night to deliver a baby, or assuaged a dangerous fever with some exotic medicine from her bag. Even as she struggled with the limits of her profession, she managed to edge her own troubled son onto a viable path. During a marriage full of unlikely turns, she and John allowed each other to flourish in their own particular ways.

Of Carrie's personal effects, which must have included untold numbers of letters from John, not a single one has surfaced save for a volume of her Sajous's medical encyclopedia. That manual came into the possession of a California doctor, who kept it until his own death many years later. At his estate sale, a curious browser opened the cover to find Dr. Leiberg's signature on the inside flap. Upon further inspection, a beautifully pressed spray of ginkgo leaves slipped from the weighty tome. Whether Carrie or John snipped the branch in remembrance of the fossil ginkgoes that he collected while exploring an ancient Dakota forest during one of his first botanical adventures cannot be known, but the fragile leaves offer a plant enthusiast's testimony to one more use of a good book.

➤⟫—⟪◄

From that fossil-rich prairie along the Northern Pacific line to the alpine ridges of the Bitterroot, the waves of civilization that followed John Leiberg's restless journeys have changed aspects of everything he saw. Nevertheless his writings suggest nothing that has happened in the succeeding century would have surprised him—not the outsized footprint of human activity or its cascading effect on our climate; not the gradual comprehension of the microbiological complexity of forest soil or the alarming cycles of wildfire; not the polarized disputes over resources and public land or the politicized distortion of the science that could help to resolve them. Were he alive today, he would be wrestling with our current problems, buoyed by the knowledge that their proper analysis begins with exactly the kind of baseline measurements and cogent observations he so doggedly compiled. Traveling as Gulliver again, he would be incorporating the thrill of microscopic details into theories on a grand scale, trusting that the persistent efforts of many others before and after him might illuminate a more expansive landscape: one where human and natural elements are weighed together, where experience informs future decisions. That is the legacy in which he dreamed of playing a role.

Evidence of a more tangible Leiberg presence survives at the south end of Lake Pend Oreille. After John and Carrie departed from Lakeview Ranch in 1906, the new owners never completed their electric transit line and eventually sold the property. For some years afterward, vendors offered a colorized postcard of the Leibergs' rustic cabin backed by the grandeur of the cliffs that extended north from Bernard Peak to Green Monarch. The photogenic setting carried the title "Idlewild," the name applied to the bay below the original homestead. Leiberg Point was renamed Blackwell Point in honor of succeeding residents, who built a much fancier house nearby. The Blackwells attempted to make the Leiberg orchard commercially profitable, but the place never quite paid its way. During World War II, the United States Navy, moving to take advantage of the remote deep waters of Lake Pend Oreille, constructed a submarine research facility that swallowed the original ranch. Naval engineers located their sewage treatment facility, consisting of four large round underground concrete tanks, on the terrace where most of the fruit trees had grown.

It took more than a few hundred yards of concrete to erase all traces of the Leibergs from that terrace, however. Each spring, pear and apple trees, vigorous sports from John and Carrie's original plantings, still flower along the rough escarpment above Idlewild Bay, and double rows of plums lead toward the vanished foundations of their cabin and barn. At the tip of the peninsula, interpretive signs describe the great Ice Age floods, gauging the depth of the Purcell Lobe's icy finger as it ground against Green Monarch Ridge to dam Glacial Lake Missoula. John Leiberg surely would be gratified to know that geologists have redubbed the site Jökulhlaup Point—an Icelandic word that describes the sudden failure of a glacial dam and the roaring deluge that follows.

This book represents a continuation of work initiated by four people who were attracted to the Leibergs' story. Ann Ferguson explained Carrie Leiberg's photographs and kept pecking away to uncover the larger story. Bitterroot fire ecologist Steve Arno wrote about the importance of the original forest reserve surveys. Art Zack applied John Leiberg's survey data to the Idaho Panhandle forests. Sarah Walker traced his routes through the Clearwater and traveled to the New York Botanical Garden and National Archives to pry open John's voluminous correspondence. All four of these researchers generously shared years of work, and I cannot thank them enough.

Shanda Dekome and colleagues from the Panhandle National Forest teamed with Kurt Pavlat, LeAnn Abell, and Idaho Bureau of Land Management staff to support further investigation.

Special thanks to Jean Teecher, Louise Conley, and Christy Walton for sharing memories of Carrie; to Joe Guarisco and Jeanne Debons for the maps and artwork; and to Lynn Camsuzou for finding the ginkgo.

Many other individuals have offered advice and inspiration, including Kathy Ahlenschlager, Dewey Almas, Felix Aripa, Joe Arnett, Bob Betts, Bruce Bjornstead, Steve Box, George and Patrick Braden, Roy Breckinridge, Bill Brusstar, Pam Camp, Francis Cullooyah, Kirk and Madeline David, Peter Dunwiddie, Charles Ferree, Carl Fiedler, Pete Gardner and Idaho Fish and Game, Dean Garwood, Karen Golinski, Karen Gray, Linda Hackbarth, Bill and Holly Hillegass, Larry Hufford, Gene Kiver, Peter Lesica,

Chris Loggers, Gary Luke and the staff at Sasquatch Books, Philip Maechling, Rich Merkel, Mary Nisbet, Jim Nisbet, Dr. George Novan, Robin O'Quinn, Stephen Pine, Rusty Russell, Tom Sandberg, Joe Schwarz, Kris Runberg Smith, Dr. Nan Smith, Tom Weitz, and Judge and Tina Wynecoop.

Thanks also to the following institutions and archives: Bonner County Historical Museum, Sandpoint, ID; Farragut State Park, Athol, ID; Library of Congress, Washington, DC; Museum of North Idaho, Coeur d'Alene, ID; National Archives and Record Administration, Washington, DC; Native Plant Societies of Washington, Idaho, Oregon, and Montana; New York Botanical Garden, Bronx, NY; Northwest Museum of Arts and Culture, Spokane, WA; Oregon State University Herbarium, Corvallis, OR; Ownbey Herbarium, Washington State University, Pullman, WA; Smithsonian Institution Archives, Washington, DC; Spokane Public Library, Spokane, WA; University of Oregon Archives, Eugene, OR; US National Herbarium, Washington, DC; and Washington State University Library Special Collections, Pullman, WA.

Archives and works frequently cited are identified by the following abbreviations:

NARA: Correspondence between Frederick Coville and John and Carrie Leiberg, Record Group 54, NC 135. National Archives and Record Administration, Washington, DC.

NYBG: Elizabeth Britton Collection, New York Botanical Garden, Bronx, NY

SIA: Smithsonian Institution Archives, Washington, DC

USNH: US National Herbarium, Smithsonian Institution, Washington, DC

WSU: Charles V. Piper Papers, Cage 317, Manuscripts, Archives, and Special Collections, Washington State University Library, Pullman, WA

Author's Note

p. ix: oral accounts from around Lake Pend Oreille: George and Patrick Braden, conversation with the author, November 7, 2015.

Introduction

p. xi: "My wife has been very ill": Leiberg to Britton, August 21, 1890, NYBG.

p. xii: "I have the preservation of the forest much at heart": Ibid., February 10, 1890.

p. xiii: "You can send anything": Ibid., December 28, 1889.

p. xiii: "We try to bear good or ill": Ibid., February 5, 1890.

Chapter One: First Ride

p. 1: "My father was a sea captain": Leiberg to Britton, April 14, 1891, NYBG.

p. 1: "How my heart used to thump": Ibid., May 9, 1890.

p. 2: hunting pirates: "Former Member of Soldiers' Home Passed Away at Florence," *Roseburg Register* (Roseburg, OR), June 17, 1913.

p. 2: "excellence of character": "Married," *Le Mars Sentinel* (Le Mars, IA), January 9, 1877.

p. 2: "popular station agent": "Seney Notes," *Le Mars Sentinel*, June 9, 1879.

p. 2: "The desire to collect and preserve plants": Leiberg to Britton, January 13, 1890, NYBG.

p. 3: "Masters of Science": Leiberg to Engelmann, May 24, 1890, George Engelmann Papers, Missouri Botanical Garden Library, St. Louis, MO.

p. 6: "It is a rather novel and strange arrangement": Leiberg, "Recent Fossil Flora," 146.

p. 8: "ascertaining the prospects of mineral wealth": Leiberg, "Notes on Forest Region," 88.

p. 8: "this species forms parklike forests": Ibid., 90.

p. 9: "In one part of the meadow": Ibid., 92.

p. 9: "For a while every trail": Ibid., 95.

p. 10: Caroline's girlhood ambition: Jean Teecher, Louise Conley, and Christy Walton, correspondence with Ann Ferguson, Sandpoint, ID, August 2017.

p. 10: "keeping house": 1880 census, Mankato, Blue Earth County, Minnesota.

p. 11: "When the filthy hovels": "More Lady Doctors," *Chicago Daily Interocean*, March 1, 1882.

p. 12: "Mining is an occupation": Leiberg, "Notes on Forest Region," p. 95.

Chapter Two: The Lake

Unless otherwise indicated, all quotations in this chapter are from John Leiberg's letters to Elizabeth Britton, NYBG.

p. 17: "When I first came": March 29, 1890.

p. 19: "sheepskins": January 13, 1890.

p. 19: "You see I am not a lover of crowds": May 21, 1889.

p. 20: "Idaho Mining and Prospecting": Book B, 47–48, Recorder's Office, Kootenai County, Idaho.

p. 20: "snow on the Leiberg trail": October 27, 1896.

p. 22: "There are different ways to explore": May 24, 1890.

p. 23: "deep forests over high ridges": Ibid.

p. 23: "I cannot tell you of the dense and gloomy forests": April 13, 1889.

p. 23: "he hung stout hand-sewn canvas bags": February 19, 1889.

p. 23: "To examine these mountains thoroughly": April 5, 1889.

p. 23: "well nigh impossible": February 19, 1889.

p. 25: "Camp Lakeside, at the south end": Leiberg, "From North Idaho."

p. 26: "Dear Madam. I shall be very glad": July 8, 1888, NYBG.

p. 27: "Can you tell me": December 12, 1889.

p. 28: "I have made no promises": February 19, 1889.

p. 28: "Along the face of this granite wall": October 1, 1889.

p. 30: "With every change": March 14, 1891.

p. 30: "Forms new to me on all sides": May 24, 1890.

p. 30: "I do not yet know": May 10, 1890.

p. 30: "May the mosses": January 1, 1890.

p. 30: "How to Study the Mosses." Britton, *The Observer* 5 (1894): 113–117.

p. 31: "The microscope is not": advertisement, *The Observer* 7 (1896): 15.

p. 31: "Even with such modest equipment": March 2, 1889.

p. 31: "air box": April 23, 1890.

p. 31: "when one does not have access": May 23, 1890.

p. 31: "I also enjoy": Ibid.

p. 32: I should be glad to accept": April 16, 1889.

p. 32: "He has the advantage": May 9, 1890.

p. 33: "I mean to work up": January 13, 1890.

Chapter Three: Family Practice

Unless otherwise indicated, all quotations in this chapter are from John Leiberg's letters to Elizabeth Britton, NYBG.

p. 35: "Many thanks": Carrie Leiberg to Britton, April 8, 1889, NYBG.

p. 37: "I only hope my boy": January 13, 1890.

p. 37: "I enclose a characteristic letter": January 21, 1890.

p. 37: "a picnic trip": May 21, 1889.

p. 38: "The vein they came from": March 2, 1889.

p. 38: "by large expeditions": April 13, 1889.

p. 38: "I discovered the key": January 13, 1890.

p. 39: "You see we are turning the 'Wheel'": July 23, 1889.

p. 39: "All the money": March 29, 1890.

p. 39: "A London fog": August 3, 1889.

p. 40: "great conflagration": August 21, 1889.

p. 40: "Three days of rain": September 5, 1889.

p. 40: "They are now reaping": February 10, 1890.

p. 41: "Least of all would she indulge": August 21, 1889.

p. 41: medical school graduation certificate: Carrie E. Marvin, Degree of Doctor of Medicine. Miscellaneous Records, Book 1: June 20, 1888, p. 197, Bonner County Recorder's Office (Coeur d'Alene, ID).

p. 41: "The dear little chick": Carrie Leiberg to Britton, February 5, 1890, NYBG.

p. 42: "Every year I love him better": Ibid., March 28, 1890.

p. 42: "You are right about it being lonesome": March 8, 1890.

p. 42: "a perfect helpmate": January 13, 1890.

p. 43: "It is a terrible thing": Carrie Leiberg to Britton, February 5, 1890, NYBG.

p. 43: I watch him, sometimes": Ibid., October 13, 1893.

p. 44: "by far the great majority": January 13, 1890.

p. 44: "It was *very* desolate": Carrie Leiberg to Britton, March 28, 1890, NYBG.

p. 45: "Somehow your letters always give me a sense": Ibid.

p. 45: "If I do, my friends will be flooded": Ibid.

p. 45: "Herewith I send you a likeness": May 29, 1890.

p. 46: an imposing tall woman: Jean Teecher, Louise Conley, and Christy Walton, correspondence with Ann Ferguson, Sandpoint, ID, August 2017.

p. 46: "stretching out on the ground": June 2, 1890.

p. 47: "all the elementals of Rosicrucian lore": Ibid.

p. 47: "Fact: the discovery of the real nature": March 29, 1890.

p. 47: "Everything is wild, lonely": July 1, 1890.

p. 48: "I spend every moment of my time": March 31, 1891.

p. 49: "I should so much like to have it": Carrie Leiberg to Britton, January 4, 1891, NYBG.

p. 49: "he is so large, so strong, so vigorous": Ibid.

p. 50: "Have no doubt this is due": August 1, 1890.

p. 51: "At present Mrs. L is in Spokane": October 22, 1891.

p. 52: Dr. Latham served as the obstetrics specialist: Cochran, *Seven Frontier Women*, 193.

p. 52: lauded for her work: "Mary Latham," *The Spokane Spokesman Illustrated Annual*, January 1, 1892, p. 37.

p. 53: "It would have squared": August 19, 1892.

p. 54: "Your correspondence and knowledge": October 10, 1892.

p. 54: *"This is confidential"*: Ibid.

p. 55: "What are the probable chances?" Leiberg to Holzinger, December 27, 1892, Record Unit 220, Box 9, Folder 20, SIA.

Chapter Four: Crossing the Columbia Plateau

Unless otherwise noted, all quotations in this chapter are from Leiberg, *Journal, Sandberg-Leiberg Expedition, 1893*, USNH.

p. 57: "When one looks over": Leiberg to Britton, February 23, 1893, NYBG.

p. 61: "under whose direction": Coville to Leiberg, May 5, 1893, Entry 26R, Botany Book 2, NARA.

p. 62: "This work made an extraordinarily 'busy man'": Leiberg to Britton, September 16, 1893, NYBG.

p. 66: first known specimen of cheatgrass: Mack, "Invasion of *Bromus tectorum*."

p. 69: "'kitchen middens': Leiberg to Britton, September 16, 1893, NYBG.

p. 70: Ephrata Fan: Bruce Bjornstead, personal communications with the author.

p. 75: The first ascent of Mount Stuart: Becky, *Cascade Alpine Guide*, 300.

p. 77: Ecologist Richard Mack: Mack, "First Comprehensive Botanical Survey," 118.

Chapter Five: Tracks

p. 82: a full-page article: Leiberg, "Petrographs."

p. 83: Indian Meadows: Nisbet, *The Mapmaker's Eye*, 75.

p. 84: hidden beneath a mass of humus: Leiberg to Britton, October 12, 1893, NYBG.

p. 84: Carrie Leiberg brought her camera: Carrie Leiberg photographs, Francis Gilbert Hamblen Collection, Northwest Museum of Arts and Culture, Spokane. These prints are glued into a photographic album and attributed to Dr. Leiberg. There is no record of the original negatives.

p. 85: leave both the lichens and the petroglyphs alone: Boreson and Peterson, 60–63.

p. 85: "He said his wife": Carrie Leiberg to Britton, October 3, 1893, NYBG.

p. 87: "other parties": Leiberg to Coville, October 30, 1893, Coville Papers, Record Unit 7272, Box 3, SIA.

p. 87: "more thorough and closer work in the field": Ibid., November 6, 1893.

p. 90: "As I view them": Leiberg to Rose, April 2, 1896, Record Unit 221, Series 1, SIA.

p. 90: he would in time complete a monograph on the family: Coulter and Rose, "Monograph."

p. 90: "the vast difference between studying plants": Leiberg to Britton, March 6, 1894, NYBG.

p. 91: "biological life zones": Sterling, *Last of the Naturalists*, 298.

p. 91: "hungry for the giant old mossbacks": Leiberg to Britton, February 24, 1894, NYBG.

Chapter Six: High Lava Plains

p. 93: "the industrial armies": Leiberg to Coville, April 25, 1894, Entry 26Q, Box 5, NARA.

p. 94: "I have several horse trades on tap": Ibid., April 29, 1894.

p. 94: "prefer to have the farmer's boy": Sterling, *Last of the Naturalists*, 199.

p. 95: "Whenever I am fortunate enough": Leiberg to Coville, May 15, 1894, Entry 26Q, Box 5, NARA.

p. 96: "a most striking and peculiar": Leiberg to Rose, no date, Record Unit 221, Series 1, SIA.

p. 96: "The roots are dried": Leiberg to Coville, May 8, 1894, Entry 26Q, Box 5, NARA.

p. 97: "cous" was applied to several different biscuitroot: Nisbet, *Ancient Places*, 59–80.

p. 98: "the country passed through": Leiberg to Coville, May 29, 1894, Entry 26Q, Box 5, NARA.

p. 98: "one could see, even miles away": Ibid.

p. 99: Local farmers were employing strychnine: Ibid., May 15, 1894.

p. 100: "My intention is to give this tract": Ibid., June 22, 1894.

p. 101: "We are all right in every way": Ibid., June 29, 1894.

p. 101: "Not much of a desert": Ibid., July 16, 1894.

p. 102: "an elegant object": Ibid.

p. 102: arcs of eruptive activity: Orr, *Oregon Geology*, 114.

p. 102: "The forest fires have not damaged": Leiberg to Coville, July 16, 1894, Entry 26Q, Box 5, NARA.

p. 104: a number of thermal springs: Ibid., August 6, 1894.

p. 104: the vast Basin and Range province: Orr, *Oregon Geology*, 78–79.

p. 105: The expedition naturalist, Dr. John Strong Newberry: Stevenson, "John Strong Newberry."

p. 105: "'Wo-Kash'—the food pounded from seeds": Leiberg to Coville, August 26, 1894, Entry 26Q, Box 5, NARA.

p. 106: the farmers living in the vicinity of Nampa: Ibid., October 2, 1894.

p. 107: Dr. Carrie Leiberg of Hope, Idaho had been appointed: "An Educated Lady," *The Medical Fortnightly*, 6, no. 12 (November 15, 1894): 683; "Dr. Carrie Leiberg," *The Railway Surgeon*, 1 no. 13 (November 20, 1894): 316.

p. 107: "The analogy between railway injuries": Northrop, "Railway Surgery," 28.

Chapter Seven: The Coeur d'Alenes

All quotations from p. 111 to p. 130 are from Leiberg, Journal and Itinerary. Idaho, 1895–1896.

p. 113: "We have received a package": Coville to Leiberg,
   March 11, 1895, Entry 26R, Botany Book 10, NARA.

p. 114: "Will you accept seven months' commission": Ibid., May
   28, 1895.

p. 114: "Your work will cover the following": Ibid., June 3,
   1895.

p. 117: "People can speak two languages": Felix Aripa,
   conversations with the author, 2014.

p. 125: All quotations from p. 125 to p. 130 are from Leiberg,
   "General Report upon a Botanical Survey of the Coeur
   d'Alene Mountains."

Chapter Eight: Basin and Range

p. 133: "Every working botanist": Leiberg to Piper, December
   16, 1895, WSU.

p. 134: "Sheep and cattle are rapidly destroying": Ibid.,
   January 4, 1896.

p. 134: "It was very thoughtful and I *greatly appreciate* it":
   Ibid., February 5, 1896.

p. 136: "the matter seemed utterly hopeless": Leiberg to
   Coville, January 2, 1896, Entry 26Q, Box 6, NARA.

p. 136: "Not necessarily an official statement": Ibid., January
   5, 1896.

p. 136: "efforts to introduce [him] to the notice of public men":
   Ibid., March 9, 1896.

p. 137: "I will not cease to hold": Ibid.

p. 137: a patient whom she identified as "Mrs. J.": Leiberg,
   Carrie, "A Double Pregnancy," 289.

p. 139: "the death and explusion of the first embryo": Ibid.

p. 139: Carrie assembled the best scenic photographs: Carrie
   Leiberg to Coville, March 23, 1896, Entry 26Q, Box 6,
   NARA.

p. 142: "You will at once recognize the importance": Coville to Leiberg, May 6, 1896, Entry 26R, Botany Book 15, NARA.

p. 143: "This will be no picnic excursion": Leiberg to Coville, May 19, 1896, Entry 26Q, Box 6, NARA.

p. 143: "the effects of tie and lumber cutting": Ibid.

p. 143: "And in *no* case": Ibid.

p. 143: "It is evident that they contemplate": Coville to Leiberg, June 2, 1896, Entry 26R, Botany Book 15, NARA.

p. 144: he did venture West that summer: Pinchot, *Breaking New Ground*, 100–104.

p. 145: with its long slopes: Leiberg to Coville, June 9, 1896, Entry 26Q, Box 6, NARA.

p. 145: "sweet and more pleasant to the taste": Leiberg to Rose, June 9, 1896, Record Unit 221, Series 1, SIA.

p. 146: "is particularly conscious to compass a large amount": Carrie Leiberg to Coville, June 1, 1896, Entry 26Q, Box 6, NARA.

p. 146: "The check for July for John B. Leiberg": Ibid., August 13, 1896.

p. 148: "is such a favorite food": Coville, "Notes on the Plants," 96.

p. 148: "Your list is much larger": Leiberg to Coville, June 17, 1897, Entry 26Q, Box 6, NARA.

p. 149: "terribly filthy water": Ibid., September 22, 1896.

Chapter Nine: Solitaire

p. 152: "who had grown up from childhood": Sonnenkalb, *Reminiscences*, 36–37.

p. 152: "over gently rolling land": Sonnenkalb, *Field Notes*.

p. 153: "road to Solitaire and Leiberg Ranch": Ibid.

p. 153: "Dr. C. E. Leiberg has made fine improvements": Ibid.

p. 154: "self-willed obstinate tenderfeet": Leiberg to Coville, October 5(a), 1896, Entry 26Q, Box 6, NARA.

p. 155: a prompt answer: Ibid., November 28, 1896.

p. 156: "in a state of profound collapse: Leiberg, Carrie, "A Case of Placenta Praevia," 377.

p. 157: "As we had remained constantly in attendance": Ibid., 377.

p. 158: "The dawn of the new year found her just alive": Ibid., 378.

p. 159: "It won't be long": Leiberg to Coville, February 27, 1897, Entry 26Q, Box 6, NARA.

p. 160: "I have seen the trees my friend ordered": Carrie Leiberg to Settlemeir Nursery, March 1, 1897, Bonner County Historical Society (Sandpoint, Idaho).

p. 160: a marriage license to John B. and Carrie E. Leiberg: April 15, 1897, Records, St. Croix County (WI).

p. 160: "Confidentially, there is a very good prospect": Leiberg to Britton, May 1, 1897, NYBG.

p. 161: "a brief account to the principal kinds": Coville to Leiberg, April 10, 1897, Entry 26R, Botany Book 17, NARA.

p. 162: "It is evident the law against fires": Leiberg to Coville, April 19, 1897, Entry 26Q, Box 6, NARA.

p. 162: "If correctly reported, this marks the beginning": Ibid., May 7, 1895.

p. 164: "My arrangement with Mr. Gannett": Coville to Leiberg, June 25, 1897, Entry 26R, Botany Book 17, NARA.

p. 164: "The only words of advice I have for you": Ibid.

Chapter Ten: From the Priest to the Bitterroot

p. 167: "The war is on": Pinchot, *Breaking New Ground*, 109.

p. 169: dispatched a crew: Arno, "Forest Explorers," 17.

p.170: Great Lakes eastern white pine companies: Smith and Weitz, *Wild Place*, 34.

p. 170: "the most valuable body of timber in the interior": Pinchot, *Breaking New Ground*, 124–25.

p. 171: "Met Leiberg": Pinchot, *Journals*, Personal Notebook I, Library of Congress.

p. 171: specific issues in the Priest River complex: Smith and Weitz, *Wild Place*, 41–43.

p. 171: "There is probably not a body": Pinchot, *Breaking New Ground*, 125.

p. 172: "In a region so difficult to traverse": Leiberg, "Priest River Reserve," 217.

p. 172: "It has been deeply sculptured and eroded": Ibid., 218.

p. 173: "these flats and bogs are important conservators": Ibid., 220–221.

p. 176: "Destruction of a Mixed Forest": Ibid., 241.

p. 176: "Burnt White Pine Forest": Ibid., 239.

p. 176: "Fires Started by Road Supervisor": Ibid., 236

p. 176: "Squatter's claim in White-Pine Timber": Ibid., 244.

p. 176: "a great many quartz claims": Ibid., 242.

p. 178: "My summer has been pretty trying": Leiberg to Coville, September 30, 1897, Entry 26Q, Box 6, NARA.

p. 178: "I have heretofore imagined": Ibid.

p. 178: a proposal to introduce Angora goats: Ibid., October 6, 1897.

p. 179: "Short, stout, and elegant": Ibid.

p. 180: "There were a lot of Snakes, Flatheads, and Nez Perce": Ibid.

p. 181: "This summer has demonstrated": Ibid.

p. 181: "It is owning to sickness": Leiberg to Coville, November 11, 1897, Entry 26Q, Box 6, NARA.

p. 183: "Whilst I do not apprehend": Leiberg to Coville, November 13, 1897, Entry 26Q, Box 6, NARA.

p. 183: Two local witnesses: Leiberg homestead application, November 3, 1897, Application No. 1283, Land Entry File D11–371986327E, NARA.

p. 184: "destined to be one of the greatest": "On a Trip Inspecting Fruit," *Lewiston Teller* (Lewiston, ID), August 27, 1897.

Chapter Eleven: Further

p. 189: geologist Joseph T. Pardee shook his discipline: Pardee, "Glacial Lake Missoula."

p. 190: J Harlan Bretz pointed to that outsized lake: Bretz, *Glacial Drainage.*

p. 190: "The existence of the lake": Leiberg, "Forestry of the Bitterroot," 356–57.

p. 192: California silviculturists: McKelverey and Johnson, "Historical Perspectives."

p. 193: "by far the most noteworthy": Leiberg, "Bitterroot Forest Reserve," 317.

p. 193: "This shrub is of rare occurrence": Ibid., 401.

p. 194: "for many years the Lochsa Basin": Ibid., 373.

p. 195: "When you come we will try to get hold of the Lewis and Clark": Coville to Leiberg, October 6, 1898, Entry 26R, Botany Book 17, NARA.

p. 198: ponderosa pine bark for sweet cambium: Leiberg, "The Cascade Range," 280.

p. 199: "A remarkable and striking example of surface denudation": Ibid., 282.

p. 199: "Do you recollect the strange looking marsh umbellifer": Leiberg to Rose, October 6, 1899, Record Unit 221, Series 1, SIA.

p. 200: overgrazed by sheep: Leiberg, "Forest Conditions in the Northern Sierra," 51–52.

p. 200: "I had such a large area of country to cover": Leiberg to Coville, April 3, 1901, Entry 26Q, Box 6, NARA.

Chapter Twelve: Silver Against Gold

p. 203: "Kootenai in the Lead": *Coeur d'Alene Press* (Coeur d'Alene, ID), June 30, 1900.

p. 206: she lunched with a garden club: "Seen and Heard Around Town," *Kootenai County Republican* (Sandpoint, ID), July 13, 1900.

p. 207: transacted business with the board: *The Silver Blade* (Rathdrum, ID), July 14, 1900.

p. 207: The margin against Carrie Leiberg: Shiach, *Illustrated History*, 775–777.

p. 208: "I think you will appreciate": Coville to Gifford Pinchot, September 24, 1900, Entry 26R, Botany Book 28, NARA.

p. 208: sowed thousands of apple seeds: Leiberg to Coville, April 3, 1901, Entry 26Q, Box 6, NARA

p. 209: "doubtless some new mosses will turn up": Leiberg to Britton, June 2, 1901, NYBG.

p. 210: "The yellow pine forest in the reserve": Leiberg, "Forest Conditions in the San Francisco Mountains," 28.

p. 211: "The real surface regulator of run-off in this reserve": Ibid., 31.

p. 212: "The fundamental idea": Pinchot, 190.

p. 212: garnered broad public attention: Newspaper articles on Leiberg's Forest Reserves reports:
"Devastation of California Forests," *Washington Times*, (Washington, DC), October 17, 1902; "Northern Sierra Nevada Forest Conditions," *Greenville News* (Greenville, SC), October 18, 1902; "Timberlands of the Sierra Nevada Range," *Washington Times*, (Washington, DC), April 22, 1903; "Forestry Conditions in the Cascade Forest," *Hood River Glacier*, (Hood River, OR), October 8, 1903; "Study of Forest Conditions," *Allentown Call* (Allentown, PA), July 18, 1904; "Forests of Arizona," *Williams Weekly Journal-Miner*, (Williams, AZ), July 20, 1904; "Information in Reference,"

Prescott Weekly Journal (Prescott, AZ), July 20, 1904; "Forests of Arizona," *Williams News*, (Williams, AZ), July 23, 1904.

p. 213: "The long drawn out 'agony'": Leiberg to Rose, June 3, 1902, Record Unit 221, Series 1, SIA.

p. 213: "The Bitterroot Reserve, with its few and difficult trails": Leiberg to Coville, November 29, 1902, Entry 26Q, Box 6, NARA.

p. 214: "Even the best and most prudent of men": Ibid.

p. 214: "Am no longer at Stuart": Leiberg to Piper, November 5, 1902, WSU.

p. 215: "Some of our western plants are remarkably local": Ibid.

Chapter Thirteen: The World Awaits

p. 217: "a mere skinning of the easily accessible places": Leiberg to Piper, March 18, 1903, WSU.

p. 219: John should pick up an elementary Spanish textbook: Coville to Leiberg, April 1, 1903, Entry 26R, Botany Book 34, NARA.

p. 220: a newspaper column identified John: "Livingston," *Butte Daily Post* (Butte, MT), September 26, 1903.

p. 220: he applied to the Bureau of Insular Affairs: Leiberg to Bureau of Insular Affairs, December 28, 1903, Record Group 350, Bureau of Insular Affairs, Document 9560, NARA.

p. 220: "Service satisfactory": Ibid.

p. 221: "before opening the Yakima Indian Reservation": "New Forest Reserve," *Tacoma Daily News* (Tacoma, WA), August 4, 1905.

p. 221: "One of my constituents": McLeary to Secretary, October 9, 1905, and Secretary to McLeary, October 11, 1905. Record Group 350, Bureau of Insular Affairs, Document 9560, NARA.

p. 222: "At the time of the granting of the divorce": "Claims Divorce Illegal," *Minneapolis Journal*, December 5, 1905.

p. 222: they renounced any further claims to the Marvin estate: James Marvin probate papers, Minnesota Historical Society (Minneapolis, MN).

p. 222: a $5,000 down payment: "The New Electric Line," *Northern Idaho News* (Sandpoint, ID), January 26, 1906.

p. 223: republished Leiberg's 1897 *Science* article: "Strange Indian Rock Carvings," *Spokesman Review*, March 11, 1906.

p. 224: "plenty of chances for playing Izaak Walton." Leiberg to Coville, June 7, 1907, Entry 26Q, Box 6, NARA.

p. 224: He told a reporter that he planned to build: "Will Build Big Bungalow," *Springfield News* (Springfield, OR), January 11, 1907.

p. 224: "If my wife can stand the climate": Leiberg to Rose, December 23, 1906, Record Unit 221, Series 1, SIA.

p. 225: "Our stay and extent of work": Leiberg to Coville, May 18, 1907, Entry 26Q, Box 6, NARA.

p. 225: "all depending on how Mrs. L. views it": Ibid., June 7, 1907.

p. 225: arranging his plant collections: "Fine Plant Collection." *Sunday Oregonian* (Portland, OR), February 23, 1908.

p. 226: "Many and diverse changes have occurred": Leiberg to Britton, October 8, 1908, NYBG.

p. 227: some remarkable species of leaf lichens: Ibid, January 19, 1910.

p. 227: "You have added greatly to my pleasure in life." Ibid., January 20, 1910.

All quotations between p. 227 and p. 229 are from Leiberg, "Diabetes Mellitus."

p. 230: "It is wonderful to see the change": Leiberg, Carrie; "Tecknic of the Leiberg Treatment."

p. 231: Then he simply went missing: "Fear is Felt for Marvin," *Oregonian*, September 24, 1911.

p. 231: "I am a logger": "B. K. Worker's Mind Blank as to Past," *Eugene Daily Guard* (Eugene, OR), November 6, 1911.

p. 232: a blow on the head: "Marvin Refuses to Talk," *Oregonian*, November 7, 1911.

p. 233: he had passed bad checks: "Fearing Insanity Fugitive Gives Up," *San Francisco Call*, September 23, 1908.

p. 233: headed south to the McKenzie River: "Mother Seeks Key to Son's Memory," *Oregonian*, November 7, 1911.

p. 233: George Lewis finally gave an extended interview: "Dual Man Fears Return of 'Other,'" *Morning Oregonian*, November 10, 1911.

Chapter Fourteen: The Doctor Calls

p. 237: "It is our intention": Leiberg to Britton, January 1, 1912, NYBG.

p. 238: John continued to consult: Leiberg to Coville, June 10, 1912, and July 6, 1912, Entry 26Q, Box 6, NARA.

p. 238: "The study of these parasites": Ibid., March 28, 1913.

p. 238: "a menagerie more extensive and remarkable": Ibid.

p. 239: "I have studied these as they never have been studied": Ibid., April 4, 1913.

p. 239: "I have never heretofore particularly esteemed": Ibid., May 10, 1913.

p. 239: "Do you know, Mr. Coville": Ibid.

p. 240: "solar energy, when *broken up and refracted*": Ibid., May 31, 1913.

p. 241: Albert Einstein's 1905 paper describing Brownian motion: Einstein, "Investigations."

p. 241: "Then on the last day of July": "'Rattlesnake King' Dies after Most Strange Career," *Roseburg Review* (Roseburg, OR), June 17, 1913.

p. 243: admitted to the local hospital: "Seriously Ill," *Eugene Morning Register* (Eugene, OR), October 16, 1913.

p. 243: He passed away there on October 28: "Died," *Eugene Guard* (Eugene, OR), October 29, 1913.

p. 243: "Dear Miss Harrison": Carrie Leiberg to Harrison, November 6, 1913, Entry 26Q, Box 6, NARA.

p. 244: "I am writing tonight": Ibid., November 18, 1913.

p. 244: "a notable collection of cryptogams": *Annual Report, Smithsonian Institution, 1915*.

p. 244: "It is a great shock to us to learn of the death of your husband": Britton to Carrie Leiberg, November 28, 1914, NYBG.

p. 245: John's will in probate court: Probate files 2496–2528, Probate Records, Lane County, Oregon; Oregon State Archives, Salem, Oregon.

p. 245: "a man who communed with nature": "Life of Study Revealed," *Eugene Morning Register*, February 26, 1914.

p. 245: "I am exceedingly anxious to send a letter": "Address of Circus Manager," *Portland Oregonian*, October 26, 1914.

p. 246: "Bernard Marvin, whose strange case": "Memory Lapsed Years; Restored," *Oakland Tribune*, January 22, 1915.

p. 246: a well-publicized 1887 incident: "Has Been Dreaming," *New Brunswick Daily Home News* (Bangor, ME), March 16, 1887; "Blank in his Life," *Boston Globe*, March 17, 1887.

p. 247: "magnificent mansion": "McKenzie River Ranch Sold," *Oregon Daily Journal* (Portland, OR), January 25, 1917; "McEwen Ranch Deal Big," *Oregonian*, January 28, 1917.

p. 247: "Leiberg deserted his family": "Case Involves Farm Title," *Oregon Daily Journal* (Portland, OR), March 29, 1917; "Leiberg Estate Involved in Suit," *Eugene Daily Guard* (Eugene, OR), March 31, 1917; "Wife is Accused of Inducing

Man to Leave Wife, Family," *Oregon Daily Journal*, May 31, 1917.

p. 248: a decision exonerating Carrie Leiberg: "Leiberg Marriage Found to be Valid," *Eugene Daily Guard* (Eugene, OR), April 8, 1918.

p. 248: information about land: "John B. Leiberg Wanted," *Morning Oregonian*, September 12, 1918.

p. 249: Carrie remained interested in gardening: Jean Teecher, Louise Conley, and Christy Walton, correspondence with Ann Ferguson, August 2017.

p. 249: Bernard seemed a little odd: Ibid.

p. 250: "Bernard was looked upon as a prodigy": "Pioneer Resident Visits Hope," *Pend Oreille Review* (Sandpoint, ID), August 23, 1929.

p. 250: Thekla accompanied Carrie to Eugene: "Personals," *Eugene Daily Guard* (Eugene, OR), August 22, 1934.

p. 250: she passed away three years later: "Carrie Leiberg," *Eugene Register-Guard* (Eugene, OR), May 28, 1937.

p. 251: "untrammeled by narrow creeds or dogmas": Leiberg to Britton, January 13, 1890. NYBG.

p. 251: a beautifully pressed spray of ginkgo leaves: Lynn Camsuzou, personal correspondence with the author, September 2016.

Annual Report of the Board of Regents of the Smithsonian Institution 1915. Washington, DC: Government Printing Office, 1916.

Arno, Stephen F. *Flames in our Forest: Disaster or Renewal?* Washington, DC: Island Press, 2002.

———. "The Forest Explorers: Probing the Western Forest Reserves, 1897–1904." *Forest History Today* Fall 2012: 16–25.

Arno, Stephen F., and Romona P. Hammerly. *Northwest Trees: Anniversary Edition.* Seattle: Mountaineers Books, 2007.

Arrington, Leonard J. *History of Idaho.* Volume 1. Moscow: University of Idaho Press, 1994.

Ayers, H. B. *Cascade Forest Reserve.* Nineteenth Annual Report of the US Geological Survey 1897–98, Part V. Washington, DC: Government Printing Office, 1899.

Beckey, Fred. *Cascade Alpine Guide: Climbing and High Routes: Volume 1.* 3rd ed. Seattle: Mountaineers Books, 2000.

Björk, Curtis R. "Distribution Patterns of Disjunct and Endemic Vascular Plants in the Interior Wetbelt of Northwest North America." *Botany* 88, no. 4 (2010): 409–428.

Bjornstead, Bruce. *On the Trail of the Ice Age Floods.* Sandpoint, ID: Keokee Books, 2006.

Bonta, M. M. *Women in the Field: America's Pioneering Women Naturalists.* College Station, TX: Texas A&M University Press, 1991.

Boreson, K., and W. R. Peterson. "The Petroglyphs at Lake Pend Oreille, Bonner County, Northern Idaho." USACE Technical Report, December 1985.

Bretz, J. H. *Glacial Drainage on the Columbia Plateau.* The Geological Society of America Bulletin 34, no. 3 (1923): 573–608.

Britton, Elizabeth G. "Contributions to American Bryology: An Enumeration of Mosses Collected by Mr. John B. Leiberg, in Kootenai County, Idaho." *Bulletin of the Torrey Botanical Club* 16, no. 4 (April 8, 1889): 106–112.

_____ . Correspondence with Carrie and John Leiberg. Britton Collection. New York Botanical Garden, Bronx, NY.

———. "How to Study the Mosses." *The Observer* 5, no. 3 (March 1894): 82–86.

———. "A Supplementary Enumeration of Mosses Collected by Mr. John B. Leiberg, in Kootenai County, Idaho." *Bulletin of the Torrey Botanical Club* 18, no. 2 (February 1891): 49–56.

Camp, Pamela, and Jon G. Gamon. *Field Guide to the Rare Plants of Washington.* Seattle: University of Washington Press, 2011.

Chamberlain, Edward B. "John B. Leiberg Obituary." *The Bryologist* 18, no. 3 (May 1915): 47–48.

Cochran, Barbara F. *Seven Frontier Women and the Founding of Spokane Falls.* Spokane, WA: Tornado Creek Publications, 2011.

Coulter, J. M., and J. N. Rose. "Monograph of the North American Umbelliferae." *Contributions from the US National Herbarium* 7, no. 1 (December 31, 1900): 9–256. Washington, DC, 1900.

Coville, Frederick V. Correspondence with Carrie and John Leiberg. Record Group 54, NC 135, National Archives and Record Administration, Washington, DC.

———. "Notes on the Plants Used by the Klamath Indians of Oregon." *Contributions from the US National Herbarium* 5, no. 2 (June 9, 1897): 87–108.

———. Papers. Record Unit 7272. Smithsonian Institution Archives, Washington, DC.

Cox, Elizabeth M. "Women Will have a Hand in Such Matters from Now On: Idaho's First Women Lawmakers." *Idaho Yesterdays* Fall 1994: 2–9.

Einstein, Albert. "Investigations on the Theory of Brownian Movement." Reprint, New York: Dover Publications, 1956.

Fernow, Bernard E. *A Brief History of Forestry in Europe, the United States, and Other Countries.* Washington, DC: American Forestry Associations, 1913.

Fiedler, Carl E., and Stephen F. Arno. *Ponderosa: People, Fire, and the West's Most Iconic Tree.* Missoula, MT: Mountain Press Publishing Company, 2015.

Gray, Karen. "*Rhizomnium nudum* in Idaho." *Sage Notes: Idaho Native Plant Society* 21, no. 4 (Fall 1999): 15–16.

Hackbarth, Linda. *Trail to Gold: The Pend Oreille Route.* Coeur d'Alene, ID: Museum of North Idaho, 2014.

Himmelwright, Abraham Lincoln. *In the Heart of the Bitter-Root Mountains: The Story of the Carlin Hunting Party September–December 1893.* New York: G. P. Putnam's Sons, 1895.

Kenny, Michael. *The Passion of Ansel Bourne: Multiple Personality in American Culture.* Washington, DC: Smithsonian Institution Press, 1986.

Lange, Erwin F. "Pioneer Botanists of the Pacific Northwest." *Oregon Historical Quarterly* 57, no. 2 (June 1956): 109–173.

Langille, H. D., Fred G. Plummer, Arthur Dodwell, Theodore Rixon, and John B. Leiberg. "Forest Conditions in the Cascade Range Forest Reserve, Oregon." *United States Geological Survey Professional Paper No. 9.* Washington, DC: Government Printing Office, 1903.

Larsen, T. A. "Idaho's Role in America's Woman Suffrage Crusade." *Idaho Yesterdays* 18 (Spring 1974): 2–15.

Leiberg, Carrie E. "A Case of Placenta Praevia." *Charlotte Medical Journal* 10, no. 3 (1897): 377–78.

———. "A Double Pregnancy." *The Medical Sentinel* 4, no. 7 (July 1896): 289.

———. "Superfoetation." *Medical Standard* 18, no. 7 (July 1896): 251.

———. "Tecknic of the Leiberg Treatment of Diabetes." *The American Journal of Clinical Medicine* 17, no 8 (August 1910): 900–901.

Leiberg, John B. "The Bitterroot Forest Reserve." *Twentieth Annual Report of the United States Geological Survey*, Part 5. Washington, DC: Government Printing Office, 1900.

———. "The Cascade Range and Ashland Forest Reserves and Adjacent Regions." *Twenty-first Annual Report of the United States Geological Survey to the Secretary of the Interior, 1899–1900*, Part 5. Washington, DC: Government Printing Office, 1900.

———. Catalogue. Idaho, 1895. US National Herbarium, Smithsonian Institution, Washington, DC.

———. Catalogue of Plants Collected. Cascades, Umpqua, Siskiyou Mountains, 1899. US National Herbarium, Smithsonian Institution, Washington, DC.

———. Catalogue of Plants Collected. Coeur d'Alene Mountains, 1895. US National Herbarium, Smithsonian Institution, Washington, DC.

———. Catalogue of Plants Collected. Oregon, 1894. US National Herbarium, Smithsonian Institution, Washington, DC.

———. Catalogue of Plants Collected. Priest River Forest Reserve, 1897. US National Herbarium, Smithsonian Institution, Washington, DC.

————. Catalogue of Plants Collected. San Francisco
Mountains Forest Reserve in 1901. US National Herbarium,
Smithsonian Institution, Washington, DC.

————. Catalogue of Plants Collected. San Jacinto, San
Bernadino and San Gabriel Forest Reserves in Southern
California, 1898. US National Herbarium, Smithsonian
Institution, Washington, DC.

————. Correspondence. Record Units 220 and 221,
Smithsonian Institution Archives, Washington, DC.

————. Correspondence with Frederick Coville. Record Group
54, NC 135, National Archives and Record Administration,
Washington, DC.

————. Correspondence with Frederick Coville. Record Unit
7272, Smithsonian Institution Archives, Washington, DC.

————. "*Delphinium viridescens* and *Sambucus leiosperma*,
Two New Plants from the Northwest Coast." *Proceedings of
the Biological Society of Washington* 11 (March 13, 1897):
39–41.

————. "Diabetes Mellitus: A Personal Experience." *The
American Journal of Clinical Medicine* 17, no. 6 (June 1910):
654–658.

————. "Effect of Forest Destruction on Mineral Resources."
The Forester 4, no.2 (1898): 34–36.

————. "Forest Conditions in the Absaroka Division of the
Yellowstone Forest Reserve, Montana, and the Livingston
and Big Timber Quadrangles." *United States Geological
Survey Professional Paper No. 29*. Washington, DC:
Government Printing Office, 1904.

————. "Forest Conditions in the Little Belt Mountains
Forest Reserve, Montana, and the Little Belt Mountains
Quadrangle." *United States Geological Survey Professional
Paper No. 30*. Washington, DC: Government Printing Office,
1904.

———. "Forest Conditions in the Northern Sierra Nevada, California." *United States Geological Survey Professional Paper No. 8.* Washington, DC: Government Printing Office, 1902.

———. "Forest Conditions in the San Francisco Mountains Forest Reserve, Arizona."*United States Geological Survey Professional Paper No. 22.* Washington, DC: Government Printing Office, 1904.

———. "Forestry of the Bitterroot Reserve." *Nineteenth Annual Report of the United States Geological Survey to the Secretary of the Interior, 1897–98.* Part 5. Washington, DC.: Government Printing Office, 1899.

———. "From Northern Idaho." *Botanical Gazette* 13, no. 6 (June 1888): 164–65.

———. "General Report on a Botanical Survey of the Coeur d'Alene Mountains in Idaho during the summer of 1895." *Contributions from the US National Herbarium* 5 (1897):1–85. Washington, DC: Government Printing Office.

———. "Is Climatic Aridity Impending on the Pacific Slope? The Testimony of the Forest." *National Geographic Magazine* 10 (May 1899): 160–181.

———. Journal. Sandberg-Leiberg Expedition, 1893. US National Herbarium, Smithsonian Institution, Washington, DC.

———. Journal and Itinerary. Idaho, 1895. US National Herbarium, Smithsonian Institution, Washington, DC.

———. "Notes on Some of the Rarer Plants Found in Blue Earth and Pipestone Counties, Minnesota During the Summer of 1882." *Bulletin of the Minnesota Academy of Natural Sciences* 3 (1883): 37–38.

———. "Notes on the Flora of Western Dakota and Eastern Montana Adjacent to the Northern Pacific Railroad."

Bulletin of the Minnesota Academy of Natural Sciences 3 (1884): 63–69.

———. "Notes on the Forest Region of Northern Idaho." *Bulletin of the Minnesota Academy of Natural Sciences* 3 (1885): 88–95.

———. "On the Carpels of *Opulaster malvacea* (Greene)." *Bulletin of the Torrey Botanical Club* 22 (1895): 271–272.

———. "Petrographs at Lake Pend d'Oreille Idaho." *Science* 22 (1893): 555–556.

———. "Present Conditions of the Forested Areas in Northern Idaho Outside the Limits of the Priest River Forest Reserve and North of the Clearwater River." *Nineteenth Annual Report of the United States Geological Survey to the Secretary of the Interior, 1897–98.* Part 5. Washington, DC: Government Printing Office, 1899.

———. "The Priest River Forest Reserve." *Nineteenth Annual Report of the United States Geological Survey to the Secretary of the Interior, 1897–98.* Part 5. Washington, DC: Government Printing Office, 1899.

———. "San Bernardino Forest Reserve." *Nineteenth Annual Report of the United States Geological Survey to the Secretary of the Interior, 1897–98.* Part 5. Washington, DC: Government Printing Office, 1899.

———. "San Gabriel Forest Reserve." *Nineteenth Annual Report of the United States Geological Survey to the Secretary of the Interior, 1897–98.* Part 5. Washington, DC: Government Printing Office, 1899.

———. "The San Gabriel, San Bernardino, and San Jacinto Forest Reserves." *Twentieth Annual Report of the United States Geological Survey*, Part 5. Washington, DC: Government Printing Office, 1900.

———. "San Jacinto Forest Reserve. *Nineteenth Annual Report of the United States Geological Survey to the*

Secretary of the Interior, 1897–98. Part 5. Washington, DC: Government Printing Office, 1899.

———. "Southern Part of Cascade Range Forest Reserve." *United States Geological Survey Professional Paper No. 9.* Washington, DC: Government Printing Office, 1903.

———. "Some Notes upon the More Recent Fossil Flora of North Dakota, and an Inquiry into the Causes That Have Led to the Development of the Treeless Areas of the Northwest." *Bulletin of the Minnesota Academy of Natural Sciences* 3 (1883): 145–151.

———. "Some Notes upon *Tripterocladium leucocladulum* C. Mull." *Bulletin of the Torrey Botanical Club* 19 (1892): 7–9.

———. "Southern Part of Cascade Range Forest Reserve." *United States Geological Survey Professional Paper No. 9.* Washington, DC: Government Printing Office, 1903.

———. "Two New Species of Mosses from Idaho." *Bulletin of the Torrey Botanical Club* 20 (1893): 112–116.

Lukas, J. Anthony. *Big Trouble: A Murder in a Small Western Town Sets off a Struggle for the Soul of America.* New York: Simon and Schuster, 1999.

Mack, R. N. "First Comprehensive Botanical Survey of the Columbia Plateau, Washington: The Sandberg and Leiberg Expedition of 1893." *Northwest Science* 62, no. 3 (1988): 118–129.

———. "Invasion of *Bromus tectorum* L. into Western North American: An Ecological Chronicle." *Agro–Ecosystems* 7 (1981): 145–165.

Maxon, W. R. "Obituary, Frederick Coville." *Science* 85 (1937): 280–81.

McGeary, Nelson M. *Gifford Pinchot: Forester and Politician.* Princeton: Princeton University Press, 1960.

McKelvery, Kevin S., and James D. Johnson. "Historical Perspectives on Forests of the Sierra Nevada and the

Transverse Ranges of Southern California: Forest Conditions at the Turn of the Century." USDA Forest Service Gen. Tech. Rep. PSW–GTR–133. 1992: 211–246.

Moore, Bud. *The Lochsa: Land Ethics in the Bitterroot Mountains.* Missoula, MT: Mountain Press Publishing Company, 1996.

Mosely, Bob. "Reflections on John Leiberg's Contribution to Plant Conservation in Idaho." *Sage Notes: Idaho Native Plant Society* 21, no. 4 (Fall 1999): 1–2.

Nisbet, Jack. *Ancient Places: People and Landscape in the Emerging Northwest.* Seattle: Sasquatch Books, 2015.

———. *The Mapmaker's Eye: David Thompson on the Columbia Plateau.* Pullman, WA: Washington State University Press, 2005.

Northrup, G. J. "Railway Surgery, with the Duties of Chief and Local Surgeons." *The Railway Surgeon* 1, no. 2 (June 19, 1894): 25–29.

Orr, Elizabeth L., and William N. Orr. *Oregon Geology.* 6th ed. Corvallis, OR: Oregon State University Press, 2012.

Ostler, William. *Modern Medicine: Its Theory and Practice,* Vol. 2. Philadelphia and New York: Lea Brothers and Company, 1912.

Pardee, J. T. "The Glacial Lake Missoula, Montana." *Journal of Geology* 18 (1910): 376–86.

Pinchot, Gifford. *Breaking New Ground: Commemorative Edition.* Washington, DC: Island Press: 1997.

———. Journals and Diaries. Library of Congress, Washington, DC.

———. "The Relation of Forests and Forest Fires." *The National Geographic Magazine* 10, no. 10 (October 1899): 393–402.

Pinkett, Harold T. *Gifford Pinchot: Private and Public Forester.* Urbana, IL: University of Illinois Press, 1970.

Renk, Nancy. *Driving Past: Historical Tours of Bonner County.* Sandpoint, ID: Bonner County Historical Society, 2014.

Robbins, William G. "Federal Forestry Cooperation: The Ferno–Pinchot Years." *Journal of Forest History* 28, no. 4 (October 1984): 164–173.

Russell, Bert, ed. *North Fork of the Coeur d'Alene River.* Harrison, ID: Lacon Publishers, 1984.

Sargent, Charles S. *Report on the Forests of North America.* Washington, DC: Department of the Interior Census Office, 1884.

Shiach, William S. *An Illustrated History of North Idaho, Embracing Nez Perces, Idaho, Latah, Kootenai and Shoshone Counties, State of Idaho.* Spokane, WA: Western Historical Publishing Company, 1903.

Simpson, Michael. "Forested Plant Associations of the Oregon East Cascades." USDA Forest Service PNW Region Technical Pater R6–NR–ECOL–TP–03–2007.

Smith, Kris Runberg, and Tom Weitz. *Wild Place: A History of Priest Lake, Idaho.* Pullman: Washington State University Press, 2005.

Sonnenkalb, Oscar. "Field Notes of the Survey of the Subdivisions and Meander Lines of Township No. 53 North, Range 2 West." Washington DC: Government Land Office, 1896.

———. *Reminiscense of Oscar Sonnenkalb, Idaho Surveyor and Pioneer.* Edited by Peter T Harstad. Pocatello: Idaho State University Press, 1972.

Sterling, Keir B. *Last of the Naturalists: The Career of C. Hart Merriam, 1855–1942.* Revised ed. New York: Arno Press, 1977.

Stevenson, John J. "John Strong Newberry." *American Geologist* 12 (July 1893): 1–25.

Wagner, David H. "History of the University of Oregon Herbarium." *Kalmiopsis: Journal of the Native Plant Society of Oregon* 4 (1994): 6[11].

Walker, Sarah. "Letters to Elizabeth Britton 1889–1894—John Leiberg." *Sage Notes: Idaho Native Plant Society* 21, no. 4 (Fall 1999): 4–14.

———. "Some Biographical Notes." *Sage Notes: Idaho Native Plant Society* 21, no. 4 (Fall 1999): 3.

Williams, R. S. "Mosses of the Philippines and Hawaii Collected by John B. Leiberg." *Bulletin of the Torrey Botanical Club* 42, no. 5 (Nov 13, 1915): 571–577.

Zybach, Bob. Comments on John Leiberg's Report on the Ashland and Oregon Cascade Forest Reserves. April 2006. www.orww.org/History/SW_Oregon/References/Leiberg_1899.

INDEX